HELL AND THE
VICTORIANS

HELL AND THE VICTORIANS

A study of the nineteenth-century theological controversies concerning eternal punishment and the future life

BY

GEOFFREY ROWELL

CLARENDON PRESS
OXFORD
1974

Oxford University Press, Ely House, London W. 1

GLASGOW   NEW YORK   TORONTO   MELBOURNE   WELLINGTON
CAPE TOWN   IBADAN   NAIROBI   DAR ES SALAAM   LUSAKA   ADDIS ABABA
DELHI   BOMBAY   CALCUTTA   MADRAS   KARACHI   LAHORE   DACCA
KUALA LUMPUR   SINGAPORE   HONG KONG   TOKYO

ISBN 0 19 826638 3
© OXFORD UNIVERSITY PRESS 1974

*Printed in Great Britain
by W. & J. Mackay Limited, Chatham*

*To my
Father and Mother*

Preface

OF all the articles of accepted Christian orthodoxy that troubled the consciences of Victorian churchmen, none caused more anxiety than the everlasting punishment of the wicked. The flames of hell illuminated vividly the tensions of an age in which men felt that old certainties were being eroded by new knowledge, and in which an optimistic faith in progress co-existed uneasily with forebodings of the consequences of increasingly rapid social change. A Bible whose Divine authority had been accepted rather than argued about was battered by the blasts of Germanic criticism and scientific theory, and the particular pattern of Christian orthodoxy which it had been assumed to uphold no longer carried full conviction. The distant and impersonal God, whose divine decrees of election and reprobation had the iron fixity and mechanical action of the laws of the Newtonian universe, was increasingly repudiated as an immoral tyrant; and the hell to which the wicked were consigned, far from being the declaration of God's omnipotent righteousness and justice, became a stumbling-block to Christian believers and a weapon of attack for secularists. Yet the need of hell as a moral sanction, and the underlying awareness that, however crudely expressed and distorted the doctrine might be, it did attempt to state something of importance about ultimate ethical values, meant that it could not simply be quietly discarded.

There was not simply criticism from outside, there was also a critique from within Christian theology. Theologians influenced by the pietism of Evangelicalism and Tractarianism, with its close links with the Romantic Movement, attempted to show how Christian eschatology and the Christian faith as a whole had to be given doctrinal expression in personal terms. If the critical study of the Bible cast doubt on the absolute authority of isolated, individual texts, it also meant the rediscovery of the biblical concern with the whole man, as opposed to the commonly accepted dualism of body and soul, and with a corporate as well as an individual eschatology.

Later in the century not only the doctrine of hell but also the very possibility of any future life appeared increasingly implausible. Evolutionary theory, which emphasized so strongly the continuity of human life with that of the animal realm, appeared to many to deal a death blow to any special claims on behalf of man, and to cast doubt on much traditional language about the soul and its assumed immortality. The work of psychic researchers, and of those theologians who stressed that any future life was a gift of God to the whole man and not the natural endowment of a particular, indestructible part of man, represent two different responses to this crisis.

The nineteenth-century debates about eternal punishment and the future life are not, therefore, to be dismissed as peripheral matters. They bring into sharp focus the gradual breakdown of an accepted pattern of human self-understanding, and provide a case-study of the ways in which Christian writers and thinkers still committed to that tradition of understanding criticized and attempted to renew that tradition, often at the cost to themselves of much agonizing doubt and questioning. It is not surprising that these concerns, which are so much at the centre of the Victorian crisis of faith, should have been reflected in much of the literature of the period.

I have attempted in this book to study the courses of these debates, and to show in some detail the issues involved and the arguments employed at various times in the century. In tracing the development in theological attitudes and interpretations I have endeavoured to illustrate them by quotations full enough to show the horizons within which the debates took place, and the way in which those horizons and the consequent perspectives changed in the course of the century. I have, finally, attempted a tentative assessment of the debates from a contemporary theological point of view.

My debts are naturally many and various, but I would like in particular to express my thanks to the following individuals and institutions, who allowed me to consult and quote from papers in their possession: the Dean and Chapter of Canterbury Cathedral; the Principals of Pusey House, Cuddesdon College and Manchester College, Oxford; the Helpers of the Holy Souls; the Fathers of the Birmingham Oratory; the Society of St. Margaret, East Grinstead; the Revd. Gordon Phillips, and many others who replied to my enquiries in the course of my research. I am also grateful to the Master and Fellows of Corpus Christi College, Cambridge, and to the Warden and Fellows of New College, Oxford, who gave me the financial support which made the completion of this book possible. My friends, Anthony Watkinson and Dr. John Feneley, gave me much assistance at different stages. But my chief debt is to David Newsome, who supervised the original research on which this book is based. His wise counsel, infectious enthusiasm, and sympathetic understanding of Victorian religion gave me much encouragement and sparked off many new trains of thought in my mind, which contributed much to whatever merits this book may possess.

Keble College, Oxford,
All Souls' Day, 1973.

Contents

R. F. Clarke and St. G. J. Mivart   176

IX.   Survival of the Fittest   180
      Early Protagonists of Conditionalism   182
      Missionary Theology   190
      The major works of Conditionalism   193
      Critics and supporters of Conditionalism   200

Appendix to Chapter IX
Continental supporters of the doctrine of Conditional
Immortality   208

X.   Conclusion   212

      BIBLIOGRAPHY   222

      INDEX   237

I   Introduction

HEAVEN, hell, death, and judgment are the traditional Four Last Things of Christian theology, but it would be true to say that twentieth-century theologians have, for the most part, been embarrassed at saying much about any of them. In this they stand in sharp contrast to the majority of nineteenth-century divines, who not only wrote at length on Christian eschatology, but regarded it as a central part of Christian teaching. Indeed there were few issues which figured more prominently in the nineteenth-century theological debate than those of the everlasting punishment of the wicked and the immortality of the soul. The student of English religion or literature in the nineteenth century is well aware of the major controversies on these matters associated with the names of F. D. Maurice and the contributors to *Essays and Reviews*, and the part which doubts about the doctrine of hell played in the general unsettlement of faith amongst the intelligentsia. The contributor to the Reverend Orby Shipley's collection of essays, *The Church and the World* (1866), who wrote that 'no one interested in theology could have lived through the last few years, without having the awful question of future punishment forced upon his thoughts', would have found many to agree.[1]

Hell-fire preaching was common, and not only in Evangelical circles, for much of the century, and the threat of everlasting punishment was in many instances the implicit sanction of both social morality and missions to the heathen. Evangelical journals and tracts popularized a religion of petty providentialism, in which Divine judgment was executed on the perpetrators of 'horrid wickednesses' and the offenders against Evangelical etiquette alike. Tales, like that which appeared in the *Christian Guardian* for 1814, were common.

Mary H——, of B—— C——, in Hampshire, who was living in service at Winchester, was curling her hair, and could not adjust it exactly as she wished. For this slight cause she uttered the horrid blasphemy of saying,

---

[1] O. Shipley, *The Church and the World* (First Series), 1866, p. 240. The article, 'The last thirty years in the English Church: an autobiography', was by Mrs. J. W. Lea. Cf. G. Greenwood, *A selection from the letters of the late John Walter Lea*, 1898, p. 16.

'D— the hair, and those that made it.' She instantly fell down *dead*!!!!
TAKE HEED.[2]

Such simple equations, and the very literal understanding of hell
common in many religious circles, were easy targets for the Secularists in the middle years of the century, and Secularist writers also
took a moral stand against a God who condemned men to suffer
everlasting punishment. Moncure Conway records a jingle which
was at one time common in Secularist circles:

> If you and God should disagree
> On questions of theologee,
> You're damned to all eternitee,
> Poor, blind, worm![3]

Austin Holyoake, one of the leading Secularists, warned that hell
brutalized all who believed in it.[4] As hell came increasingly under
attack it is not surprising that Christians also began to ask whether
the Bible so unequivocally taught the hell which was popularly
preached. Passages which favoured the doctrine of universal salvation were quoted against those which appeared to suggest eternal
torment, and attempts were made to reconcile the two. Belief in an
infallible Bible undoubtedly contributed to the difficulties experienced by those who wished to cut loose from the popular hell of
everlasting physical and spiritual torment, and there are many
accounts of the real anguish suffered by those who were undecided
whether they could honestly preach a non-eternal hell or a doctrine of
annihilation of the wicked whilst holding to a biblical faith. Stewart
Headlam, the founder of the Christian Socialist Guild of
St. Matthew, told the Fabian Society towards the end of the century
that they probably did not know what it was 'to have been delivered
in the world of thought, emotion, imagination from the belief that a
large proportion of the human race are doomed to endless misery',
and he attributed the changed outlook to the influence of F. D.
Maurice.[5] W. M. W. Call, a clergyman and minor poet, was haunted
by the thought of 'a great part of the human race . . . kept ever-
lastingly alive, to be the victims of . . . insane concentrated malignity

[2] *Christian Guardian*, vi, 1814, 169. For other examples cf. x, 1818, 335–6; xiv, 1822,
38; xx, 1828, 118.
[3] M. D. Conway, *Autobiography*, 1904, ii. 322n.
[4] A. Holyoake, *Heaven and Hell: where situated?*, n.d.
[5] F. G. Bettany, *S. D. Headlam*, 1925, p. 20.

on the part of God', and eventually resigned his orders.[6] The Calvinist preaching of eternal punishment at the York Street Congregational Church in Walworth caused agonies to Edward White, later to be the leading exponent of the doctrine of conditional immortality, and also disturbed Robert Browning.[7] Tennyson recalled a Calvinist aunt who would say to him, 'Alfred, Alfred, when I look at you, I think of the words of Holy Scripture—"Depart from me, ye cursed, into everlasting fire"'.[8] John Stuart Mill's reaction to those who attempted to defend God's goodness in condemning men to everlasting punishment, by arguing that the goodness of God was qualitatively different from that of man, is well known: 'I will call no being good, who is not what I mean when I apply that epithet to my fellow creatures; and if such a being can sentence me to Hell for not so calling him, to Hell I will go.'[9]

There can be no doubt that the doctrine of everlasting punishment was a major concern of Christians for the greater part of the nineteenth century, yet by the end of the century, to such an extent had opinion changed, that Gladstone could express his alarm that the doctrine was no longer preached.

A portion of Divine truth, which even if secondary is so needful, appears to be silently passing out of view, and . . . the danger of losing it ought at all costs to be averted . . . It is not now sought to alarm men by magnifying the power of God, and by exhibiting the strictness and severity of the law of righteousness. The anxiety now is to throw these subjects into the shade, lest the fastidiousness of human judgment and feeling should be so offended as to rise in rebellion against God for his harshness and austerity.[10]

The change of emphasis can be clearly seen in one family in the contrast between the preaching of everlasting punishment by Bishop Samuel Wilberforce, and the universalism upheld by his son, Basil.[11] How this change occurred, and the different answers which were given to the question of the fate of the wicked, are matters with which we will be subsequently concerned.

[6] W. M. W. Call, *Reverberations revised*, 1875, pp. 5, 10, 12, 35–6.
[7] F. A. Freer, *Edward White, his life and work*, 1902, pp. 4–7.
[8] Hallam Tennyson, *Tennyson: a memoir*, 1897, i, 15.
[9] J. S. Mill, *Examination of Sir William Hamilton's Philosophy*, 1865, p. 103. Cf. *Three Essays on Religion*, 1874, pp. 113–14.
[10] W. E. Gladstone, *Studies subsidiary to the works of Bishop Butler*, 1896, pp. 199, 201.
[11] C. E. Woods, *Archdeacon Wilberforce: his ideals and teaching*, 1917, p. 152; A. R. Ashwell and R. G. Wilberforce *The life of Samuel Wilberforce*, 1880–2, ii, 32.

It would be a mistake, however, to imagine that the theological
debates of the nineteenth century were concentrated on the doctrine
of hell to the exclusion of other areas of Christian eschatology. There
was considerable discussion of the future life as such, ranging from
philosophical discussions of immortality to the speculations about the
life of heaven of popular religious literature. George Eliot, whilst
herself rejecting belief in a future life, is well known for her comment
to F. W. H. Myers that God, immortality, and duty were the inspir-
ing trumpet-calls of men, and Tennyson told Bishop Lightfoot that
the 'cardinal point of Christianity is the life after death'.[12] Perhaps
the greatest interest was taken in the question of immortality in the
1870s, a time when churchmen became increasingly conscious of
the challenge of a critical agnosticism. John Morley wrote that the
problem of immortality was a living issue in the seventies, but had
ceased to be so by the eighties and nineties: men were then more
interested in the rights of nations and imperial policy.[13] Certainly the
seventies saw considerable discussion of the doctrine of conditional
immortality, as well as the publication of articles on the connection
between mind and brain, and symposia on the future life and everlasting punishment in the *Nineteenth Century* and the *Contemporary
Review*. Evolutionary theory, with its emphasis on the connection
between man and the animal world, made it increasingly difficult to
assume immortality as a cardinal doctrine of natural religion, as had
been done in the previous century. In 1870 T. H. Huxley read a
paper before the Metaphysical Society in which he stressed the close
links between man's mental processes and activity in the brain, and
in another Metaphysical Society paper two years later Mark Pattison
reviewed sceptically the evidence for a future life. Whereas in the
eighteenth century, he wrote, 'the soul was not thought of as an
assumption; it counted as a fact', and the defender of natural religion
had no need to prove the immortality of the soul, now anyone who
wished to speak of 'soul' or 'mind' could only do so after a 'volumin-
ous preamble'. The old arguments for immortality—the universality
of the belief, the instinctive testimony of the conscience, and
arguments based on moral and psychological considerations—no
longer carried any weight.[14] Reluctant doubters, like Henry Sidgwick,

[12] F. W. H. Myers, *Essays Modern*, 1883, p. 269; H. Tennyson, op. cit. i. 321n.
[13] F. W. Hirst, *Early life and letters of John Morley*, 1927, i. 305.
[14] Mark Pattison, 'The Arguments for a future life' (Metaphysical Society Papers,
xxv), p. 4 and *passim*.

felt keenly the uncertainty which had replaced the old faith in immortality. For Sidgwick there was a close connection between immortality and morality, and he wrote to J. B. Mozley in 1881 of his fears about the consequences of the loss of faith in immortality.

While I cannot myself discover adequate rational basis for the Christian hope of happy immortality, it seems to me that the general loss of such a hope, from the minds of average human beings as now constituted, would be an evil of which I cannot pretend to measure the extent. I am not prepared to say the dissolution of the existing social order would follow, but I think the danger of such dissolution would be seriously increased, and that the evil would certainly be very great.[15]

F. W. Newman, the Cardinal's brother, valued his uncertain belief in immortality because of the strength it gave him to love, but came eventually to all but abandon it as subversive of true morality and a distraction from man's proper concerns.[16]

It is not surprising that Tennyson's poem, *In Memoriam*, with its hope of a future life, and its awareness of the difficulties caused to a belief in immortality by the new scientific theories, should have enjoyed such popularity. The hope of a future life stood very much at the heart of Tennyson's faith, and he once told an inquirer that 'if faith means anything at all, it is trusting to those instincts, or feelings, or whatever they may be called, which assure us of some life after this'.[17] E. B. Mattes has suggested that Tennyson drew much on Bishop Butler and Wordsworth for his earlier thinking about immortality, but she is less convincing in her suggestion that sections 40, 63, and 73 may have been based on the arguments of the Reverend Isaac Taylor's *Physical Theory of Another Life* (1836).[18] Certainly Taylor's emphasis on a spiritual body, and on the activities of man in the future life extending throughout the universe, was presented in a quasi-scientific guise and was likely to be attractive to Tennyson, but there is no evidence that he ever read the work, and the reference to the spirit's work in the future state being one of nurturing and teaching others is one which was a commonplace of many works besides that of Taylor.[19] To those oppressed by anxiety about

---

[15] A. and E. M. Sidgwick, *Henry Sidgwick*, 1906, p. 357. Cf. pp. 471–2.

[16] W. Robbins, *The Newman Brothers*, 1966, p. 159n.

[17] H. Tennyson, op. cit. i. 495.

[18] Eleanor B. Mattes, *In Memoriam: the way of a soul*, New York, 1951, pp. 40–43.

[19] *In Memoriam*, xl. Isaac Taylor (1787–1865) was Sir William Hamilton's rival for the chair of philosophy in Edinburgh in 1836. He is now chiefly remembered for his *Natural History of Enthusiasm* (1823). George Eliot read his *Physical Theory of Another*

eternal punishment the tentative faith of *In Memoriam* was an
attractive alternative, and trust in 'the larger hope' became a keynote
of much that was written on the subject. The great preacher,
F. W. Robertson of Brighton, considered 'the most satisfactory
things that have ever been said on the future state' were to be found
in the poem, and Henry Sidgwick wrote appreciatively of the strong
appeal of Tennyson's 'defence of "honest doubt"' and of his attempt
to integrate scientific knowledge with his appreciation of nature.[20]
The Queen herself found solace in the poem after the death of the
Prince Consort.[21]

In Memoriam, although the most considerable, was not the only
poem concerned with the future life to influence the thought of the
nineteenth century. Newman's *Dream of Gerontius* (1865) presented
an understanding of purgatory which was acceptable to many outside
his own communion, whilst the Evangelical Edward Bickersteth's
rambling work, *Yesterday, Today and Forever* (1866), hinted at an
eschatology in which the problem of hell was overcome by the
annihilation of the wicked. Bickersteth comforted bereaved parents
with the belief that 'a babe in glory is a babe for ever', and his saints
and angels were permitted the luxury of Victorian tears.

> Yes, there are tears in heaven, Love ever breathes
> Compassion; and compassion without tears
> Would lack its truest utterance: saints weep
> And angels: only there no bitterness
> Troubles the crystal spring.[22]

Life in 1841 with a 'rapture . . . as intense as any schoolgirl over her first novel'. (G. S.
Haight (ed.), *The George Eliot Letters*, 1954, i. 93, 21 May 1841). Taylor argued against a
reductionism of either mind or body, and held that a body, conceived as some tangential
point between mind and matter, was necessary for man's future life. The body could be
ethereal or ponderous. Limitations of language, sense-perception, and memory would be
overcome in the future state, and the society of the future life would be co-extensive with
the universe. The prospect that there would come a time when man's expanded powers
of knowledge would have progressed to the point of comprehending God was overcome
by Taylor's postulate that God's infinite powers were in a progressive relationship with
the created world and thus 'the Infinite Perfections shall never have exhausted those
combinations of which the finite and created system is susceptible'. (*Saturday Evening*,
1832, p. 471; cf. *Physical Theory of Another Life, passim*).

[20] H. Tennyson, op. cit. i. 298n.; *Henry Sidgwick*, pp. 539–40.

[21] G. E. Buckle, *The Letters of Queen Victoria*, 2nd series, iii, 1928, p. 438, (7 Aug.
1883); cf. C. Tennyson: *Alfred Tennyson*, 1949, pp. 336–8.

[22] E. Bickersteth, *Yesterday, Today and Forever*, 1866, pp. 46, 114. The poem had
gone through seventeen editions by 1885. (Cf. H. N. Fairchild, *Religious Trends in
English Poetry*, iv, 1830–80, Morningside Heights, New York, 1957, p. 22n.) P. J.
Bailey's *Festus*, originally published in 1839, and later much expanded, was another

Earlier in the century Robert Pollok's poem, *The Course of Time* (1827), with its dramatic portrayals of heaven, hell, and judgment, enjoyed considerable popularity, and the death-bed and graveyard poetry of the eighteenth century was still widely read. James Montgomery, the hymn-writer, asked, of Robert Blair's poem, *The Grave*: 'Where is the person, owing to the universal interest of the subject, and the striking delineations of character with which the poem abounds, who has passed the tender age of childhood without having been deeply affected by its first perusal?'[23] When Blair's poem was republished in 1858, F. W. Farrar was able to assume in his preface that not only it, but Edward Young's *Night Thoughts*, and the prose works by James Hervey and Charles Drelincourt, *Meditations amongst the tombs* and *The good Christian's preparation against the fears of death*, were standard reading.[24] Death was regarded as possessing a peculiar poetry of its own, and the emotions which it aroused were taken as revelatory of truth about the human condition.[25] Evangelicalism and romanticism were closely linked here, and it is no accident that Young's *Night Thoughts*, which had such a powerful influence on the Romantic Movement on the Continent, should also have been regarded by Charles Wesley as more useful than anything apart from Scripture. If Romanticism saw death as the occasion of significant emotion, Evangelicalism gave death a moral significance. The death-bed was the place where the elect testified to their faith and demonstrated their trust in God. Henry Venn, in *The Complete Duty of Man* (1812), which became one of the standard Evangelical works of moral guidance, urged parents to let their children have experience of Christian death-beds.

If an opportunity could be found of bringing your child to the bedside of a departing saint, this object would infinitely exceed the force of simple instruction. Your child would never forget the composure and fortitude, the lively hope and consolation painted on the very countenance of the Christian; nor his warm expressions of love, and gratitude to the Saviour, for a heaven of peace within, and assurance of pardon, instead of gloomy

---

poem with an eschatological theme, which won the approval of Tennyson, D. G. Rossetti, Matthew Arnold, W. S. Landor, and the New England Transcendentalists. Cf. Robert Birley, *Sunk without Trace*, 1962, pp. 172–208.

[23] J. Holland and J. Everett, *Memoirs of the Life and Writings of James Montgomery*, 1854, i. 38–9.
[24] F. W. Farrar, Preface to R. Blair, *The Grave*, 1858, pp. xi–xii.
[25] Cf. *Tait's Magazine*, xxii, 1855, 'The Poetry of Death', pp. 157–9.

thoughts and foreboding apprehensions, or stupid insensibility to any future existence, the general case of dying men.[26]

There came in some circles to be almost an approved etiquette of dying, which, if followed, was taken as indicating the dying man's salvation. Richard Whateley, the Oriel 'Noetic' and later Archbishop of Dublin, who disapproved of such an outlook, commented on some of its features in his book, *The Future State* (1829). A good death was popularly regarded, he wrote, as one for which there was ample time for preparation, with the sick man having been warned beforehand. A clergyman should be in attendance and the Sacrament received, and the sick man should then express his confidence in his salvation. If the death was then easy and painless, it might be taken as a sign of salvation.[27] The didactic use of death-beds was also found in the High Church tradition, as can be seen in the three volumes of *Death-bed Scenes* by John Warton. His gruesome description of the death of the infidel Mr. Waring is typical.

Mr. Waring . . . was stretched upon the bed of death, and now almost a lifeless corpse. His eyes were closed; his face was black and ghastly; his throat gurgled horribly, as the breath forced a passage through it. I seized his hand, and pressed it. He opened his eyes convulsively, and shut them instantly. He attempted to speak, but no intelligible sound escaped from his lips. Nevertheless his mind was manifestly not yet gone; and I hoped that he still possessed the sense of hearing. I knelt down, therefore, and began in a loud and solemn tone that most beautiful, affecting, and divine prayer, which is prescribed for the sick at the point of their departure. His lips moved, as if he were trying to accompany me. This sign of God's gracious goodness towards him, in the midst of his dreadful agony, for a moment overpowered me, and of necessity I stopped. He began to speak, and I put my head close to catch his words. He said, 'It is very comfortable to me;' and that was all which I could distinctly understand . . . When he had entirely ceased, I resumed the prayer; his lips moved again for a short time, and then became motionless altogether. I grasped his hand, and asked him, if he died in the faith of Jesus Christ. He gave me no sign. Unwilling to witness his last moments, I withdrew; ejaculating to Heaven a petition for the salvation of his soul, and [was] at length relieved by tears.[28]

[26] H. Venn, *The Complete Duty of Man*, 1812, pp. 308–9.

[27] R. Whateley, *The Future State*, 1829, pp. 238–74. Death-bed piety was even to be found in the comparatively uncongenial Unitarian tradition, as a popular tract shows. *Advice from Farmer Trueman to his daughter Mary upon her going into service* (Unitarian Society for promoting Christian Knowledge Tracts, v), 1792, pp. 63–89.

[28] J. Warton, *Death-bed Scenes*, i, 1827², pp. 51–2. As a young man Pusey read Warton (cf. Pusey MSS. E. B. Pusey to Maria Barker, early Oct. 1827).

Not only was death used didactically in this way, the tradition of graveyard musings, most notably represented by James Hervey, continued in articles with such titles as 'Contemplations in P-N churchyard' and 'The Village Churchyard' by Aliquis, which were characteristic of Evangelical journals in the earlier part of the century.[29] Its influence is reflected later in the century in those planners of the new cemeteries who wished to make them morally improving places.[30]

A common theme of Evangelical eschatology was the discussion of the details of the future life. In particular the question whether friends would recognize each other in heaven exercised many writers and preachers. On the one hand it was argued that the doctrine was not scriptural, and that the enjoyment of heaven was linked to the presence of God, who was all in all, and not to the continuation of earthly friendships; but, on the other, it was maintained that the very idea of a future life involved a continuous identity, and that the joy of heaven included gratitude for past mercies, and on both these counts recognition was likely.[31] It was generally concluded that the blessed would recognize one another, and a concern with this question led to the heaven of much popular religious writing being conceived in very sentimental and anthropomorphic terms. Curious arguments were produced in favour of the belief, such as that which asserted that, if the blessed did not recognize each other, how would it be possible for those 'out of every nation and kindred and people and tongue' to praise God according to their nationality?[32] The heavenly reunion was also used as an ethical sanction. 'How can we, who have sainted friends, continue to live in an unregenerate state?' asked one writer, and another invoked the loss of a child: 'Reader, have you a little white-robed warbler in the celestial choir? Are you content to see his face no more for ever? If you die in your present unregenerate state, where your child is you can never come!'[33] Even the Queen and Prince Albert took an interest in the debate. An account in the *Northern Whig* of the last hours of Prince Albert reported that, in the six months before his death, as a consequence of the death of the Queen's mother, he and

---

[29] Many examples of such series are to be found in the *Christian Guardian*, 1809–35.

[30] J. C. Louden, *On the laying-out, planting and management of cemeteries*, 1843, p. 1.

[31] There is a good summary of the arguments on both sides in the *Memoir of James Montgomery*, iv, 1855, pp. 16–20.

[32] *The Recognition of Friends in Heaven: a symposium*, 1866 p. 112.

[33] pp. 306, 308–9.

the Queen had read together a book called *Heaven our Home*. This work had portrayed heaven as an 'etherialised, luminous, material habitation', and had been emphatic both that there would be a reunion of friends in the future state, and that those already departed were much concerned with those still on earth. 'A heaven from which *saint-friendship* and *social intercourse* among those who are in glory are excluded', the author had proclaimed, '*is* not and *cannot* be a suitable abode for us, who have received from God's own plastic hand those *social affections* which we are to possess for ever.'[34]

The religious circles in which the doctrine of the heavenly reunion was popular generally approved of the extraordinary portrayals of the future state in the three so-called 'Judgment Pictures' of John Martin (1789–1854). These were displayed in London in 1855 as 'The most sublime and extraordinary pictures in the world', and attracted large crowds both there, and when they went on tour in subsequent years to the provinces and to the United States.[35] The three pictures were 'The Last Judgment', 'The Great Day of His Wrath', and 'The Plains of Heaven'. The first two were enormous canvasses of apocalyptic terror, and the third portrayed a celestial landscape in iridescent blues and golds peopled with white-robed figures.[36]

No discussion of nineteenth-century ideas concerning the future life would be complete without a mention of the Spiritualist movement, even though this had little direct influence on the doctrine of more orthodox religious thinkers. Where it was valued, it was so largely because it appeared to offer empirical evidence for a future life, and where it was ignored, it was frequently on the grounds that the reported psychic phenomena were the result of satanic agency. In any case it cannot be pretended that the picture of the future life generally presented by Spiritualism was other than banal. The *Saturday Review* sarcastically commented in 1856 that the Spiritualist heaven was a progress through 'a picture gallery of our own deeds, self-delineated'.

[34] *The Last Hours of HRH Prince Albert of Blessed Memory* (reprinted from *The Northern Whig*), n.d., p. 6; [W. Banks] *Heaven our Home*, 1861, pp. iii, 12. The Queen's reading of *Heaven our Home* was taken to be an indication of her leaning towards Spiritualism. (E. Longford, *Victoria, R.I.*, 1964, p. 337). For another example of royal interest in the subject cf. J. Fleming, *Recognition in Eternity* (a sermon preached before the Prince and Princess of Wales, 1892).

[35] T. Balston, *John Martin, 1789–1854*, 1947, pp. 233–53.

[36] 'The Great Day of His Wrath' is now in the Tate Gallery; the other two 'Judgment Pictures' are in the possession of Mrs. Charlotte Frank.

What a picture indeed! All the socks that never came home from the wash, all the boots and shoes which we left behind as worn-out at watering places, all the old hats which we gave to crossing-sweepers have had their pictures taken! (in the spiritual world). What a notion of heaven—an illimitable old-clothes shop, peopled by bores, and not a little infested with knaves.[37]

It was not very surprising, considering the theological debate over the question of everlasting punishment, that mediums generally assured their hearers that such a hell did not exist.[38]

Spiritualism enjoyed considerable popularity in England in the mid-1850s, after the visit of the American medium, Mrs. Hayden, in 1852 had provided the first links with the American movement. In 1853 it was said that nothing was talked about 'but table-movings and spirit rappings', and that one could not dine out without being invited to join in a table-turning session.[39] The movement advanced again after 1859, when the American medium, D. D. Home, came to England for a considerable period. Interest in Spiritualist phenomena was not confined to the middle-class society in which, for the most part, Home and the other American mediums moved. As Dr. Gauld has pointed out, by the mid-1860s Spiritualism had established itself in working-class areas, particularly in the industrial towns of Lancashire and Yorkshire, where it drew a number of its adherents from nonconformity, and Methodism in particular.[40] It was also capable of gathering in those who had previously been renowned for their atheism, as happened at Keighley in Yorkshire. The *Westminster Review* commented on this group, that their behaviour was not inconsistent, for their Spiritualism, as their atheism, was the result of what they considered to fit best with empirically demonstrable facts.[41] In 1870 the London Dialectical Society conducted the first serious inquiry into the phenomena of Spiritualism, and during the 1870s F. W. H. Myers and Henry Sidgwick carried out a series of investigations with a number of mediums. With the foundation of the Society for Psychical Research in 1882 the study of psychic phenomena was finally established in a serious way.[42]

[37] *Saturday Review*, 19 Aug. 1856, p. 269.
[38] Cf. *Spiritual Magazine*, v, 1864, 281–3.
[39] Alan Gauld, *The Founders of Psychical Research*, 1968, p. 67; *Saturday Review* 19 Aug. 1856, p. 268.
[40] Gauld, pp. 74–7.
[41] *Westminster Review*, N.S. xxi, 1862, 89–91.
[42] For a full account cf. Gauld, *passim*.

Some of the concern of Victorian divines with death and questions
related to the future life may well be connected with the fact that
more clergy were ministering in urban situations, where overcrowd-
ing and disease meant a more frequent confrontation with death.
They could not help being aware also that many of those whom
they buried were only nominally Christian, if that, and Anglican
clergy agonized over the legal requirement to use the Prayer Book
burial service for all but suicides. When the new city cemeteries
came into existence, the breaking of the traditional connection of
church and churchyard, linked together at the centre of a community, made clear what was already known to be the case, that in
the towns death no longer occurred within a strong community
framework with a traditional mourning ritual well established, as
was characteristic of village society. New and elaborate mourning
patterns—mutes, black feathers, crape, mourning jewellery—were
developed by the more prosperous middle classes, only to be copied
slightly later by those lower in the social scale. The conspicuous
character which they gave to funerals only served to emphasize the
fact of human mortality in an age with a high death rate. The
cholera epidemics were often devastating, but quite apart from these,
the death rate was high, so that it was possible for a man like Isaac
Williams to begin the dedication of his autobiography to his children
with the phrase 'If any of you should live to manhood'.[43] In 1840 the
annual death rate per 1,000 persons in England and Wales was 22·9;
by 1880 it had only fallen to 20·5, and in 1900 it was still 18·2; but by
1935 it had decreased to 11·7. The decrease first showed itself in
1875, but this was not the case as far as the infant mortality figures
are concerned. In 1840 there were 154 infants of under a year old
who died out of 1,000 live births, and this figure remained fairly
constant until 1900. Only after that did it decrease to the 1935
figure of 57 per 1,000 live births.[44] Evangelical addresses to children
on the subject of death become more comprehensible against this
background, and it would probably be fair to say that, by the time a
child reached the age of ten, it was likely that he would have
experienced at least one death in the family and quite possibly more.[45]

    [43] Isaac Williams, *Autobiography*, 1892, p. vii.
    [44] B. R. Mitchell, *Abstract of British Historical Statistics*, Cambridge, 1962, Tables
12 and 13.
    [45] For notable examples of Evangelical addresses to children on death cf. 'On Death—
addressed to Youth', *Christian Guardian*, i, 1809, 480ff.; 'Address on Death of Miss W.,
to Manchester Sunday School children', ibid., xxi, 1829, 264–6.

The changes in the understanding of Christian eschatology during the nineteenth century, and their relation to the whole history of this area of Christian theology, will be considered in more detail later, but there are certain general considerations, in addition to the ones already mentioned, which must be alluded to here. Since, as we have seen, the doctrine of everlasting punishment was one of the central points of debate, it is not surprising that changing ideas about punishment in the realm of penal theory should have had repercussions on the theological debate. The doctrine of hell was framed in terms of a retributive theory of punishment, the wicked receiving their just deserts, with no thought of the possible reformation of the offender. In so far as there was a deterrent element, it related to the sanction hell provided for ensuring moral conduct during a man's earthly life; in eternity, although it was generally considered that the blessed would know of the sufferings of the damned, the only purpose such knowledge could serve would be to increase the thankfulness of the blessed for having escaped the torments of hell. Quite apart from the difficulties of reconciling an impersonal, retributive hell with the personal God of love of the Christian gospel, many became uneasy about a doctrine which was so clearly retributive in an age whose understanding of punishment was increasingly influenced by the theories of Bentham and the Utilitarians, with their emphasis on deterrence and reformation. Interestingly enough this uneasiness appears more in terms of the general way in which hell was questioned, than in the specific citation of Bentham's ideas, though Edward White, the leader of the conditional immortality school, explicitly attributed the questioning of the traditional school of eschatology to the triumph of Benthamite ideas of punishment.[46] By Benthamite criteria hell was not a successful punishment, for it manifestly did not prevent sin and crime; as an evil, which all punishment was held to be, it inevitably compromised the goodness of God; and an infinite punishment, which was imposed because the offence had been committed against an infinite Being, did not tally with Bentham's contention that in punishment regard should be paid to the intentions and understanding of the offender. It is possible that the speculations of some divines on the possible varying degrees of punishment in hell may have been influenced by Bentham's insistence on the need for varying the intensity and duration of punishment, and his principle of frugality, though we must

[46] E. White, *Life in Christ*, 1878 ed., p. 501.

not forget that there was an earlier tradition of varying punishments in hell, worked out according to the theory of *contrapasso*, the punishment tallying exactly in kind with the crime committed.

At the same time as Benthamite influence was making itself felt, it must not be forgotten that there were those who stood by a retributive theory of justice. Fitzjames Stephen asserted that it was morally right to hate criminals, and it was not surprising that, in another context, he proclaimed that Christian love stopped short at the gates of hell, and hell was 'an essential part of the whole Christian scheme'.[47] Carlyle was likewise an ardent opponent of what he called 'Benevolent-Platform fever' and urged 'hearty hatred' instead of 'general morbid sympathy' for the criminal. The 1860s, in fact, saw a general hardening of attitudes in penal theory. Sir Henry Maine, the legal member of the Council of India, believed that the 'sentimental theory of punishment' had all but collapsed, and that too much attention to the reformatory aspect of punishment had increased the number of criminals. In this he was supported by the 1863 House of Lords' Select Committee on Prison Discipline, and by the fact that only one M.P. criticized the 1865 Prisons Act as representing a 'return to the greater severity of past time'.[48] The old effort to make a distinction between the deserving and the undeserving poor appeared in a new guise when H. A. Bruce, the Liberal Home Secretary, spoke in 1869 of reclaimable and irreclaimable criminals, of whom the former should be given every assistance and encouragement to reform, whilst the latter should be hunted down without mercy. Some divines made a similar distinction between sinners who would repent given an adequate opportunity—for instance, the heathen and those from particularly unfavourable environments— for whom future probation ought to be allowed, and those so sunk in sin that no future probation would change them, and who ought therefore to be annihilated, or consigned to hell, depending on the particular eschatology adopted.

In the more specifically theological realm the eschatology which nineteenth-century Christianity inherited was an eschatology of the immortality of the soul, though alongside this there had also developed a secular eschatology of the progress of the world. The notion of progress had also been taken up into some of the thinking concerning immortality, where the destiny of man was conceived as

[47] Quoted in Sir Walter Moberly, *The Ethics of Punishment*, 1968, pp. 84, 329.
[48] Cf. W. R. L. Burn, *The Age of Equipoise*, 1964, pp. 179–93.

INTRODUCTION   15

an unending progress rather than an arrival at a static perfection.
As A. O. Lovejoy has pointed out, this concept is already fore-
shadowed by Henry More, the Cambridge Platonist, with his insistence that the dead passed through a series of carefully graduated
stages, rather than leaping immediately from terrestrial imperfection
to celestial beatitude, and Addison and Leibniz stood in the same
tradition, with their hope of man's perpetual progress to ever new
pleasures and perfections.[49] Paul Tillich has commented on this
notion of progress, which remained powerful throughout the nineteenth century, suggesting that its roots lay in the replacement of a
static, hierarchical society by a bourgeois society, whose functioning
was dependent on the ability of man to go beyond his allotted place.
In order to achieve such an ordered social progress it was important
for a man to be able to presuppose that the operations of nature
were both regular and calculable. But this reliability was only
achieved by the abolition of all critical 'boundary line concepts' so
that only a reasonable religion remained.

Thus the existential elements of finitude, despair, anxiety, as well as grace
were set aside. What was left was the reasonable religion of progress,
belief in a transcendent God who exists alongside of reality, and who does
not do much in the world after he has created it. In this world left to its
own powers moral demands remain, morals in terms of bourgeois
righteousness and stability. Belief in the immortality of the soul also
remains, namely, the ability of man to continue his improvement pro-
gressively after death.[50]

It was an immortality of self-realization, rather than an immortality
of salvation, to which man looked forward, and so we find that in
many nineteenth-century works on eschatology the future life is
envisaged as a time of ever-increasing powers of mind and knowledge
of the universe, attendance at some celestial university. Like all
immortalist doctrines, however, it presupposed the existence of an
isolable soul, an essential man, which, divorced from the material
world, was able to be as truly man as man in the body. It was also an
individualist doctrine, which allowed little place for any eschatology
which spoke of the destiny of the universe as a whole.

Much Christian eschatology in the nineteenth century was the

[49] A. O. Lovejoy, *The Great Chain of Being*, New York (Harper Torchbooks ed.),
1960, pp. 246–8.
[50] P. Tillich, *Perspectives on 19th and 20th Century Protestant Theology*, 1967,
pp. 47, 48.

eschatology of debased Calvinism, and the reaction to it was in part the reaction to a determinist theology of divine decrees. Already in the eighteenth century Methodism had taken its stand against Calvinist exclusivism, proclaiming that Christ died for all, and thus making it clear that the gospel was universal and was to be preached to all men. Although, as can be seen from John Wesley's controversy with William Law, universal redemption did not imply universal salvation, both were linked in their refusal to limit God's redeeming love. The reaction against exclusivist theologies was helped eventually by the missionary movement. Large numbers of Christians became aware of the immense numbers which had to be considered as destined for hell if an exclusivist theology was to be maintained, and more liberal positions were adopted.[51] The discovery by many missionaries that threats of hell were not necessarily the most effective way of proclaiming the gospel also played its part in making the Calvinist hell less credible.

But perhaps the most important change in eschatology was the more personal understanding of Christianity which was characteristic of the nineteenth century. This new emphasis clearly owed something to the subjectivism of the romantic movement and idealist philosophy, but it also represented the recovery of an emphasis on the existential elements of religion, and sharpened the protest against an eschatology which was conceived as the end-term of a mechanical process. Although it could degenerate into sentimentalism, it could equally well be transformed into revivalist fervour, or into the appeal of a Newman for that personal holiness without which no man could see God. Maurice's insistence that salvation was salvation from sin and not from punishment is part of the same outlook.

The changes in eschatology and the interest of the nineteenth century in the theme of the future life are undoubted, and, since the debate about hell played such an important part in the Victorian crisis of faith, it is not without interest to survey the way in which the changes in eschatology arose. How did the various denominational traditions of Christianity react to the challenges to accepted orthodoxy in this area of belief, and in what way did their reactions

---

[51] Cf., as a protest against exclusivist theologies, the article, 'By whom will Heaven be tenanted?' in the Unitarian *Christian Reformer* (vii, 1840, 97–101). This argues that, according to Congregationalist theologians who professed a Calvinist theology, 10,500,000 persons would be saved and 938,000,000 damned.

reflect inherent tensions in the established pattern of Christian eschatological teaching? This is the major concern of the chapters which follow. Inevitably the opinions which are discussed are, for the most part, those of the theologically informed, which in practice tends to mean the clergy, or at least those with an official position within a denomination, but it is possible from time to time to take a wider view by a consideration of the public reaction to some of the more notable controversies. The debate itself was largely concentrated between the years 1830 and 1880, and this is, consequently, the period which is given the greatest attention, but in several instances, notably Unitarianism, it has been necessary to have an earlier starting point. Since almost every divine who published a volume of sermons during the century included one or two on the theme of death and the future life, a truly comprehensive treatment would be impossible, but, by drawing on more systematic works on the subject, and a detailed consideration of the major controversies, with an examination of related correspondence, a reasonably accurate picture may be obtained.

II   The Historical Development
of Christian Eschatology

THE pattern of the nineteenth-century debates about eschatology
was not determined by critical attacks on the doctrines of everlasting
punishment and the immortality of the soul alone; it also reflected
the particular tensions inherent in the accepted eschatology of
Western Christendom. Any account of the development of eschatology in the nineteenth century must, therefore, be prefaced by a
brief survey of the history of Christian eschatology in order that these
tensions may be fully understood.

The Christian understanding of the Last Things emerged out of
the faith of Judaism, and the eschatology of the New Testament
reflects the already divergent traditions of Jewish eschatology. In the
New Testament period Judaism both made affirmations about the
hoped for future of the individual and the community, and was also
an eschatological faith in a wider sense, in that it was centred on
definite, saving acts of God in the past, which were the basis of
faith in God's future saving activity. Israel's hope for the future
could be conceived in narrowly nationalistic terms, by which God
would fulfil the covenant relationship which he had established with
his people by subduing their enemies, and establishing them in a
position of political and material power. But it was also possible for
this eschatological hope to have a wider reference. The emphasis
could fall not on what God was going to do for Israel in the future,
on the basis of what he had done for Israel in the past, but on what
God would do for all men through Israel in the future, on the basis
of what he had done for Israel in the past. Whilst this belief was slow
to develop, it is clearly to be found in the Old Testament, and
emerges as a hope for the world, which was to be realized with the
coming of the Messiah.

Alongside this corporate hope, and this cosmic eschatology, there
developed gradually, first a sense of the responsibility of the individual for his own actions, and then a growing conviction that the
relationship which had been established between God and the individual believer was such that God would maintain it even in the

face of death. The belief that the individual found his future in the continuance of that covenant between God and his people, in which he had also shared, was undoubtedly part of the reason why it was only comparatively late in the development of Judaism that an individual hope of a life beyond death emerged. Moreover, the persistent struggles of the prophets with various forms of the cult of the dead may also have contributed to a suspicion about such doctrines.[1] As was to be expected with a doctrine which remained closely linked with a covenant theology, the hope of the future life was at first a hope for the righteous alone; and even that was tentative. It was the Maccabean revolt, with its accompanying martyrdoms, which strengthened this hope of a future life for the righteous. As men came to believe that the suffering of the martyrs would be recompensed in a life beyond death, so in the apocalyptic literature of the period this hope of a future life became more general, and part of God's vindication of his people. Inasmuch as the future life was linked with the redressing of the moral balance there was a corresponding development of belief in the future life of the wicked. Not only would those faithful to God receive a reward for their faithfulness after death; the enemies of God's people would also receive their just deserts. The development of this theme in apocalyptic literature, with its dramatic revelations of God's powerful intervention at the end of the world, removed the decisive Divine judgment from the course of events within this world to the final resolution of the issues of good and evil at its end, a point which was also the beginning of the Messianic age. The development of Jewish eschatology was undoubtedly influenced from Persian sources, and two recurring themes are to be traced to them, the myth of the end of the world by fire, and the division of world history into aeons ending in a catastrophic apocalypse.[2]

In Judaism at the time of Christ two conceptions of the future life were current, the resurrection of the body and the immortality of the soul. The resurrection of the body was characteristic of traditional, Palestinian Judaism, and was in accordance with its opposition to a dualistic picture of man as consisting of body and soul. Man was an 'ensouled body', whose power of living was derived entirely

---

[1] Cf. R. Bultmann (ed.), *Life and Death* (Kittel Bible Key Words), E. T. 1965, p. 11 and *passim*.

[2] Cf. M. Eliade, *Cosmos and History* (Harper Torchbooks ed.), New York, 1959, p. 124.

from God, the source of all life. When a man lost that power of life when God 'took away his breath', man died, and the only existence he might then have as an individual was a shadowy existence in *Sheol*, the place of departed spirits. As sickness was seen as a weak form of life, so death was considered as the weakest form of life, if it was to be considered as life at all. To hope for a future life was, therefore, to expect that God would raise the dead from this shadowy form of existence, or indeed from non-existence, by once more bestowing on them his power of life. In this resurrection of the dead men would share in an eternal life bestowed by God, in a state in which their historical continuity would be maintained, but in which their being would be transformed. It was an apocalyptic hope in a moment of divine intervention when God's power would be decisively manifested, and men would be raised to a new life in a renewed heaven and earth, though there were many different conceptions as to who would be raised, the stages by which the resurrection would be accomplished, and the precise details of the resurrection life.[3] By contrast in Hellenistic Judaism the future life was thought of in terms of the immortality of the soul, and the resurrection of the body was rarely mentioned. The future life was dependent, not so much on God's dramatic intervention at the last day, as on the events of this life which carried with them their appropriate rewards and punishments, and which led to a future life immediately after death. It was at once a more spiritualized and individualized eschatology, in which the future of the individual was seen apart from both his bodily existence and the future of the world.

Primitive Christianity inherited both these eschatologies, and many of the tensions inherent in traditional Christian eschatology may be traced to attempts to harmonize these two understandings. In Christianity they were brought into relationship with the Christian belief that in Jesus God had decisively intervened on behalf of his people, and had made this clear above all in raising Jesus from the dead. Resurrection from the dead was, however, an event which belonged strictly to the last times of God's decisive action, and, if Jesus had been so raised, these had, therefore, begun. Yet manifestly God's purposes were not yet fulfilled, for the end of the world had not yet come. What is more, Jesus himself had looked

---

[3] Bultmann, pp. 44-5; cf. W. Pannenburg, *Jesus—God and Man*, E. T. 1968, pp. 88ff.

forward to a glorious consummation, 'the coming of the Son of Man'. The faith of the early Christian communities was therefore directed towards the expected triumphant return of Christ. As long as this was the case, it was possible for questions concerning the future of the individual after death to be subsumed under the end of the world and the fate of mankind as a whole, which was imminently to be decided by the return of Christ. Indeed, it seems that, in some circles of Christian believers at least, it was apparently supposed that no Christians would die before the return of Christ. When this did occur it caused bewilderment, as we see from Paul's attempts to deal with the problem in I Thessalonians.[4] As Christian hopes of an early return of Christ remained unfulfilled adjustments had to be made in Christian eschatology, and there are indications in the New Testament of a growing acceptance of an 'age of the Church' as part of the divine plan. The effect and extent of this changed outlook has been very differently estimated. Martin Werner has argued that it produced a radical transformation of Christian teaching, holding that the earliest believers regarded themselves as the elect of the last generation, whose peculiar privilege it was to share in the millennium, the thousand-year reign of the Messiah, but that this idea was made untenable when Jesus did not immediately return in glory. 'The idea of an ordained Messianic salvation-period' was then necessarily 'merged in that of the subsequent blessedness of the Kingdom of God, as an eternal consummation'.[5] The future of the individual became more important, and, at the very least, some account had to be given of the intermediate state between death and the resurrection at the Last Day. The basic choices were really limited to two. According to one theory the individual soul remained in a state of suspended animation, 'slept', until the Last Day when the resurrection took place and it was reunited with its body, which meant, as far as the individual was concerned, that the moment of death and the day of resurrection appeared coincidental. The alternative view held that the soul remained conscious in the intermediate state, during which time it was almost invariably considered to experience a foretaste of its future destiny. It was thus possible to develop an eschatology on the lines of that already adumbrated in Hellenistic Judaism, with its

[4] 4: 13ff.
[5] M. Werner, *The Formation of Christian Dogma*, E. T. 1957, p. 284. Cf. J. Daniélou: *A History of Early Christian Doctrine*, i, E. T. 1964, pp. 377–405, for the importance of millenarianism in Jewish Christianity.

picture of a judgment at death followed by immediate rewards and punishments, with the Last Day and the resurrection playing a minor role.

For Christianity the tension between the two eschatologies was perhaps more acute than in Judaism, for the figure of Christ was central to Christian eschatology, whichever of the two patterns was adopted, and controlled the ways in which they could be related. The Resurrection of Christ meant that the resurrection of the body became a cardinal affirmation of the Christian faith, and thus an eschatology of the immortality of the soul could never entirely dispense with the resurrection at the Last Day. Moreover, the gospel tradition quite clearly emphasized the return of Christ in glory and in judgment at the end of time. On the other hand, there were indications in the gospels, and particularly in St. Luke, with his recording of the parable of the rich man and Lazarus, and Jesus' promise of an immediate entry into paradise to the penitent thief, which indicated a judgment and a future life which began, not at the Last Day, but at the moment of death. St. Paul also spoke variously of the resurrection at the Last Day as the final consummation to which the Christian looked forward, of death as a sleep, and of death as a departing to live with Christ, and these are never completely integrated. It would, therefore, be wrong to suppose that a coherent eschatology could be derived from the New Testament, and rash, in the light of the already existing differences within Judaism, to suppose that there was originally a coherent pattern which was subsequently confused as a result of the hope of the immediate return of Christ being disappointed. Rather there were originally conflicting eschatologies, into which the figure of Christ was fitted, and which were only somewhat uneasily related, although the forms which traditional eschatology finally assumed were undoubtedly influenced by the need to adjust to a situation in which the expectation of the immediate return of Christ had been disappointed.[6]

The linking of the two eschatologies remained awkward. If, as came to be generally accepted, a man entered on his future life immediately after death, and experienced in that life a foretaste of his ultimate destiny, the resurrection hope only played a minor role. In the Hellenistic Church the influence of both Gnostic and Platonist ideas contributed to a view of man which exalted the soul over the

[6] Cf. P. Althaus, *Die Letzten Dinge*, Gütersloh, 1964[9], pp. 141–4; Werner, pp. 291–2; cf. S. G. F. Brandon, *The Judgment of the Dead*, 1967, pp. 74, 110–12.

body, and emphasized the redemption of the soul apart from the body as the essential part of man's salvation. It was not surprising that the particular judgment of the individual soul at death became more important than the Last Judgment, and that the future of the individual was treated in isolation from that of the world. An image, such as the renewing fire of judgment, which was originally associated with the Last Day, later became linked with the particular judgment after death, and so contributed to the development of theories of purgatory: the purifying fire through which all had to pass who wished to achieve the sanctity necessary for communion with God. The judgment at the Last Day was reduced to a declaratory judgment on the individual, when the sentence already passed at the particular judgment was made fully known, and to a judgment on the nations. A clear example of the substitution of the particular judgment of death for the judgment of the Last Day can be seen in the fifteenth-century devotional classic, *The Imitation of Christ*, in which 'the coming of the Son of Man' is specifically referred to the moment of death: 'Plenty of people die quite suddenly, without any warning; the Son of Man will appear just when we are not expecting him.'[7] The Bull *Benedictus Deus* (1336) of Benedict XII stated definitively that it was possible for a man to experience fully heaven or hell immediately after death. These are late examples, but they show the final stages in the evolution of the accepted eschatology of Western Christendom. The pattern which was established was, that after death the departed soul immediately underwent the particular judgment, and was assigned to heaven, hell, or purgatory, there to remain, experiencing joy or pain as the case might be, until the Day of Judgment. At the Day of Judgment the resurrection took place and souls were once more united with their bodies to be assigned either to heaven, to enjoy the perfection of bliss, or to hell, to suffer just punishment. The punishment suffered in hell consisted both of the deprivation of God (*poena damni*) and positive torment (*poena sensus*), and the punishment would be apt—'the pattern of a man's sins will be the pattern of his punishment', as the *Imitation of Christ* puts it.[8]

Eschatology in the Western Church was also affected by the theological debates about election to grace and the possibility of the

---

[7] *Imitation of Christ*, I. xxiii. 3.

[8] I. xxiv. 3; cf. Aquinas: *Summa Theologica*, II. ii. lxi. 4. This paralleling of punishment and sin, known as *contrapasso*, is, of course, strikingly exemplified in Dante.

existence of a 'pure church'. The Latin genius for legal understanding also played its part. *Extra ecclesiam nulla salus,* with its
particularist emphasis, was characteristic of the west, in contrast to
the broader and more universalist tradition of Origen and the
Cappadocian Fathers, who hoped for an ultimate restoration of all
things. Doctrines of the atonement, which presented Christ's death
in terms of a judicial transaction between two Persons of the Trinity,
and which used the language of satisfaction, influenced the development of the doctrine of purgatory. This was at times presented
almost exclusively in the quantitative terms of the nature and
amount of the satisfaction it was left for man to make in addition to
that achieved by Christ on Calvary. The same legalist emphasis
influenced the doctrine of hell, through the argument that, since sin
is an offence against an Infinite Being, the punishment of it must
necessarily be infinite. This argument, which frequently appears in
the nineteenth-century debates, was clearly derived from feudal
practice, where the status of person against whom the offence was
committed was often of more importance in determining the punishment than the offence itself. Inevitably the tangling of ideas of satisfaction with eschatology produced an emphasis on an impersonal and
quantitative approach to many of the major theological issues. In
addition, questions of celestial and infernal map-making, and of the
exact nature of the punishments of hell, tended to oust the genuine
theological concerns of man's relationship with God, and to sever the
connection of eschatology and life in such a way as to make eschatology merely the ultimate sanction of virtue. This impersonal approach
was reinforced by a theology which attempted to deal with the
question of evil by speaking of the moral perfection of the universe
in aesthetic terms, as Augustine did in speaking of the necessity of
shadows to bring out the beauty of a picture when justifying the
torments of hell as part of the goodness of God's creation.[9]

The Western eschatological synthesis, as it had been developed
by the end of the Middle Ages, was never entirely satisfactory either
in relation to the New Testament or in internal consistency. The
assimilation of the Last Day to the day of a man's death played its
part in the development of the *ars moriendi,* the art of dying well,
which was characteristic of much late medieval popular devotion. If
death and judgment were all but coincidental, the state in which a
soul was at the moment of death became of vital importance in

[9] John Hick, *Evil and the God of Love,* 1966, pp. 93–5.

whether it would be assigned to heaven or to hell. To die well became almost more important in some respects than to live well.[10] The Last Judgment became in practice an ethical symbol of the ultimate accountability of all mankind, rather than that which was the consummation of the individual and the world. The primitive sense of the communion of saints, the unity of the whole Church in heaven and on earth in Christ, remained, but the expressions of that sense of communion, such as the remembrance of the departed at the eucharist, were altered in emphasis. The solemn commemoration of the departed combined with a prayer for their well-being became supplication for those in purgatory to be delivered from their torment.

The effect of the Reformation on the accepted eschatological pattern was, in general, to alter the details of the picture whilst leaving the outlines intact. Purgatory, of course, disappeared because of its association with indulgences, and its connection with ideas of satisfaction which offended against the principle of justification by faith. If Christ saved absolutely and entirely, then ideas of a further satisfaction to be made through suffering in purgatory were inadmissible. Similarly requiem masses and prayers for the dead, which seemed to make man's salvation dependent on human works and not on faith in Christ could not be countenanced. Luther attempted to recover the primitive perspective with its emphasis on the importance of the Last Day, though his acceptance of death as the separation of soul and body meant that he still had to include an intermediate state in his eschatology. The soul, he argued, was, during this time, in a deep, dreamless sleep, without consciousness or perception, though yearning to be reunited with its body. Just as a man asleep is still alive, though he may appear lifeless, so the soul in this condition could be described as alive to God. But the day of resurrection would be the day of the resurrection of the whole man, and not just of the body only.[11] By contrast Calvin, who was more influenced by Platonism, was firmly opposed to ideas of the sleep of the soul, and even wrote a treatise, the *Psychopannychia* (1542), against it. Biblical references to death as a sleep were not to be taken literally, but as metaphor which showed how the bitterness of death had been mitigated for the believer. The intermediate state

---

[10] For the fifteenth-century obsession with death cf. J. Huizinga, *The Waning of the Middle Ages*, 1965 ed., pp. 134–46.

[11] P. Althaus, op. cit. pp. 146–8; ibid. *The Theology of Martin Luther*, E. T., Philadelphia, 1966, pp. 404–25.

was a period of waiting, but one in which the soul shared in the experiences of joy and sorrow, though in a temporary and provisional way.[12]

The disappearance of purgatory in the Reformed confessions of faith left Protestants in the position of maintaining that all men were divided into two categories, those whose ultimate destination was heaven and those whose ultimate destination was hell. This absolute alternative, whilst it corresponded to the experience of the 'twice-born' religiously, and to the doctrine of predestination, was to others at variance with common human experience. Most men were neither so transparently good, or so transparently believing, that they could be said unequivocally to be destined for heaven, nor, on the other hand, were most men so clearly evil that they were destined for hell. The doctrine of purgatory corresponded, at one level of experience at least, more exactly with the way men lived, than an absolute alternative. This makes it the more surprising that there is little evidence to show that the absence of a doctrine of purgatory contributed to a decline of belief in hell until the nineteenth century.[13]

It must not be forgotten, however, that the absolute choice of Protestant eschatology reflected the intense personal experience of those who framed it. As Basil Hall has written of Calvin:

Because of his consciousness that God dominated him, Calvin became a man mastered by the idea of God's sovereignty; he lived for God; all things, all men existed for God alone, and this world was but the theatre of God's glory where in all things man must say 'soli Deo gloria'. For Calvin there is no liberty of second causes, and there are no fortuitous accidents . . . What is new with Calvin is the absolute and unqualified assertion of God's sovereignty and man's total corruption as fundamental to right belief.[14]

It was this which was the background to the doctrine of predestination, which was intended 'to replace the authority and finality of the Roman Church and its sacramental system by the objective fact of God's eternal decree in Christ, which also provided a full

---

[12] Cf. H. Quistorp, *Calvin's Doctrine of the Last Things*, 1955, *passim*; Althaus, *Die Letzten Dinge*, pp. 148–9.

[13] D. P. Walker, in his study of seventeenth-century discussions of hell, argues that the disappearance of purgatory must have been personally painful to many Protestants, but is only able to cite two examples. *The Decline of Hell*, 1964, pp. 59–60.

[14] B. Hall, *John Calvin, Humanist and Theologian*, 1956, p. 20.

personal assurance of salvation'.[15] But, where this personal experience was lacking, the eternal decrees of God could only appear as the basis of a determinist system, from which there was no possibility of escape, and which appeared to operate independently of a man's personal choices and motives. Calvin believed in double predestination, that is that some men were predestined to reprobation as well as the elect being predestined to salvation, but he was always careful to talk of the workings of Divine Providence with a reserve which acknowledged their mystery.[16] His successors were not always so careful, and Beza's assertion of supralapsarianism, the doctrine that maintains that God decreed the election and reprobation of individual men before the Fall of Adam, had the effect of abolishing any possible connection between moral choice and salvation and left men faced with an inscrutable and apparently arbitrary Providence. A man who did not have the experience of knowing himself lifted out of a morass of sin and despair by God's sovereign grace could only consider himself reprobate, or search desperately for some sign that he might be numbered amongst the elect. The government of the universe could easily appear mechanistic and impersonal, and an emphasis on predestination was certainly difficult to hold with any evolutionary or developmental view of personality.

Doctrines of predestination pressed to the extreme can easily become antinomian, and the idea that the elect were free from the moral law was always a danger in Calvinist circles. It was moreover difficult to find a place for the painstaking search for sanctity in a thorough-going predestinarian theology. It is not, therefore, surprising that pietist groups, who were concerned with both sanctification and a more personal and 'enthusiastic' religion, often reacted against the impersonal determinism of Calvinist theology, and adopted a theology which was Arminian in its basic position. In other words, they rejected the Calvinist doctrine that the salvation won by Christ was for the elect only, a position which Calvinists maintained on the grounds that it would be an infringement of God's omnipotence to hold that Christ died for some men who were not subsequently saved. Against this Arminians argued that to restrict the salvation won by Christ's atoning death to those men already predestined to salvation limited God's love, and believed rather that Christ died for all men, but whether a man would in fact be saved depended on his response to Christ's offer of salvation, and

[15] p. 21.   [16] For Calvin on predestination, cf. *Institutes*, III. 21. 5.

his intention to live a holy life. Sanctification was not just the evidence of justification, but was the making actual of the righteousness which Christ made possible in a man's life. It pointed, therefore, to a developmental understanding of salvation, and hence to the possibility of the intermediate state being seen as a time of sanctification.

Although Luther in particular, and to some extent Calvin, had attempted to restore a theological importance to the Last Day, both Protestant orthodoxy and the mainstream of pietism reverted to an emphasis on the day of death as the decisive point in eschatology. Suspicion of the millenarian excesses of the Anabaptists, and other representatives of the 'radical Reformation', combined with the influence of the older tradition of eschatology, contributed to this, as did the highly individualist aspect of the doctrine of justification by faith. As J. P. Martin has written, in Protestant orthodoxy, 'the unity of the possession of salvation and its consummation was essentially only for the individual. The basic importance of the consummation of the Kingdom as a collectivity disappeared'. The result was an individualized eschatology, the Last Judgment seen as a condemnation of the ungodly, and a direct linking of the bliss of heaven with the moment of death.[17] It is not surprising that this very anthropocentric eschatology gave an increasingly important place to the immortality of the soul as the major part of Christian teaching about the future life. It harmonized with the optimism of the eighteenth century concerning man, and it provided common ground with Deism, as is indicated by Bishop Butler's use of it to open his argument in the *Analogy of Religion*.[18] In the late seventeenth and early eighteenth centuries arguments based on the immortality of the soul were more frequently employed as an ethical sanction than those based on the Last Judgment, and this may in part account for the violence of the reaction to the denial of man's natural immortality by Henry Dodwell at the beginning of the eighteenth century.[19]

The common affirmation of immortality by both Christians and adherents of rational religion in the eighteenth century meant that it was this aspect of belief about a future life which was the least likely to come under attack. Controversy centred upon the doctrine

---

[17] J. P. Martin, *The Last Judgment in Protestant Theology from Orthodoxy to Ritschl*, 1963, pp. 12, 15–16.

[18] pp. 44–45; G. R. Cragg, *From Puritanism to the Age of Reason*, 1966 ed., p. 66.

[19] Cf. F. Brokesby, *Life of Mr. Henry Dodwell*, 1715, II, p. 608.

of hell, which, apart from anything else, was so grossly offensive to the optimism characteristic of eighteenth-century natural religion. The topic had already been the subject of debate in the seventeenth century, and Dr. D. P. Walker, in his book *The Decline of Hell*, has both recounted the main controversies and analysed the arguments involved. Many of these same arguments recur in the nineteenth-century disputes, though it is interesting to note that it was still possible for the French preacher, Lacordaire, to maintain in the early 1850s that objections to the doctrine of hell were a new thing.[20] It may well be that one of the reasons for Lacordaire's remarks is the secrecy that surrounded any discussion of hell, for the denial of hell was regarded as subversive, because of its importance as the chief moral sanction. Men were wary of publishing their doubts about hell because of the personal risk involved in admitting to disbelieving in hell, and because of genuine moral scruples concerning the collapse of the fabric of society if such views became widespread.[21] Nevertheless the theological tradition which had looked to a restoration of all things as the ultimate goal of the history of the world and of man had never been entirely forgotten, though it had often been the preserve of sectarian groups outside the main body of the Church. The reprinting of the works of Origen in the late fifteenth and early sixteenth centuries, and the use made of them by Erasmus in his own works, made one of the classic statements of this tradition widely available, and Walker has suggested that this was one of the contributory factors in the criticism of the doctrine of hell. This theological tradition certainly had an influence on groups like the Philadelphians, and the radical pietists in Germany, whose hope of universal salvation was made more widely known in England in the eighteenth century through the writings of William Law.[22]

In the seventeenth century, alongside this older theological tradition, which was critical of the doctrine of hell, a growing minority began to question the justice of everlasting punishment, because of their doubts concerning the whole of the retributive theory of punishment. Since, after the Last Day, hell could no longer be said to serve any deterrent purpose, as men had been judged and finally assigned to heaven or hell, everlasting punishment could only be justified on the grounds that it was a just retribution

[20] Lacordaire, *Oeuvres*, IV, Paris, 1861, pp. 544–5.
[21] D. P. Walker, op. cit., pp. 4–7.
[22] p. 13.

for the enormity of the offence. This in itself was generally estimated on the old feudal ground that an offence against an Infinite Being merited infinite punishment. But, although the retributive theory of punishment was logically of more importance in upholding the doctrine of hell, it was the deterrent value of hell as a future possibility used to ensure virtuous living in the present which was more commonly preached. This deterrent aspect had also been attacked in the seventeenth century, and on grounds which were also to reappear in the nineteenth-century controversies. As Walker has pointed out, there were three main grounds of attack: that savage punishments were both self-defeating and ineffective; that virtue induced as a result of such threatened punishment was unworthy of the name; and that nobody who admitted to believing in hell seriously considered it, in all its horror, as a possibility for himself.[23]

Two other points also emerged from these early debates, which were to be echoed many times in later discussions. The first concerned the close connection between eternal punishment and the Atonement maintained by some theologians. To deny hell was more than likely to involve the denial of the divinity of Christ, for, it was argued, that the expiation offered by Christ was infinite in character, and therefore was sufficient to satisfy the infinite punishment demanded for an offence against an Infinite Being. But in order that the expiation achieved by Christ should have this infinite character it was necessary that he should be fully divine. Therefore Arians and Socinians, who denied the full divinity of Christ, also consistently denied the need for an infinite expiation, and man's liability to suffer the pains of an infinite hell, and orthodox controversialists were quick to see the implications of the Arian and Socinian denial of hell for other areas of theology. Those who denied hell were held to belittle sin and to threaten the moral foundations of society, a charge later brought against Unitarian divines. The second point to emerge was the defence of hell as a truth which men must accept simply because God had revealed it, and comparisons were often drawn with the doctrine of the Trinity, as a doctrine which was believed though not fully comprehensible. Again this argument was to recur in later discussions, but it is unlikely that those who found hell morally abhorrent were likely to find it any less so by being told it must simply be accepted.[24]

[23] pp. 40–3.   [24] pp. 26–8.

Eschatology was, thus, not a new subject of controversy in the nineteenth century, but there is little doubt that it was discussed more publicly, and perhaps with more vehemence, than in any previous age.

III The Contribution
of the Unitarians

FOR most of the nineteenth century Unitarianism served as a kind of halfway house for those who found themselves no longer able to accept orthodox Christian belief and who did not as yet wish to pass entirely into agnosticism. Its radical tradition and theological liberalism meant that many of the questions which were to agitate churchmen and dissenters alike in the course of the century had already been openly debated and discussed within Unitarianism in the late eighteenth and early nineteenth centuries. These early controversies provide an illuminating background to the more widely known disputes in the orthodox denominations.

The stand of Unitarians on the position that Trinitarian orthodoxy was a corruption of original Christianity had affinities with the older desire for a pure Church, but Unitarian theology could be coloured either by Deist influence, or by a biblicism, which differed from that of Evangelicalism only in interpretation. The central feature of Unitarian theology was, of course, the denial of the Divinity of Christ coupled with an affirmation of the Unity of God, a doctrine which Unitarians thought was imperilled by both traditional Trinitarianism and theories of the Atonement which apparently opposed Christ to the Father. This emphasis on the Divine Unity was carried over into eschatology, where any ultimate dualism was rigorously eschewed, and either annihilationism or universal restoration was advocated, though many Unitarians were too much children of their age to forego entirely notions of future retribution.

The links between the denominational Unitarianism of the late eighteenth and early nineteenth centuries, and the Socinianism of the sixteenth and seventeenth centuries are tenuous, but both held an unorthodox eschatology. The annihilationist doctrine put forward by the earliest Socinians is thought to have been derived from the combined influences of the speculations of Jewish and Anabaptist circles in Italy and Erasmian biblical criticism.[1] Later Unitarians, however, preferred a universalist to an annihilationist eschatology,

[1] *The Decline of Hell*, pp. 73–6.

and their theology was marked more by the influence of John Locke and the Arians and Deists of the Enlightenment than by the older Socinian tradition. Indeed, as Basil Willey has suggested, Unitarianism often differed from Deism only in its greater organization and the character of its adherents. 'Deism was largely the perquisite of "gentlemen", Unitarianism was bourgeois. Deism was professed by isolated free-thinkers, while the Unitarian Congregation, having evolved by perceptible stages from the older forms of dissent, retained a strong group consciousness as a religious fellowship.'[2]

As a distinct denomination Unitarianism began in 1773, the year in which Theophilus Lindsey, then the incumbent of Catterick in Yorkshire, seceded from the Church of England after the Feathers Tavern Petition had failed to secure any relaxation in the requirement of clerical subscription to the Thirty-nine Articles. Even though Unitarian tenets had long been widespread amongst both the General Baptists and the Presbyterians, Lindsey had no desire to ally himself with these groups and preferred to set up a new denomination on the basis of Unitarianism alone. He hoped that this would encourage other Establishment clergy to join him. His expectations of an exodus from the Church of England were not, however, fulfilled, though by 1778 he had gathered enough adherents to be able to open a chapel in Essex Street in London.[3] Eight years later the New College at Hackney was opened with Joseph Priestley as one of the lecturers. The college acted as a magnet to students in other dissenting colleges who were finding their traditional Calvinism restricting and irksome, and its radicalism soon became a byword. Occasions like the entertaining of Tom Paine to dinner gained the college considerable notoriety, and seemed to prove that the fears of orthodox believers, that Unitarianism was next door to infidelity and the bedfellow of a seditious radicalism, were justified.[4]

THE INFLUENCE OF HARTLEY AND PRIESTLEY

Although Theophilus Lindsey was the founder of Unitarianism as a denomination, the shaping of Unitarian thology was not his work, but that of Joseph Priestley, celebrated equally as a scientist, philosopher, and divine. Priestley's influence was such that, as

---

[2] *The Eighteenth-Century Background*, 1950, p. 183.
[3] T. W. Belsham, *Memoirs of Theophilus Lindsey*, 1873[2], p. 67.
[4] J. Kenrick, *A biographical memoir of Charles Wellbeloved*, 1860, pp. 21–9; cf. D. P. Walker, *The Decline of Hell*, pp. 4–6.

James Martineau remarked, he set out the pattern of Unitarian orthodoxy for generations to come, and the order of his own theological inquiries became established as the conventional pattern of Unitarian theology, which always began with the question about the person of Christ and ended with Universal Restoration.[5] Priestley did not adopt universalism until the end of his life, although he had long been familiar with it from its place in the work on which, more than any other, he based his theology, David Hartley's *Observations on Man*.[6] Priestley had first come to know this from a reference he had discovered in Doddridge's divinity lectures, and ended by rating Hartley next to Scripture. It was from Hartley that Priestley derived his characteristic materialist psychology.[7]

Hartley stands, as Basil Willey has said, 'in the apostolical succession of the English physico-theologians'.[8] He had originally been destined for the Church, but had turned instead to medicine when his doubts on eternal punishment did not allow him to proceed to ordination. His *Observations on Man* appeared in 1749. In the earlier part of the work Hartley discusses the nature of man and the nature of mental phenomena. Following Locke he maintains that all mental phenomena are grounded in the physical in such a way that the mind is only formed and operates as a consequence of external stimuli, and he uses Newton's theory of 'Vibrations' as an explanatory model of the association between the mental and the physical. In terms of this associationist psychology whatever changes occur in the brain-substance a corresponding change ensues in a man's ideas, though Hartley denies that the two changes are identical.[9] When, at the end of the second volume of the *Observations*, Hartley discusses the possibility of a future existence after death, he makes use of this associationist psychology to support his belief in a future life. Not only does he reproduce many of the familiar eighteenth-century arguments for immortality—man's knowledge of conscience and morality, the common desire for a future life, the metamorphoses undergone by various species of animals, and the restitution of man's

[5] J. Martineau, *Miscellanies*, 1852, pp. 16–17.

[6] A. Gordon, *Heads of English Unitarian History*, 1895, p. 125; *DNB* Article, 'Priestley'.

[7] J. T. Rutt (ed.), *Works of Joseph Priestley*, iii, 1817, 10.

[8] *Eighteenth-century Background*, p. 136.

[9] Although both Priestley and James Mill adopted Hartley's associationist psychology, neither took over his theory of vibrations. For an account of the theory, cf. Willey, pp. 141–2.

faculties after periods of sleep or madness—he also argues for the existence of 'all that great *Apparatus* for carrying us from Body to Mind, and from Self-love to the pure love of God, which the doctrine of Association opens to view'.[10] Because it is arguable that the associationist analogy could equally well apply to animals, Hartley does not feel able to deny that they may possess the necessary qualities for a future existence, and he is even willing to extend this hope to vegetables, if they can be shown to have sensation, though he confesses that, in his own view, man's distinctive attributes give him a greater possibility of a future life.[11] He maintains that his position is not only rational, but is confirmed by the Christian revelation.

Hartley's associationist psychology inevitably influenced his understanding of the future life. Any meaningful future existence must be a corporeal one, for the body is necessary to the complete man, and this existence will only be fully achieved at the Last Day, when the body will be raised. Those admitted immediately to the bliss of the new life will inhabit either a re-paradised earth or the air, and although this life will be a corporeal one, the role of the body will be reduced to that of a 'mere Instrument and Inlet to the refined Pleasures of Benevolence and Piety'.[12] This will not be the case with the wicked. Their bodily senses will suffer directly, instead of acting merely as attenuated channels of sensation for the mind; for, as sensuality forms so great a part of vice, 'it may be necessary . . . that actual Fire should feed upon the elementary body . . . in order to burn out the Stains of Sin'.[13] The bodies of the wicked will, however, survive this torment. Hartley is quite clear that the purpose of this punishment is primarily reformatory, and that the wicked will eventually be brought to a final state of ultimate happiness in relationship with God. Although their punishment will be long, because any great change takes time, and although it will be severe, for 'Men are not carried from Worldly-mindedness to Heavenly-mindedness, nor advanced from lower Degrees of the last to higher, in general, but by passing through Pain and Sorrow', its purpose is the same as that of the evils of this present life: 'viz, to meliorate and perfect our natures, and to prepare them for ultimate happiness in the love of God, and of his works'.[14]

Because of his belief that the fullness of man's future life will only be achieved at the Last Day, Hartley gives considerable attention to

---

[10] D. Hartley, *Observations on Man*, 1749, ii, 387.   [11] pp. 391–2.
[12] p. 399.   [13] Ibid.   [14] pp. 405, 413, 419.

the nature of the Intermediate State. His conception of this is determined by the important place which he assigns to the body in his understanding of man. The Intermediate State, he suggests, must be one in which the soul is either completely insensible, or more or less fixed in a passive state, the good experiencing more pleasure than pain, and the wicked the reverse.[15] It is in no sense a place of trial or purification, for that requires the possibility of change, which can only be effected through the mind's receiving of the impressions mediated by the bodily senses.

The happiness of which Hartley speaks as man's ultimate destiny springs entirely from God's infinite goodness, happiness and perfection, in which he wishes all men to share. To this end the universe has been framed, so that, whether a man experiences good or evil, pleasure or pain, he will eventually be brought to 'the ultimate unlimited happiness of the love of God and of his works'. Calvinist ideas of double predestination were abhorrent to Hartley, even though his own scheme was in many ways an optimistic version of one aspect of Calvinism, the inevitable working out of a divine decree. All men were made for 'eternal and infinite Happiness', but they came to enjoy it in different ways: 'one by passing through much Pain, the other by passing through little, or perhaps none; one by an Acceleration in one period of his existence, the other in another'.[16] Hartley's philosophy is one of necessity, which leaves no place for the possibility of a man's ultimately rejecting the goodness, happiness, and perfection, which God intended him to share. Such a rejection would mean the experiencing of pain and evil, and Hartley believed that these worked mechanically on a man to bring him eventually to the point at which he returned to his true end, the pursuit of the happiness willed for him by God. Hartley claimed that his philosophy allowed a place for free will, but, as Professor Vereker has emphasized, Hartley understood free will in an idiosyncratic way as man's freedom to follow the currently strongest desire. What that desire was, was determined entirely by the external sensations passively received by the brain.[17]

Although Hartley advocated universal salvation, he was at pains, like most universalists, to stress that his doctrine did not involve an antinomian freedom from moral restraint, and was fully compatible with moral effort. The limited future punishment, which he pro-

[15] pp. 402-3.   [16] pp. 421-2.
[17] Cf. Charles Vereker, *Eighteenth-Century Optimism*, Liverpool, 1967, pp. 68-9.

posed, he believed to be a more effective sanction than eternal punishment.

> If there be no Punishment in another State, besides what is absolutely eternal, Men of very low Degrees of Virtue will hope to escape this, and consequently to escape with Impunity; Whereas, if there be a purging Fire, into which all the Wicked are to be cast to remain and suffer there according to their Demerits, far beyond what Men will generally suffer in this Life, and if there be only a few, that are admitted to Happiness after the Expiration of this Life, without such future Purification; what Vigour and Earnestness should we use to escape so great a Punishment, and to be of the happy Number of those, whose Names are written in the Book of Life.[18]

The future perfection at which men will all ultimately arrive, is unlikely to be reached without some kind of suffering. For Hartley, with his belief in the capacity of suffering to work mechanically to bring men back to the true path of virtue, a purgatorial process fits neatly into his scheme. Such a purgatory, in which suffering is directly productive of virtue, may be described as 'morally dynamic', in contrast to a purgatory in which men suffer punishment as part of the satisfaction required by divine justice. Hartley's purgatory takes place after the Last Day, and this is a feature of Unitarian theology throughout the early part of the nineteenth century. By his linking of a mechanistic, materialist psychology to an optimistic theism, Hartley maintained 'a confident faith in the necessity of progress towards perfection',[19] but it was at the expense of an impersonalism which was reflected in the aridity of much Unitarian theology.[20]

Hartley, as his wife protested, was 'by no means a Dissenter', though the adoption of the greater part of his system by the Unitarian, Joseph Priestley, meant that, after his death, he was often regarded as such. Although Priestley did not adopt universalism until the end of his life, he took over Hartley's materialism much earlier, though he dispensed with the mythology of vibrations. From 1772 he advocated a theory, propounded originally by Boscovitch, that matter consisted of points of force, which enabled him to deny that there was any real distinction between body and

---

[18] Hartley, ii, 432–3.   [19] Willey, pp. 153–4.

[20] Owen Chadwick sums up this side of Unitarianism as 'preaching rational religion, unpoetic common-sense, anti-evangelical, suspicious of fervour and enthusiasm, calm in religious life and arid in religious thought'. On the other side were Unitarian 'Bible-Protestants' 'distinguished from evangelical dissenters only by the conviction that the Trinity was not a doctrine of Scripture'. (*The Victorian Church*, i, 1966, 396–7.)

soul, mind and matter. His advocacy of it was in part a protest against a quasi-Gnostic dualism, which depreciated matter because of its sluggishness and solidity, and therefore held it to be incompatible with 'thought' or 'sensation'.[21] As with Hartley, Priestley's materialism meant that many of the arguments for man's natural immortality were unconvincing to him, and he consequently made a primary appeal to revelation in upholding belief in a future life. The doctrine of the resurrection of the body was the clear alternative to doctrines of the natural immortality of the soul, and Priestley supported an extremely literal interpretation of this, and was primarily responsible for the reduction of Christianity in Unitarian thought during the early nineteenth century almost to the theme of the revelation of a future life, confirmed by the resurrection of Christ. As J. J. Tayler wrote, looking back from the viewpoint of later idealist Unitarian theology, in the philosophy of Priestleian Unitarianism,

everything in man's mind is originally external, and the evidence for the most important truths rests primarily on the deposition of the sense taken up by the great law of association, and wrought out by it mechanically to a given result. It is obvious how readily such principles coalesce with those views of religion which, distrusting the impulsive suggestions of the mind within, look for assurance in the testimony of historical facts alone, and place all the hope of a future life on the attested resurrection of Jesus.[22]

It is not very surprising that Priestley eventually adopted universalism. Apart from his acquaintance with it in Hartley's *Observations*, he upheld a *laissez-faire* faith in progress, which looked to a future paradise, achieved by the granting of greater liberties to man in his present state of growth. As he wrote in his *Essay on Government*: 'Whatever was the beginning of the world, the end will be glorious and paradisaical, beyond what our imaginations can now conceive'.[23] With the future life conceived in terms of a glorified, corporeal existence, to be enjoyed in a restored and purified world, political hope and eschatological expectation were frequently combined. Confidence in the possibility of human progress towards a more perfect society was joined to the hope of a perfect resurrection life after death.

[21] Cf. the old Stoic theory of the soul as compounded of a refined and subtle matter, which was held by Tertullian. (*De Anima*, vii.)
[22] J. J. Tayler, *A retrospect of the religious life of England*, 1845, p. 435.
[23] Cf. Willey, p. 195.

EARLY UNITARIAN CONTROVERSIES

Unitarianism was inevitably attacked by orthodox Christian controversialists, and its early years of denominational existence were marked by a series of disputes, mainly with Calvinist divines, which ranged over all the main areas of disagreement, including the future life. In 1793 Andrew Fuller, the leading theologian of the Particular Baptists, published an attack on Unitarians under the title of *The Calvinistic and Socinian systems examined and compared*, which was probably provoked by the spread of Unitarian doctrines amongst several Baptist congregations.[24] A Unitarian reply came from John Kentish. At Bristol, John Prior Estlin, the minister of Lewin's Mead Chapel, published a number of sermons and theological works, which drew from Joseph Cottle the polemical *Essays on Socinianism*. Richard Wright, an itinerant Unitarian preacher and a strong universalist, who had formerly been a General Baptist minister at Wisbech, aroused the wrath of Calvinist incumbents and dissenting ministers alike. Hostile witnesses said that his preaching was weak, but his expositions of Unitarian doctrine are exceptionally clear, and his missionary journal is a valuable record of the pattern of dissenting congregations affected by Unitarianism up and down the country. Thomas Belsham, the organizational genius of early Unitarianism, was perhaps the most renowed of all the controversialists, and in 1800 he threw down a challenge to Evangelical orthodoxy by an attack on William Wilberforce's *Practical View*, an attack that was met by a future Archbishop of Dublin, William Magee, in his *Discourses and Dissertations on the Scriptural Doctrines of the Atonement and Sacrifice*. Lant Carpenter, Estlin's successor at Bristol and the mentor of James Martineau, replied for the Unitarians. At a less theologically literate level there were a number of controversies, such as that between Thomas Thrush and Charles Wellbeloved on the Unitarian side, and Francis Wrangham, the bibliophile Archdeacon of Cleveland, on the orthodox one. It was a dispute which led Sydney Smith to comment that, had he a lawsuit

---

[24] e.g. that at York, which met under the leadership of David Eaton, a cobbler, and proved to their own satisfaction that Calvinism and Scripture were incompatible. In 1802 Eaton came to London and opened a bookshop on the premises where the universalist, William Vidler, had once carried on business. In 1806 he played a leading role in the establishment of the Unitarian fund, and from 1814 co-operated with Charles Wellbeloved in the production of an annotated Bible with marginal corrections and notes for the unlearned.

to win, he would fee Mr. Wellbeloved to plead for him, and double-fee Mr. Wrangham to plead against him.[25]

Although these controversies took place over the space of thirty years, the positions taken up by both sides remain very much the same. In the field of eschatology the main points of disagreement concerned the immortality of the soul, the intermediate state, and future punishment, and, bearing on these topics, the nature of God and the nature of sin.

The question of immortality most frequently arose as a simple protest by the Unitarians against the accepted orthodoxy. For the most part their orthodox opponents were content to reaffirm their traditional position without troubling to counter Unitarian arguments in detail, preferring to concentrate on disagreements over future punishment. The Unitarian writers, with varying degrees of emphasis, maintained the resurrection of the body as the distinctively Christian doctrine, and unanimously asserted that the Christian possessed a far firmer basis for his belief in a future life than those whose arguments were merely those in support of natural immortality. Estlin took the standard eighteenth-century line of attributing general belief in a future life to a revelation in antiquity, since the belief appeared to be coeval with man, but he insisted that such a belief, regardless of its origins, remained, even according to the most plausible arguments in its favour, vague and shadowy. The Christian by contrast stood on firm ground. '*Information from God*, *positive* and *definite*, and confirmed by the resurrection of Jesus Christ from the dead, is the *only satisfactory* ground of belief that the grave is not the termination of our existence but that we are formed for immortality.'[26] Other grounds for belief in a future life, such as the existence of a virtue and wisdom which remained unfulfilled in this life, man's capacity for unlimited happiness, and the general desire for immortality (which Estlin believed to be strongest in the virtuous), were, in Estlin's opinion, no more than tenuous hints compared with the clarity of the Christian revelation.

Estlin did not discuss the mode of man's immortality, but many other Unitarians were prepared to do so. David Eaton's congregation at York rejected any idea of the immortality of the soul as

---

[25] Cf. *Freethinking-Christians Magazine*, i, 1811, 391; L. R. Carpenter, *Memoirs of the life of the Reverend Lant Carpenter*, Bristol, 1842, p. 344; J. Kenrick, *Memoir of Wellbeloved*, 1860, p. 152.

[26] J. P. Estlin, *Familiar Lectures on Moral Philosophy*, 1818. ii, 332.

unscriptural. It was, they argued, merely a prop for Deists, who, as long as they could invoke the arguments of natural religion to establish immortality, would never be brought to pay serious attention to the testimony of Scripture.[27] Richard Wright stressed man's affinity with the animal realm, and followed Hartley and Priestley in advocating a materialist anthropology. There was, he argued, no more reason to suppose man immortal on natural grounds than to suppose that animals had a future life. As far as man was concerned any future life was solely dependent on 'the pure goodness and sovereign will of God', who would at the Last Day bestow immortality on man by raising him from the dead. A miraculous event, it is true, but one that would be no more miraculous than man's original creation.[28] The hope of immortality established on these grounds, and not by the erroneous, 'mathematical' proofs of natural religion, Wright regarded as more conducive to virtuous living than either the deterrent of eternal punishment or the absolute certainty of a future life.[29]

More than any other Unitarian controversialist of this period, Wright elaborated the doctrine of the resurrection of the body, and in this, as in his eschatology generally, he was frequently very literal in his interpretation of the biblical imagery. For instance, he commented on 'the lake of fire':

If the phrase *lake of fire* was only a metaphor to represent the burning wrath of their own minds as preying upon the wicked, how could the judge bid them depart into it—how could they be said to be cast into it—when, according to that hypothesis, they would have it in them, and carry it along with them? It appears then that as this globe has been the centre of their crimes—the rock on which they have built their happiness—here they will be judged, and there they will have their punishment.[30]

Wright argued that the common neglect of preaching and teaching about the resurrection of the dead in orthodox Christian circles was the result of a refusal to acknowledge the primitive theology, which taught, he claimed, that Christ did not become Son of God until the

[27] D. Eaton, *Narrative of the proceedings of the society of Baptists at York*, York, 1800, p. 133; for the very different attitude of the seventeenth-century latitudinarians, cf. G. R. Cragg, *From Puritanism to the Age of Reason*, 1966 ed., pp. 66–7.
[28] R. Wright, *An essay on a future life*, Liverpool, 1819, p. 11.
[29] pp. 26f.
[30] R. Wright, *An abridgement of five discourses*, Wisbech, 1798, p. 71.

Resurrection. He also pointed to the way in which death and immortality had replaced the Last Judgment and the resurrection of the dead in the accepted scheme of Christian eschatology.

In the reputed orthodox system, a future life is neither dependent on or necessarily connected with the resurrection from the dead; for it supposes man to be naturally immortal, that, though his body dies, he continues to live as a real conscious being, that he has a future existence either in heaven or hell without a resurrection; that the righteous enjoy a state of happiness and glory immediately after death, far superior to what could be attained in this life, and would continue to enjoy it for ever, though there should be no resurrection ... In fact, death is made the great deliverer, that which frees the christian from the prison house of clay, from the fetters of mortality, and introduces him to blessedness and glory.[31]

More frequent than disputes about the immortality of the soul were those about eternal punishment. Whilst both orthodox Christians and Unitarians were agreed that there was to be a future life, and only differed about its mode, there was no such agreement about eternal punishment, a doctrine which was held to have a much greater immediacy, because of its deterrent value, than arguments about immortality and resurrection. Much of the debate was concerned with the nature of punishment. Orthodox Christians insisted that it was retributive, 'vindictive', as they frequently described it; Unitarians, on the whole, denied it. At one point the Baptist, Andrew Fuller, specifically stated that the punishment of the finally impenitent contained no element which was aimed at the final good of the offender, though he was careful to add that he did not mean by this that God punished sinners for the sake of inflicting pain on them. Rather, he held that it was necessary for the good of the Universe that some 'should stand, like Lot's wife, as *pillars of salt*, or as everlasting monuments of God's displeasure against sin; and that while their smoke shall rise up for ever and ever, all the intelligent universe shall *hear and fear and do no more so wickedly!*'.[32] Coleridge, in a letter to Estlin, stood out firmly for retributive punishment.

[31] R. Wright, *The Resurrection from the dead an essential doctrine of the Gospel*, Liverpool, 1820, p. 18. J. P. Martin makes the same observation on the eschatology of Protestant Orthodoxy, and ascribes it to the influence of Calvin and the failure of the Last Judgment as an adequate ethical sanction. (*The Last Judgment in Protestant Theology from Orthodoxy to Ritschl*, 1963, pp. 16, 47.)

[32] A. Fuller, *The Calvinistic and Socinian systems examined and compared as to their moral tendency*, 1794², p. 124.

I believe that punishment is essentially vindictive, i.e. expressive of abhorrence of sin for its own exceeding sinfulness: from all experience as well as *a priori* from the constitution of the human Soul I gather that without a miraculous intervention of Omnipotence the Punishment must continue as long as the Soul, which I believe, imperishable. God has promised no such miracles—he has covenanted no such mercy—I have no right therefore to believe or rely on it—It *may* be so; but woe to me! if I presume to believe on it.[33]

On the Unitarian side Lant Carpenter insisted that punishment was reformatory. Retributive punishment can have no place in God's intentions, and, 'when suffering has done its work, and the deep stains of guilt have been removed as by fire, suffering will be no longer continued'.[34]

Cottle, in his reply to Estlin, emphasized the deterrent effect of eternal punishment. He accused the Unitarians of extinguishing 'hell with a Trope' and confuting 'Heaven with a Syllogism', and of proposing nothing less than a 'Pandemonian Irruption' in their vision of the impenitent being finally admitted into heaven. Were their ideas to triumph, the consequences would be dire.

The world, with all the warnings of heaven, and the restraints of religion, presents a melancholy spectacle, where outrage and wrong are rampant, though repressed by the influences of human laws, and the threats of future retribution; but what an appalling image would society present if all the salutary checks founded on *Satan* and *hell* were wholly removed, and men believed, as Socinians tell them, that, in the eternal world there is no place found for 'the Devil and his Angels'; that, whatever their rebellion against God may be, it will not obstruct their future happiness for 'the mansion of the blessed' will be the *ultimate* portion of *one* and *all*.[35]

Unitarians justifiably claimed that such language belonged more to a religion of fear than to one of love, and maintained that the real debate concerned the character of God and the nature of sin. Richard Wright pointed out that the doctrine of grace, which was so emphasized by Evangelical opponents of Unitarianism, could easily lead to antinomianism, and be just as subversive of morality as Unitarian universalism. Moreover, he argued, it was a curious argument which accused a doctrine whose prime aim was the extirpation

[33] E. L. Griggs (ed.), *Letters of S. T. Coleridge*, iii, 1959, 467. (5 Apr. 1814.)
[34] Lant Carpenter, *An Examination of the Charges made against Unitarians and Unitarianism . . . by the Rt. Rev. Dr. Magee, Bishop of Raphoe*, Bristol, 1820, p. 282.
[35] J. Cottle, *Essays on Socinianism*, 1850 ed., pp. 114, 149.

of sin of encouraging it.[36] If the upholders of hell could point to its supposed deterrent value in the restraining of sin and revolution, it was equally possible for universalists to point to its abuse by the upholders of various kinds of totalitarian rule. 'Have not all persecuting popes, bloody inquisitors, all the tyrants and destroyers of mankind, under the Christian name, professed to believe the doctrine of endless punishment?' Wright asked,[37] and he compared those who argued for an endless hell from the use of the same word— αἰώνιος—to characterize both hell and heaven, to men,

... who living in countries groaning under the yoke of tyranny, in the enjoyment of great advantages, and fattening on the tears and blood of the oppressed multitude, oppose the amelioration and happiness of whole nations, lest *they* should lose any of their exclusive privileges by a change in the situation of the multitude.[38]

The connection between Unitarian and radical is clear.

Some Unitarians saw beyond the deterrent argument of the orthodox, with its frequent political overtones, to the more fundamental problem of the effect of evil on a man's character. Estlin, for instance, although he believed that all would eventually be saved, allowed that the characters of the wicked would have been so marred, that they would lack a certain capacity for the enjoyment of the bliss of heaven. They would be in the same position as a blind man before a beautiful view, or a deaf man at a concert.[39] Estlin attempted to reconcile his universal, graduated heaven with scriptural references to everlasting punishment, by suggesting that 'the *punishment*, the *penalty*, or the *loss* of the wicked, will be strictly speaking, *everlasting*', as a result of their not having obtained their happiness at the same time as the righteous.[40]

The conflict about the character of God and the nature of sin was in many ways more important than the attempts of men like Estlin to do justice to certain aspects of traditional eschatology. John Kentish provides us with a good early statement of the Unitarian understanding of God:

Pure, unlimited benevolence is, in our judgment, the most glorious perfection of the Divine character. We believe, according to the language of the

---

[36] R. Wright, *An abridgement of five discourses . . .* .p. 37.   [37] p. 43.
[38] R. Wright, *The Eternity of Hell Torment indefensible*, n.d., p. 11.
[39] J. P. Estlin, *Sermons*, Bristol, 1802, p. 259.
[40] pp. 233–4. Cf. the theories of T. R. Birks, below, p. 125 f.

favourite Apostle, that 'God is Love'; we consider all his moral excellencies, his justice, truth and holiness, as modifications of this principle. Happiness we regard as the grand object of his works and dispensations and conceive of his glory as resulting from the diffusion of this happiness.[41]

Richard Wright underlines this position. He argues that, even if it is true that Christians have the privilege of being the first-fruits, all will eventually be drawn into the orbit of God's love, and it is because love is God's supreme characteristic that he is able to achieve this.

Why do sinners continue in rebellion against God? ... Surely [Dr. Ryland] would reply, Because they are strangers to *his* love; if they saw his loveliness and perceived his love to them they would certainly love and obey him. Can they then be brought to love and obey God by having their minds inspired with tormenting fear? I think the Dr. will say, No; nothing short of a sense of the love of God can do that; *we love him because he first loved us.*[42]

From this understanding of God Unitarians were able to stigmatize the God of Calvinism as immoral, and understandably rejected by large numbers of men as incredible. To Thomas Belsham it seemed that William Wilberforce portrayed God as 'a Being who first forms his creatures with a nature radically depraved, and then condemns the majority of them to eternal misery, for being what he himself made them'. 'Can it be surprising,' he asked, 'that such a God as this is not the object of love?'[43] David Eaton, likewise, accused Calvinists of being callously insensitive to the horrors of a doctrine which stated that 'the greatest part of the human race are brought into existence without any will of their own, and by a chain of fixed events, or by the effects of Adam's sin (a crime they had no concern in) hurried through life to eternal perdition, independent of good and evil conduct'. Even though God's honour might possibly be saved by the theory that, as God is perfectly just, he can do nothing unjust, and so his predestination of a large part of creation to destruction might be right, 'is it right to sport with their miseries, and to insult them in their low and fallen condition, by calling them to believe this and that, believe and obey his will or be damned for not

[41] J. Kentish, *The Moral Tendency of the Genuine Christian Doctrine*, Exeter, 1798², p. 11.

[42] *Eternity of Hell Torments*, p. 18.

[43] T. W. Belsham, *A Review of Mr. Wilberforce's Treatise entitled 'A Practical View'*, 1800, p. 120.

obeying, when he knows they have no power to comply with the smallest injunction? Is this right, or good, or just?'.[44]

The most common orthodox reply to such charges was the accusation that Unitarians believed in a sentimentalized God because they had a defective understanding of sin. Andrew Fuller, for instance, suggests that the Unitarians were in the habit of using palliating terms to describe sin, so that it would be viewed with pity rather than with blame: 'Sin is so trifling an affair it seems, and the punishment against it of so little consequence, that we may be quite resigned and indifferent, whether we go immediately to heaven, or whether we first pass through the depths of hell!'[45] Fuller goes on to accuse Kentish of depicting a God who was no more than the projection of the self-interest of the individual and to deny that God desires the final happiness of each man. Were this true, it would be necessary to believe that it was on this principle that God destroyed the inhabitants of Sodom, as well as Cain, Balaam, Saul, and Judas, 'and all those who in every age have lived *foaming out their own shame*'.[46] A God such as Kentish describes, is 'such as the most depraved being must approve of', for '*sinners can love those who love them*'. By contrast, 'a Being, the perfections of whose nature require him to promote the good of the creation in general, will be loved by those, and those only, who value the general good, and who no otherwise desire the happiness of any creature, not even their own, than as it is included in the well-being of his moral empire'.[47] Not only is Fuller's doctrine harsh, it manifests that impersonal quality which was always a danger with Calvinism.

Cottle's attack on Unitarianism emphasizes other points. He questions whether the effects of sin on a man's character really are as evanescent as some Unitarian writers appeared to suggest. Can there be any grounds for morality, he asks, if there is to be no final separation of good and evil? Like most anti-Unitarian writers he believes Unitarians to have a defective understanding of sin and a low idea of heaven; they march up to heaven's gate proclaiming 'We are worthy!'.[48]

As we have seen from the history of Christian eschatology, the state of the soul between death and the final resurrection constitutes

[44] *Narrative of Proceedings*, p. 71.
[45] *Calvinistic and Socinian Systems*, p. 15.
[46] *Socinism indefensible on the grounds of its moral tendency*, 1797, p. 70.
[47] p. 76.   [48] *Essays on Socinianism*, p. 120.

a problem for any scheme of eschatology which conceives of the future life only in terms of the general resurrection at the Last Day. Many Unitarians followed the lead of Hartley and Priestley in coping with this difficulty and put forward theories of the sleep of the soul, or the soul's continued existence in a fixed, passive state, or else looked to what was tantamount to a new creation at the day of resurrection. The soul, they believed, would be cleansed from the pollution which it had acquired during its earthly life, and this many Unitarians considered would take place during the millennial reign of Christ. 'Christians' or 'the righteous' would enjoy this, whilst the wicked were cleansed from the taint of evil before being admitted to the final beatitude at the consummation of all things. Some writers, however, amongst whom Estlin is a notable example, did not follow Hartley and Priestley so closely. These were willing to allow that the soul might not only be conscious in the intermediate state, but might also be cleansed and fitted for eternal life during that time. If purgatory was interpreted, Estlin suggested, as meaning only that the soul continued in a disembodied state until the resurrection, and, during that time, was refined 'from the pollutions contracted by its union with an *animal and corruptible*, and prepared for a union with a *spiritual and incorruptible body*', then there would be no objection to it as a speculative opinion, so long as it was not interpreted as indicating a moral probation beyond this life.[49]

A characteristic of these early controversies on the orthodox side is the accusation made against the Unitarians that they were attempting to pry into matters beyond human understanding. Certainly, from an example Cottle gives, in which it is stated that the Garden of Eden could not have been in the polar regions because there would then have been no fruit and so no fall, they were capable of very curious speculations.[50] But this orthodox counsel of submission to the unsearchable ways of God was not much heeded. Unitarians considered that much Evangelical preaching, particularly expositions of the 'terrors of the Lord', only too strongly suggested that the preachers were emotionally unbalanced, in contrast to Unitarians, whose faith was founded 'not upon the moral and intuitive sense . . . a frame of feelings . . . preternatural communications and divine impressions, but upon argument and reason':

[49] Estlin, *Sermons*, pp. 208ff., 243; Cf. id., *A Unitarian Christian's Statement and Defence of his principles*, Bristol, 1815, pp. 82–3.
[50] *Essays on Socinianism*, p. 103.

... A judicious instructor would neither expect nor desire to produce one of those ecstatic Christians, who are sometimes mounted on 'the top of Pisgah' exulting in the prospect of the promised land, and at other times sighing and weeping in 'the vale of humiliation', and tormenting themselves with doubts and imaginary terrors: sometimes full of rapturous affection to their 'Beloved' and their souls carried out 'like the chariots of Aminadab' and at other times mourning under the 'hidings of his face' and crying out 'Why stay his chariot wheels?'[51]

These early debates, though hardly remarkable for deep theological insight, reveal the characteristic elements and emphases of Unitarian eschatology. In some writers a strong scriptural emphasis was dominant, deriving from the view that the primary reason for asserting the truth of Unitarianism was simply that it was the doctrine of the New Testament.[52] But Unitarian scripturalism was but part of a broader tradition going back to Locke's *Essay on the Reasonableness of Christianity*. It was from Scripture that Unitarians claimed they had learnt of the centrality of the love of God, which they opposed to the extremes of a predestinarian theology and a popular Calvinism which appeared to drive a wedge between God's mercy and justice. But this emphasis on the love of God, and the universalist doctrine which Unitarians professed, also reflected, both in its substance and in the manner of its expression, the characteristic optimism of the eighteenth century combined with a philosophy which was both materialist and mechanistic. The Unitarian God of love could become little more than a God of sentimental benevolence, whose purposes were achieved with the same mechanical inevitability as the God of popular Calvinism saved and damned blocks of men by his divine decree. Hartley, with his combination of moral objections to eternal punishment and a determinist philosophy, undoubtedly strengthened this aspect of Unitarian theology.[53] Yet, even when these objections have been made, it is clear that this early Unitarian eschatology reveals a growing individualism and a new insistence on the love of God as the determining factor in God's dealings with men. By contrast, against the harmony of Unitarian universalism with eighteenth-century optimism must be set its opposition to that cardinal doctrine of

[51] *Monthly Repository*, i, 1806, 40; Belsham, *Review of Wilberforce*, pp. 130–131.
[52] J. Estlin Carpenter, *James Martineau, Theologian and Teacher, a study of his life and thought*, 1905, p. 101.
[53] p. 132.

eighteenth-century natural religion, the natural immortality of the soul. As Thomas Belsham put it:

To believe in the Christian revelation . . . is to believe that Jesus of Nazareth was a teacher commissioned by God to reveal the doctrine of a future life, in which virtue shall find a correspondent reward and vice shall suffer condign punishment; and that of this commission he gave satisfactory evidence by his resurrection from the dead.[54]

The hope of a future life rested solely on divine revelation.

NEW DIRECTIONS IN UNITARIANISM

In 1839 Liverpool was the scene of a series of public debates between Evangelical Anglican clergy and three Unitarian ministers, Henry Giles, James Martineau, and J. H. Thom,[55] who declared that their intention was to argue for 'the *spiritual* character of the Faith above the verbal and metaphysical' and 'against the attainableness of salvation only by one set of opinions'.[56] The lecture on eschatology was delivered by Henry Giles. He spoke of 'beings maddened and convulsed by the visions of Calvinism': 'it was not until there was a hell without hope, that there was a heart without mercy'.[57] All sin, he declared, was personal; no man could be held responsible for Adam's sin, and the Augustinian picture of a *massa perditionis* was abhorrent. Because sin is a personal matter it left injurious consequences, consequences which might be eternal. But it is not permissible, he argued, to move from this to saying that guilt utterly destroys the happiness of a soul, or that it absolutely impedes its progress.[58] He regarded the Evangelical stress on the decisive importance of the moment of death as erroneous. 'Temporal and eternal are but distinctions of imagination; our eternal life commences, and our earthly is but the first stage, the infancy of that awful and endless existence.'[59] Hell was an importation into Christianity, which had only endured so long because of the prestigious backing of Augustine, the advantages the doctrine gave to ecclesiastical interests, and the important place it occupied in

[54] T. W. Belsham, *A Summary View of the Evidence and Practical importance of the Christian Revelation*, 1807, p. 5.

[55] The Unitarian, George Harris, had been at the centre of a similar public controversy in Liverpool in 1819–20. 'Harris kill the devil!' and 'No hell fire' were said to have been chalked on Liverpool walls for months. (Historical Society of Lancashire and Cheshire, *Proceedings and Papers*, v, 1852–3, 22).

[56] *The Unitarian Lectures at Liverpool*, Liverpool, 1839, pp. xvii–xix.

[57] xii, 5–6.   [58] p. 17.   [59] p. 19.

Calvinist theology. For Giles, if there was an eternal hell, there was a limit to both the power and love of God: 'there is no room in the same universe for a good God and an eternal hell'.[60]

The controversy excited more than usual interest because of the revelation, in a letter to the *Liverpool Albion*, that Fielding Ould, the leading Evangelical lecturer, had culled his lectures almost verbatim from Fuller's *Calvinistic and Socinian systems compared*, which had long been relegated to the theological dust-heap.[61] But quite apart from Ould's discomfiture these lectures indicate that the character of Unitarianism was beginning to change. Instead of an appeal to Scripture, there is an appeal to the 'spiritual character of the Faith', which is contrasted with the 'verbal and metaphysical'. The emphasis on the personal nature of sin likewise points to a growing concern with the subjective and the individual. In some respects this is only a reflection of the influence of Evangelicalism, and the predominant pietism of English religion, yet Evangelical critics were loud in their condemnation of Unitarian divines as men lacking the characteristic pietist virtues. Charles Jerram, an Evangelical incumbent, wrote of them, that they were 'altogether men of the world'.

They frequented theatres, balls and assemblies. They spent most of their evenings in cards. They seldom conversed on religious topics . . . Their prayers appeared to me to be dry and formal—to have in them little of humiliation and self-abasement on account of sin, and a corresponding want of earnestness in asking for forgiveness. Their thanksgivings related chiefly to the nature and attributes of God and his goodness in constituting them capable of knowing so much of him and in commissioning Jesus Christ to make known so much of his will and setting us so excellent an example of moral duties and aimiable conduct . . . As for their discourses they were mere moral essays, philosophical disquisitions, and refined in style. There was no unction in them; no appeal to conscience; no instruction for the poor, if such had constituted part of their assembly; no consolation for the afflicted.[62]

[60] p. 34. Giles also criticized popular notions of heaven, which portrayed it as an 'elysium for indolence', when it should be 'the sphere of highest action'—a recurrent nineteenth-century sentiment.

[61] The Unitarians made the most of this, the *Christian Reformer* comparing Ould and Fuller to Gilbert White's Selborne owls, which hooted in unison. William Shepherd, a local Unitarian minister, published a satirical pamphlet under the title of *The Clerical Cabbage Garden*, and sent it together with a large red cabbage to Ould. (*Christian Reformer*, viii, 1841, 675; *Theological Review*, xiv, 1877, 88–91; Shepherd MSS., Manchester College, Oxford, ix, 83.)

[62] J. Jerram (ed.), *The Memoirs and a selection from the letters of the late Charles Jerram*, 1855, pp. 41–2.

THE CONTRIBUTION OF THE UNITARIANS

That there was a large element of truth in such charges was freely acknowledged by the chief architect of the new Unitarian theology, the American divine, William Ellery Channing. In 1841 Channing, in a letter to James Martineau, set out what he considered to be the weakness of Unitarianism, and it is instructive to compare his comments with those of an earlier Evangelical critic like Jerram.

Old Unitarianism must undergo important modifications or development. This I have felt for some years. Though an advance on previous systems, and bearing some better fruits, it does not work deeply, it does not bear living springs in the soul. This is perfectly consistent with the profound piety of individuals of the body. But it cannot quicken and regenerate the world, no matter how reasonable it may be, if it is without *power*. Its history is singular. It began as a protest against the rejection of reason— against mental slavery. It pledged itself to progress, as its life and end; but it has gradually grown stationary, and now we have a Unitarian orthodoxy.[63]

Whilst Channing was prepared to admit the real genius of Priestley, he was convinced that his materialist outlook had done nothing but harm to the Unitarian understanding of man's moral nature, and had led to a false doctrine of God.

Channing's theology, as that of American Transcendentalism as a whole, reveals the influences of both pietism and German idealism; indeed, Transcendentalism has been defined as 'Unitarianism in the process of "getting religion"'.[64] Against what Emerson called 'the corpse-cold Unitarianism of . . . Harvard College', Channing asserted that scepticism in spiritual matters was irrational, unphilosophical and degrading: there was more evidence that a man possessed a soul or spirit than that he possessed a body.[65] Heaven was a union of thought and feeling with all the great and good of the human race, and consisted in 'the freed and sanctified mind, enjoying God through accordance with his attributes, multiplying its bounds and sympathies with excellent beings, putting forth noble powers and ministering, in union with the enlightened and holy, to the happiness and virtue of the universe'.[66] Such a heaven could be enjoyed during man's present earthly existence in a way that the heaven of the older Unitarian theology could not. Channing's acquaintance with German

[63] W. H. Channing, *Memoir of W. E. Channing*, 1851 ed., p. 294.
[64] C. L. F. Gordes, *The Periodicals of American Transcendentalism*, Durham (North Carolina) 1931, p. 10.
[65] W. E. Channing, *Works*, 1840[3], iv, 219.   [66] iii, 225–6.

idealism was primarily through the writings of Madame de Staël and Coleridge, and for this reason his appreciation of idealist philosophy remained second-hand and imperfect. In Kant he found confirmation of the ethical views with which he had long been familiar from the work of Price, and in Schelling and Fichte he discovered an understanding of humanity as a manifestation of the Divine, as well as an assertion of the almost unlimited powers of the human will. That Channing should have found these writers congenial witnesses to the close links between Unitarianism and pantheism, though, as Frothingham comments, Channing's sympathies with the idealism of Romantic philosophy were more on moral than on intellectual grounds. Intellectually he tenaciously upheld the old evidence-type theology, with its reliance on miracles as attesting the mission of Christ; and it was perhaps this dual appreciation of idealism and the older Unitarian theology which gave him such great influence amongst his fellow Unitarians.[67]

Dissatisfaction with a dry, rationalist theology, a desire for a religion of the heart, and a concern with 'practical theology' was a common feature of much English religion in the early nineteenth century. Unitarianism, which had perhaps been drier than other denominations, was no exception. The young James Martineau, repelled by the crudities of Evangelical theology during his ministry in Liverpool, was nevertheless haunted by the piety he had known in the works of Wilberforce and Hannah More and the hymns of the Wesleys, and it was this piety which drove him to demand, in his preaching, the effort which the determinism of his associationist psychology was unable to justify.[68] It was through reading Channing that Martineau first discovered a way of reconciling his Unitarian theology with a religion of the heart. As Estlin Carpenter has put it:

From Channing, then, did James Martineau learn with new meanings, the profound lesson of religion, that 'moral perfection is the essence of God, and the supreme end for man'. It carried with it far-reaching consequences. It transformed the concept of Revelation; from the communication of objective truths by a heaven-accredited messenger, the function of Christ came to be interpreted as the manifestation of the divine character under the limits of humanity, which received its attestation from the witness of the soul within. It elevated the person of Jesus into a centre of supreme

---

[67] *Memoir of W. E. Channing*, p. 146; O. B. Frothingham, *Transcendentalism in New England*, New York (Harper Torchbooks), 1959, pp. 110–11.
[68] *James Martineau*, pp. 173–4.

reverence and affection as 'the image of God'; and enabled the disciple to preserve his moral homage undisturbed, in spite of the plainest intellectual limitations in the object of his spiritual faith.[69]

This is clearly reminiscent of that concern for sanctification as the primary object of religion which was so characteristic of both Evangelicalism and Tractarianism, and it marks the abandonment of a dry evidence-theology for an emphasis on 'the Christ of faith', and a shift of interest from the events of history and the action of God within them, to the inner light and the extension of human powers. The effect of this change was, as Frothingham wrote of the New England Transcendentalists, to claim 'for all men as a natural endowment what "Evangelical" Christianity [ascribed] to the few as a special gift of the Spirit'.[70] Although Transcendentalism as such never attained the influence in England as an organized school of thought that it did in America, the writings of its leading exponents, notably Emerson and Theodore Parker, enjoyed considerable popularity, particularly amongst Unitarians, 'reluctant doubters', and Utopian groups such as the Ham Common community.

It was not only Martineau who embraced Channing's teaching. A letter from John James Taylor to J. H. Thom in 1855 shows a similar reaction against the Priestleian tradition. On re-reading Priestley after he had become acquainted with Channing's idealism, Tayler was astonished to find how far he had drifted from the principles in which he had been brought up. He could only say that he knew of none with which he had less sympathy, and towards which he felt a more utter distaste and alienation: 'I think its intimate connection with Unitarianism in this country has been very disastrous to the *religious* influence of that system, and had not Dr. Channing and the American school come to the rescue must have ultimately led to its extinction as a form of religion altogether.'[71] The change in outlook within Unitarianism inevitably affected its eschatology. Channing himself had declared that he was dissatisfied with the evidences of immortality supplied by revelation, including the Resurrection, unless there were inward, intuitive evidences to support them, and Martineau argued that immortality must rest on moral rather than metaphysical grounds.[72] Martineau felt that the old arguments proved as much for a cat as for a man, and so could

---

[69] p. 175.   [70] Frothingham, pp. 143, 303.
[71] J. H. Thom (ed.), *The Letters of J. J. Tayler*, 1872, ii, 28. (12 Feb. 1855.)
[72] *Memoir of W. E. Channing*, p. 321.

only increase scepticism and indifference. 'The sentiment of responsibility—the experience of conscience' were specifically human, and it was from these that he argued to a belief in immortality, for they were, he reckoned, the highest experiences known to man, and it was only fitting that they should supply the evidence for the highest truth about man.[73]

Martineau set out his position more fully in a series of lectures on the gospels, which he delivered between 1840 and 1845. In these he maintained that immortality was neither revealed nor proved by Christianity. It was already an accepted doctrine based on an intuitive conviction, the natural belief that man is a composite being, whose spirit was immaterial and separable from the fortunes of the body, conjoined with the moral sense of right and wrong.[74] As a supporting argument he referred to man's inability to conceive of himself as no longer existing. 'It is far more incredible that from not having been *we are*, than that from actual being we shall *continue to be*.'[75]

Martineau's major exposition of the doctrine of the future life is to be found in his *Study of Religion* (1888). In this he argues that faith in a life after death constitutes a genuine part of Christianity, because a future life, considered as an object of thought, is transcendental like God. In other words, it is 'apprehended by us neither in the immediate consciousness by which we know ourselves, nor in the sensuous perception by which we know the world; but in virtue of an intuitive third idea, of a Divine, universal power, which relates and unites them both'.[76] It is this intuitive sense of the Divine, with which it is possible to form a personal relationship, which is the most important element in any talk of immortality. The immensities of time and space, which have so frequently been used to convey something of what immortality might mean, are no more than imagery, and it is important that they should not dominate the picture.[77] As the soul has so generally been involved in discussions of a possible future life, Martineau feels it necessary to clarify his understanding of it. Like the Transcendentalists he insists that the nub of the

[73] C. B. Upton, *Dr. Martineau's Philosophy*, 1905 (rev. ed.), pp. 193–4 (Letter of 6 Oct. 1851).

[74] J. Drummond and C. B. Upton, *The Life and Letters of James Martineau*, 1902, i, 170–1.

[75] J. Martineau, *Endeavours after the Christian Life*, i, 1843, 174.

[76] J. Martineau, *A Study of Religion*, 1888, ii, 326.

[77] pp. 326–7.

matter is 'the likest god within the soul', so that 'the soul may be said to be the individual, God the cosmical aspect of the inward principle of our existence; and they are homogeneous in our thought, except in the spheres at their disposal'.[78] The soul is the permanent term in the midst of the flux which characterises human existence. Yet the imagery which has so often been used in talking of it, has been of 'winds or mists' and 'what is all but empty and invisible', which has obscured this reference to the permanent and continuing identity of the individual. Such imagery should always be regarded as an attempt to express the purely subjective, rather than be taken as referring to something either vague or impermanent.

These ghostly terms are selected precisely because they verge upon the very zero of objectivity, and mark the extreme but vain struggle of language to take the final step into the purely subjective. Instead of first turning other people into ghosts, and then appropriating one ourselves by way of imitation, we start, I apprehend, from the sense of personal continuity, and then predicate the same of others under the figures which keep most clear of the physical and perishable.[79]

Although Martineau occasionally expressed himself in terms which verge on pantheism, he was alert to this danger and stressed both the subjective reality of each individual and the continuing existence of the personality in relation to God. Even when the language of self-surrender was used, he insisted that there was no question of the soul being absorbed into the Divine Essence: the very language of self-surrender implied the continued existence of the self which made this act of renunciation.[80] In the course of his argument Martineau also shows a critical awareness of the mathematical preconceptions involved in all talk of infinity, and he endeavoured to free his theology from quantitative ideas by drawing a distinction between the infinite and the total when what is under discussion is the relationship between God and man. Infinity in such a context is a qualitative attribute, and 'when we carry the infinitude from quantity to quality, it ceases to be altogether a totality, and becomes an intensity; and far from embracing all that is less than itself, completely excludes it'.[81] But clear as Martineau's intentions are, he perhaps fails to see, in his desire to escape from what he regards as the impersonality of quantitative language, that the quantitative reference of infinity has an importance in the establishment of the unchangeable quality of

[78] p. 352–3.   [79] p. 353.   [80] pp. 356–7.   [81] p. 362.

the relationship between God and man, which he so strongly wishes to assert as the primary characteristic of the future life.

It is, however, the arguments from moral experience which finally carry weight with Martineau, and these, he suggests, force two conclusions upon us: first, that in man's conscience, physical nature and social organisation, there are marks of a morally constituted world moving towards a righteous end; and, secondly, that the realization of that end is nowhere discoverable, 'but only the incipient and often baffled tentatives for realising it by partial approximation'.[82] The future life is thus to be understood as the end term of an evolutionary, moral process, though because man still lives in the confusion of the present, the picture of this final end is blurred and fragmented. Against the Darwinian emphasis on man's links with his animal past, which seemed to make claims of human immortality extremely doubtful, Martineau replies that the more that is learnt of evolution, the more man's immortality appears as the end term which gives the whole process meaning, and he cites with approval John Fiske's statement in *The Destiny of Man*, that he believed in the immortality of the soul, not in the way that he believed scientific propositions to be true, 'but as a supreme act of faith in the reasonableness of God's work'.[83]

In much the same way as the old, static picture of the universe as 'the great chain of being' was gradually transformed into a dynamic universe of becoming, so the older Unitarian eschatology of a future life certainly established on the basis of the Resurrection of Christ, had, by the time Martineau wrote *The Study of Religion*, been replaced by a view which was evolutionary, idealist and teleological.[84] The old determinism of Hartley and Priestley had given way to an emphasis on free will and the realization of human potential by the exercise of choice between competing alternatives.[85] The inevitable clouding of the older certainties by this stress on possibilities, whilst

[82] p. 393.
[83] John Fiske, *The Destiny of Man*, Boston, 1884, p. 116; Martineau also quotes with approval an argument frequently used at the time, that, were the law of the conservation of energy to be applied to the will and the emotions, science could provide positive proof of immortality. (Cf. A. W. Momerie, *Agnosticism*, 1884, p. 59.)
[84] The extent to which the old stress on the resurrection of the body had been abandoned can be gauged from a comment in the *Theological Review* for 1869 that, were consciousness so dependent on the existence of a material organization that it necessitated a resurrected body for a future life, one could scarcely believe in a God who was described as a conscious Spirit. (vi, 554.)
[85] *James Martineau*, p. 297.

it must have been disturbing to some, was felt by many to be a gain, and the hope of immortality could even take the place of the fear of hell as a moral sanction. As J. J. Tayler put it in 1877:

> If more of that gross, palpable, measurable certainty which we justly demand in matters of the present life, were actually attainable, and had been vouchsafed to us, not only would it have deranged the proper relation between the two worlds, and wholly unfitted us for our present disciplinary work, but it would have taken from the hope of immortality that moral character through which it exercises its most elevating influence on our present being. It would have become a mechanical impression and ceased to be a spiritual trust.[86]

F. W. NEWMAN

As the century progressed the theology of all denominations, but especially that of the Unitarians, became increasingly concerned with the possibility of a future life. The Unitarians continued to give hospitality to those whose adherence to universal restoration had excluded them from their own churches, but with the decline of Calvinism more and more universalists found it possible to remain within the orthodox denominations.[87] As theology became more liberal the old Unitarian polemic against hell became reduced to the expression of incredulity that anyone had ever believed the doctrine.[88]

One of those who found a temporary home in Unitarianism was Francis Newman, brother of the Cardinal, who, whilst he was Professor of Classics at Manchester New College in the 1840s, had developed a close friendship with James Martineau. Although his theological views were idiosyncratic his close relationship with Martineau gives him some right to be considered in the context of Unitarian eschatology.

An early work of Newman's, which attracted considerable notice in Unitarian circles when it appeared in 1849, was *The Soul, its sorrows and aspirations*. Martineau, even though he was critical of many of Newman's arguments, was deeply moved by the work, and told Newman that nothing he had ever read 'unless some scattered thoughts of Pascal's' had come home to him so sharply and

---

[86] J. J. Tayler, *Christian Aspects of Faith and Duty*, 1851, p. 252, cf. pp. 211, 246–7.
[87] One of the most interesting of these doctrinal refugees was Athanase Coquerel of the French Reformed Church.
[88] Cf. Frances Power Cobbe in the *Theological Review*, ix, 1872, 509.

'strengthened a deep but too shrinking faith'.[89] *The Soul*, which John Henry Newman described as 'a dreadful work . . . denying Scripture as a *whole* to be true', was intended to show that the only place where it was possible for a man to come to a knowledge of God was in his own soul. As Robbins comments, it reveals a belief in the two supreme realities as intensely as any of J. H. Newman's works.[90] In contrast, however, to his brother's belief in eternal punishment, Francis was highly critical of it. Though he had firmly believed in hell when a child, and had indeed read much on the subject, he could not recall ever having dreaded it. As far as he could observe there were a few good people who had a morbid fear of it, but all the wicked seemed to be of the opinion that they were not evil enough to deserve it.[91] Much confusion had been occasioned, Newman believed, by a too ready use of the phrase, 'Guilt *ought* to be punished', for were this true, it would turn mercy into a vice. A more accurate expression would be 'Guilt *deserves* to be punished', which would leave a sharp distinction between that which the offender deserved, and that which the one offended ought to inflict.[92] At the time when he wrote *The Soul* Newman still had a fervent belief in a future life, though he dismissed the argument based on the resurrection of Christ. More than one passage in the book witnesses to his belief, and bears on his brother's contention that Francis was 'an evangelical and a zealous one, and still seems like one in his way of going on'.[93]

. . . but suffice it ourselves to live with God now, if haply we may live with Him to all eternity; or at any rate, let us love Him while we live, and live only to be conformed to His Will. For if an eternity of holy obedience is infinite bliss, it can only be because every day of obedience is bliss. We therefore do not need the promise of such an eternity as any bride to be obedient and loving now: but either Heaven is an empty name and foolish delusion, or it is a Heaven on earth to be God's true servants. In any case therefore it remains to rest our souls on a faithful Creator, knowing that, 'whether we live, we live to Him, or whether we die, we die to Him. Living or dying we are His.'[94]

Ten years later Newman attempted a fuller exposition of his doctrine in a kind of prose poem, *Theism, Doctrinal and Practical*, in

[89] C. B. Upton, pp. 63–4.
[90] C. S. Dessain (ed.), *The Letters and Diaries of John Henry Newman*, 1961–, xiii, 415; W. Robbins, *The Newman Brothers*, 1966, p. 110.
[91] F. W. Newman, *The Soul*, 1849, p. 232n.   [92] p. 100.
[93] Dessain, xii, 335, cf. 415.   [94] *The Soul*, p. 238.

the course of which he discussed the problem of the future life. Although he rejected all theories which attempted to ascribe to the moment of death a special importance by isolating it from the rest of a man's life, Newman was still a firm believer in man's immortality.

> For the extinction of the righteous screams discord to Faith,
> To which otherwise holy truth sounds as melody.
> Even when the arguments for a Hereafter rise out of the personal,
> Nor savour of selfishness and overweening folly:
> But they grow with the growth of the soul, grow with depth of heart,
> With the breadth of moral survey, and with conscious nearness to God.[95]

The world is the place where the soul reaches perfection, and it is the soul which gives value to the material world. Hell is a 'frightful dream' and a 'Pagan monstrosity', yet a universalism which seems to deny the value of effort is too easy; and so in the end it is a version of the doctrine of conditional immortality which Newman finds the most satisfactory: 'The fire of his Spirit all-pervading must either melt or destroy.'[96]

Despite these two attempts to find grounds for believing in a future life in a kind of moral idealism, Newman in the end seems to have rejected the idea. He came to hold the view that belief in a future life tended to distract men from their present obligations, even though the possibility of a future life might in some cases be a beneficial influence.[97] But the shadowy hope of a future life, which he is prepared to allow, is in no way to be identified with the Christian heaven. That was too restricting for his faith in 'the improvability of human nature'.[98] As he wrote of the Christian heaven in 1886:

It is certainly too monotonous for an Eternity. The *negative* side of it sounds all right. Absence of pain, or mental disquiet, of cold and heat, of hunger and thirst, of turmoil and contention, of toil and weariness, of sin and death—thus much I understand . . . To make a new life desirable it must give us something to do, something worth striving for, and *a career by which we may improve in Virtue* . . . If we are to increase in Virtue we need occasion for *self-denial*, *self-control*, and *self-sacrifice*. But these

---

[95] F. W. Newman, *Theism, doctrinal and practical*, 1858, p. 92.   [96] p. 95.

[97] F. W. Newman, *Life after Death? Palinodia*, 1886, pp. 50–1. Cf. Robbins pp. 158–9; I. Giberne Sieveking: *Memoir of F. W. Newman*, 1909, p. 243.

[98] Robbins, p. 183.

cannot exist where there is no want, no offence, no pain. Want and pain, toil and trial, cannot be wholly banished out of *my* Heaven.[99]

Thus, even at this late stage, when he retained only a shadowy belief in a future life, Newman conceived it very much in terms of an extension of Evangelical earnestness and the imperative call of duty, at the same time as he repudiated concepts of a static beatitude and the traditional imagery of heaven. His suspicion of immortality sprang from his belief that a spiritual faith was only possible if it was rooted in moral energies directed towards the ends of human brother-hood.[100] Were belief in a future life to be allowed to draw attention away from humanitarian causes the possibility of the growth of true religion would be excluded and man would be denying his true nature. It was only by living the life that a man could know the doctrine. Immortality might be true, but it could only remain a remote possibility. In a sense for Francis, as for his brother, sanctifi-cation was the one thing needful, though its nature, means of attainment, and final end were very differently conceived.

*   *   *

Towards the end of the century Unitarianism was waning. The liberalism of its theology, if not the detail of its arguments, had become the property of almost all the major denominations, and its distinctive witness had consequently become less striking. As the specifically Christian element in it was replaced by a reduced ethical Theism, its impact was diminished. Men no longer required a religious framework in which to doubt and, if they did, they could do so within the orthodox denominations. By the 1890s even those Unitarian arguments which had rested on idealism and natural religion were uncertain. Estlin Carpenter, addressing the National Conference of Non-subscribing churches in 1897, said that the days when it was possible to claim that eternal life was a universal intuition had long disappeared. He criticized the validity of the frequently posed dilemma, 'either man is immortal or God is not just' on the grounds that it meant in practice that men had to remain agnostic about the character of God.[101]

Inevitably a theology which talked so much in terms of man's aspirations and desires, and which relied so heavily on intuition as a

---

[99] *Life after Death?* p. 34.   [100] Robbins, p. 182.
[101] J. Estlin Carpenter and P. H. Wicksteed, *Studies in Theology*, 1903, p. 141.

basis for belief, as much Unitarian and 'Theist' theology undoubtedly did, faced increasing difficulties with the rise of modern psychology, to which it was, perhaps, more vulnerable, than to the assaults of 'Science' in the middle years of the century. Above all, a denomination which had always remained largely intellectual in its approach, and which had never developed a truly popular form, had no large following, and so suffered more than most from the increasing indifference to all forms of religion.

Unitarian eschatology must be recognized as a powerful influence on that of other denominations during the nineteenth century. Most obviously this is seen in the case of F. D. Maurice, who consciously drew on his Unitarian background. More generally, however, it offered an alternative to the rigid formulations of Calvinism. At its best it was an important element in the movement away from an understanding of redemption in terms of absolute, divine 'decrees' towards a more personal emphasis. If in its early years its links with Evangelicalism were to be found in the place which both gave to the Bible, and its differences in its rationalism and general philosophical outlook, in the later period it was the philosophical aspect which was allied with certain Evangelical fervour, so that Unitarians of the older school, who remained dependent on a reinterpreted Bible used in the manner of evidence theology, appeared by comparison to be lacking in vitality. It may well be that this change was as much the consequence of the influx of doubters from an Evangelical background like Francis Newman, as it was derived from the thought of Channing and the American Transcendentalists. Whilst it is true that the subjectivism of later Unitarianism could reduce theology to cloudy talk of an emotional bias in human nature with no objective point of reference, at its best Unitarian theology, including its eschatology, stood for a new insistence on the importance of the personal. Neither must we forget that its maintenance of the doctrine of the resurrection of the body in the early period was an important challenge to traditional eschatology.

IV   Life Eternal and Death Eternal

THE dismissal of Frederick Denison Maurice from his professorial chair at King's College, London, in 1853 as a consequence of his views on eternal punishment was one of the theological *causes célèbres* of the nineteenth century. Most men at the time believed that, in his *Theological Essays*, Maurice had denied the popular view of hell, though they were generally uncertain about the positive doctrine which he maintained. The majority thought that he was a universalist, and recalled that the *Essays* were addressed to Unitarians, who certainly held a universalist eschatology. Maurice, however, insisted, in his usual cloudy phraseology, that he was not a universalist, and a careful examination of his writings confirms that, whilst he hoped for a universal salvation, he never affirmed that this would in fact be the case.

Maurice always stated that he belonged to no party; but it would be a mistake to see him as an isolated figure. In his eschatology, as in other aspects of his theology, he stood in a definite, if somewhat diffuse, tradition. The influence of Coleridge and of his father's Unitarianism can both be discerned. The teaching of the Scottish divines, Erskine of Linlathen and McLeod Campbell; the Cambridge Platonists; the mystical tradition of Jacob Boehme and William Law; all these left their mark on Maurice's theology, and must be taken into account in any assessment of Maurice's eschatological teaching.

S. T. COLERIDGE

Samuel Taylor Coleridge, poet, philosopher, and religious thinker, occupies a position of great significance in the history of nineteenth-century English theology. His wide reading embraced the idealist philosophers of the Continent, who were little more than names to the majority of his contemporaries, and he was a primary channel for mediating their ideas, as well as the very different traditions of mysticism and Unitarianism, to a wider public. He did not, however, simply pass on ideas derived from elsewhere, he also attempted to reflect creatively on the issues which they raised. It is true that he never managed to complete the *magnum opus*, of which he often spoke, and was critical of the claims of limited systems to embody universal truth, but he was at the same time passionately concerned to 'unite the insulated fragments of truth, and therewith to frame a perfect mirror'.[1] His vision, if not the details of the philosophical position adumbrated in his writings, was enduring. That this was so, was perhaps mainly the consequence of his clearly existential concern, his appeal to experience rather than to authority, and his endeavour to hold together the truths of the heart and of the head. Interpretations of Coleridge's overriding aim vary, but Professor McFarland has cogently argued that his philosophical work is to be seen primarily as a struggle with the pantheism, deriving from Spinoza, which so greatly influenced many of the German idealist philosophers and to which Coleridge himself was strongly attracted. Yet, in the end, such a pantheist philosophy did not do justice to human personality and its moral potential, and Coleridge's conviction of the primary importance of this, the 'I am' as the starting point of philosophy, outweighed the appeal of the 'it is' philosophy of a romanticized nature.[2] The bearing of this 'I am' philosophy on his thought concerning the future life may be seen in a comment on immortality in his notebooks.

Immortality! What is [it] but the impossibility of believing the contrary? The inevitable Rebounce of the I Am, itself the fearful Rebound of Life. The moment that the Soul affirms, I Am, it asserts, I cannot cease to be. For the I Am owns no antecedent, *it* is an act of Absolute Spontaneity and of Absolute Necessity. No cause existing why it *is*, no cause can be imagined why it should cease to be. It is an impossible thought so long as the I Am is affirmed.[3]

A second notebook entry presents another aspect of this position:

To me, therefore, and I believe to all men, the best proof of immortality is the fact, that the preassumption of it is at the bottom of every hope, fear and action! For a moment an instinctive certainty that we should cease to be at a given time—the *whole* feeling of futurity would be extinguished at the first feeling of such a certainty—and the whole mind would have no motive for not dying at the same moment.[4]

These assertions contrast strongly with the materialist psychology

[1] S. T. Coleridge, *Table-Talk and Omniana*, 12 Sept. 1831; quoted by Thomas McFarland: *Coleridge and the Pantheist Tradition*, Oxford, 1969, p. 49.

[2] McFarland, pp. 184-7 and *passim*.

[3] S. T. Coleridge, Notebook 39: f. 37ᵛ, quoted in J. D. Boulger: *Coleridge as religious thinker*, New Haven, 1961, p. 165.

[4] Notebook 25: f. 27ᵛ, quoted ibid.

of Priestley, according to which the future life could only be conceived in terms of the resurrection of the body by divine action.
Through his early association with Unitarianism Coleridge had
come into contact with Priestley's views, but their mechanistic
assumptions were abhorrent to him, and he came to regard Priestley's
materialism as a system, which, by dissolving all human personality
into material components, was tantamount to the *deus sive natura* of
Spinoza's pantheism.[5] Against Priestley Coleridge maintained his
belief in the soul, pointing out that materialists of all schools
admitted that man was different from the beasts, and that they based
their judgment, in part at least on the evidence of their own self-
consciousness.[6] Although he admitted that ideas of the pre-existence
of the soul were 'very intelligible poetry', he considered them to be
'very wild philosophy' and maintained an orthodox Christian viewpoint of God's creation of the soul at conception.[7] Those who denied
the immortality of the soul frequently pointed to the dissolution of
the body in death as a powerful argument against it. Coleridge
agreed that this was a telling point, yet, he insisted, there could be no
doubt that man's thoughts and affections stretched far beyond the
world of sense, and why, he asked, should the faculty of vision be
lost because the spectacles were broken?[8] But the argument which
accorded best with his own 'I am' philosophizing, and which he
described as 'the only satisfactory reply I have ever heard', depended
on man's experience of different degrees and intensities of pleasure
and pain. Man's ability to experience these variations suggested,
Coleridge argued, a concentration of the personality being possible.
Since, therefore, there was an intense feeling of pain at the moment
of death, this could be taken as an indication that the dissolution of
the body did not involve the dissolution of the soul.[9] He again had

---

[5] McFarland, p. 170.   [6] *Table-Talk*, Oxford, 1917 ed., p. 39.

[7] E. L. Griggs (ed.), *Collected Letters of Samuel Taylor Coleridge*, Oxford, 1956-9,
Letter 164. To John Thelwall, 17 Dec. 1796, (i. p. 278). 'Now that the thinking part of
Man, i.e. the Soul, existed previously to it's appearance in its present body, may be very
wild philosophy; but it is very intelligible poetry, inasmuch as Soul is an orthodox word
in all our poets; they meaning by 'Soul' a being inhabiting our body, and playing upon it,
like a Musician enclosed in an Organ whose keys were placed inwards.—Now this
opinion I do not hold,—not that I am a Materialist; but because I am a Berkleian.' At
this period Coleridge was still using Berkeley against Godwin, but he later became
dissatisfied with Berkeley's philosophy. Cf. McFarland, p. 158.

[8] *Table-Talk*, p. 395.

[9] Ibid. Coleridge echoes the popular, but erroneous, belief that dying is necessarily
accompanied by severe pain. Cf. John Hinton, *Dying*, (Penguin Books), Harmondsworth,
1967, pp. 69-72.

recourse to this curious notion of intensity in discussing the resurrection of the body. Literal interpretations of the resurrection were not, he considered, to be taken seriously, but he speculated whether it might be possible for the body 'without losing its consciousness and individuality' to be subject to a process of sublimation and intensification.[10] As an entry in the notebooks shows, he was particularly concerned to emphasize that, whatever man's final, future state might be, it was not one which involved a loss of personality.

Life begins in detachment from Nature and ends in union with God. The adorable Author of our Being is likewise its ultimate end. But even this last triumphal Crown, the summit and *ne plus ultra* of our immortality, even the union with God is no mystic annihilation of our individuality, no fanciful breaking of the Bottle and blending the contained water with the ocean in which it had been floating, the dreams of oriental Indolence, but on the contrary an *intension*, a perfecting of our Personality.[11]

Coleridge's opposition to the idea of a 'mystic annihilation' of man's personality in God is another reminder of his dislike of all that seemed to flow from pantheism. He valued the mystics highly because of their experimental religion, and their awareness of a relationship with God which transcended particular doctrinal formulations, but he also knew that they could dangerously support pantheism. In the *Biographia Literaria* he wrote:

The writings of the mystics acted in no slight degree to prevent my mind from being imprisoned within the outline of any single dogmatic system. They contributed to keep alive the *heart* in the *head*; gave me an indistinct, yet stirring and working presentment, that all the products of the mere reflective faculty partook of DEATH, and were as the rattling twigs and sprays in winter, into which a sap was yet to be propelled from some root to which I had not penetrated, if they were to afford my soul either food or shelter ... That the system is capable of being converted into an irreligious pantheism, I well know.[12]

He was likewise critical of many individual mystical writers, to whom he acknowledged a debt. For instance, he described Jacob Boehme [Behmen] as a 'poor, unlearned man' who sought the truth through 'a luminous mist, the vaporous darkness rising from his Ignorance and accidental peculiarities of fancy', and said that the

---

[10] Griggs, Letter 922, To Joseph Cottle, late April, 1814, (III, p. 485).
[11] Notebook 36: f. 65, quoted in Boulger, p. 150.
[12] S. T. Coleridge, *Biographia Literaria*, 1847 ed., i, 152.

true wonder was that 'in so many places it thins away . . . and Jacob
Behmen the philosopher surprises us in proportion as Behmen the
Visionary has astonished and perplexed us'.[13]

In view of his admitted debt to the mystics, his early espousal of
the philosophy of Hartley, and his association with Unitarianism,
it might be thought that Coleridge would have upheld universalism.
In fact he seems to have recognized that universalism could have an
effect much like pantheism, a reconciliation of all individuals and
their dissolution into one, undifferentiated whole. Although he
found many of the orthodox descriptions of hell morally intolerable,
he was also aware that man possessed a freedom of choice between
good and evil, whose consequences were not to be nullified by a
deterministic universalism.

A mere machine could be made happy, but not deserving of happiness; but
if God created a Being with a power of choosing good, that Being must have
been created with a power of choosing evil; otherwise there is no meaning
in the word *Choice*. . . . The whole question of the origin of Evil resolves
itself into one. Is the Holy Will good in and of itself, or only *relative*, that is,
as a means to pleasure, joy, happiness, and the like? If the latter be the
truth, no solution can be given of the origin of Evil compatible with the
attributes of God; . . . If the former be true as I more than believe, the
solution is easy and almost self-evident. Man cannot be a moral being
without having had the choice of good and evil, and he cannot choose good
without being able to choose evil.[14]

Coleridge considered that both Unitarianism, which asserted universal salvation, and Calvinism, which denied it, misconceived the
nature of God. Unitarianism considered Him as mere mercy, 'or
rather Goodnature, without reference to His Justice and Holiness,
. . . the deification of human passion', whereas Calvinism distorted
his omnipotence out of all proportion.[15] Both views were partial and
hence inadequate. As far as Unitarians were concerned, Coleridge
believed that their conception of God was closely linked with their
understanding of sin and forgiveness. Did they not talk of repentance as though it were the easiest thing in the world?

But repentance, perhaps, the repentance required by Scripture, the
passing into a new contrary principle of action, this METANOIA, is it

[13] Coleridge's annotations to William Law's edition of Boehme, (*c.* 1808), quoted in
Alice D. Snyder: 'Coleridge on Boehme', *Proceedings of the Modern Language Association
of America*, xlv, 1930, 617. The only works of Law Coleridge admitted reading were the
Serious Call and the *Spirit of Prayer*. (*Aids to Reflection*, 1854[7], p. 322.)

[14] *Biographia Literaria*, pp. 300, 301.   [15] p. 304.

in the sinner's own power? At his own liking? He has but to open his eyes to the sin, and the tears are close at hand to wash it away? Verily the tenet of Transubstantiation is scarcely at greater variance with the common sense and experience of mankind, or borders more closely on a contradiction in terms of this volunteer transmentation, this self-change as the easy means to salvation.[16]

Unitarianism was, he believed, the autonomous man of the Enlightenment set within a determinist system, 'the worst of one kind of Atheism, joined to the worst of one kind of Calvinism, like two asses tied tail to tail'.[17] The Unitarian concept of universal salvation Coleridge held to be fundamentally amoral. Not only did it treat man as one who was able to save himself, it also compromised his freedom by its necessitarian philosophy and involved the twisting of Scripture.

It neither states the disease, on account of which the human being hungers for revelation, nor prepares any remedy in general, nor ministers any hope to the individual . . . [It] involves the shocking thought that man will not, and ought not to be expected to do his duty as man, unless he first makes a bargain with his Maker and his Maker with him. Give me . . . a positive proof that I shall be in a state of pleasure after my death, if I do so and so, and then I will do it, not else![18]

But if Coleridge objected strongly to dogmatic universalism, he was also careful not to exclude the ultimate salvation of all, as a possibility within the providence of God, though his consciousness of the 'sinfulness of sin' made him insist strongly that such a possibility was in no way to be presumed upon. He had little use for crude notions of eternal punishment, and in the *Table-Talk* commented ironically on the divergent estimates of the dimensions of hell made by Lessius and Ribera.[19] In a correspondence with Cottle in 1814, he acknowledged that there were many passages of Scripture which suggested that all men would finally be saved, and he saw no grounds for treating these as metaphor. He doubted whether, if talk of the love of God, or gratitude, or the fear of limited punishment was insufficient to encourage virtue, it was to be expected that the notion of eternal punishment would have any greater effect. Few men considered such punishment as a real possibility for themselves, and many turned their trust in God's mercy into 'a presumptuous

---

[16] *Aids to Reflection*, p. 98.   [17] *Table-Talk*, p. 173.
[18] p. 397.   [19] p. 325.

watchword for religious indifference'. The absolute dichotomy between heaven and hell, which was characteristic of Protestant eschatology, he considered to be a real hindrance to acceptance of the doctrine of hell, and he believed that the Roman doctrine of purgatory had more effect on morality than the stark alternatives of Protestantism. He was, moreover, quite certain that it was 'a perilous state in which a Christian stands, if he has gotten no further than to avoid evil from the fear of hell!'.[20] To talk of heaven and hell meaningfully was, for Coleridge, to have plumbed the depths of the divine and the demonic, and he believed some of his experiences under the influence of opium to have been experiences of hell.

I feel, with an intensity unfathomable by words, my utter nothingness, impotence and worthlessness, in and for myself—I have learnt *what* a sin is against an infinite imperishable Being, such as is the Soul of Man—I have had more than a glimpse of what is meant by Death and utter Darkness, and the Worm that dieth not—and that all the Hell of the Reprobate is no more inconsistent with the Love of God, than the Blindness of one who has occasioned loathsome and guilty Diseases to eat out his eyes, is inconsistent with the Light of the Sun.[21]

Salvation, he believed, could not be attained without a knowledge of 'the exceeding sinfulness of sin'. 'To him who but for a moment felt the influence of God's presence, the thought of external exclusion from that presence would be the worst hell his imagination could conceive.'[22]

As Coleridge knew only too well, belief in hell could be merely belief in a mechanical scheme of salvation, a balance sheet of rewards and punishments for deeds done on earth. Yet he was prepared to admit that motives of reward had their place in Christian morality, as we can see from a letter he wrote to Sir George Beaumont, in which he attempted to balance the dangers of a mechanistic understanding with the reward language which was undoubtedly to be found in Scripture. Sir George had argued that there was a distinction between those for whom the chief incentive to a moral life

[20] Griggs, Letter 913, To Joseph Cottle, early April 1814?, (iii, p. 468). Cf. the story Coleridge cites from Jeremy Taylor, of St. Louis's encounter with 'a grave matron' whose purpose was 'with the fire to burn Paradise, and with my water to quench the flames of Hell, that men may serve God without the incentives of hope and fear, and purely from the love of God'. (S. T. Coleridge, *Notebooks*, (ed. K. Coburn), I, 1957. 872.1.12, December 1800).

[21] Griggs, Letter 933, To Joseph Cottle, 27 May 1814, (iii. p. 498).

[22] Griggs, Letter 913, (iii, pp. 468-9).

was the penalty which immorality would incur after death, and that more virtuous group of men for whom such incentives were both unnecessary and unworthy. Coleridge was certainly sympathetic to the view that a forced virtue was no virtue at all, but, in his reply, he took his correspondent to task for attempting to categorize men on these grounds, which was 'not only unpsychological but pernicious'. Christianity, he wrote, was more than a code of ethics, 'a Whim of modern date', it was 'an offer of Redemption from Moral Evil and its Consequences', and as such legitimately spoke of the reward of the redeemed state which it offered.

I recollect no instance in the *New* Testament, in which it is said—Be temperate and chaste, in order that you may enjoy the keen pleasures of which Health is the necessary condition—still less any passage which says —Be honest—and God will make you rich. But I recollect many passages in which Rewards are offered in a Future State, & Punishments threatened. —Wherein lies the Difference? In this: that in the belief of the latter there is *implied* a FAITH, a submission of the fleshly sense to the Moral Being, which is verily and indeed the *Beginning* of Wisdom.[23]

It was their inevitable uncertainty, Coleridge argued, which removed the rewards promised in the future life from the domain of selfishness. The hope of heaven was, moreover, a social hope, and it was clear, Coleridge stated, that nothing necessarily social could be absolutely selfish, even though a preaching of heaven in terms of a narrow reward for the individual alone could in practice make it a selfish conception.[24]

Coleridge's eschatology was characteristic of his 'I am' philosophy, and owed much to his acquaintance with the vivid consciousness of the mystics that man lived *sub specie aeternitatis*, and their refusal to separate man's relationship with God during this present life from the quality of any future life. He was, in consequence, opposed to both mechanistic theories of reward and punishment, and doctrines of universalism, which, in effect, did away with any real moral seriousness. His weakness as a Christian thinker was that of all theologians whose primary appeal is to experience: the absence of any real place in his thinking for the historical events of the life of Jesus. As Boulger has pointed out, for Coleridge the historical existence of Jesus at time amounted to little more than an objective

[23] Griggs, Letter 734, To Sir George Beaumont, *c.* 30 Dec. 1808, (iii, pp. 153–4).
[24] Ibid.

confirmation of eternal decrees apprehended by man's own reflection on his nature, and he had little to say about either the Incarnation or the Resurrection.[25] F. D. Maurice stood in this same tradition, and, perhaps as a result of this attitude, was little disturbed by the biblical criticism which caused deep anxiety to many nineteenth-century believers. As Dr. Vidler has pointed out, Maurice 'studied the Bible as one who already believed in [the divine] kingdom. He went to the Bible to receive light upon its constitution'.[26]

THOMAS ERSKINE OF LINLATHEN

In his history of theology in Germany and Britain in the nineteenth century Otto Pfleiderer claimed that the most significant theological writing of the period in Britain was that of the Scottish divines, Thomas Erskine of Linlathen and John McLeod Campbell. It had been their achievement, Pfleiderer claimed, to carry out a reconstruction of the doctrine of salvation in a similar way to the work done on the Continent by Kant and Schleiermacher and their followers, but Erskine and Campbell had worked independently and had developed their theology on the basis of their own study of the Bible. Their work, he wrote, had transformed the doctrine of salvation from a matter of 'forensic externality to ethical inwardness and a truth of direct religious experience'.[27]

Erskine's theology indeed grew from his own study of Scripture, but he was also influenced by other writers. He was acquainted with the experiential theology of the Moravians through the writings of John Gambold, whose theological works he edited. He may also have been influenced by the Hon. and Revd. Gerard Noel, with whom he travelled for a time on the Continent.[28] Noel's sermons, although in many ways typical of orthodox, Evangelical preaching, also exhibit a strand of that ethical inwardness which Erskine was to make his own. For instance, Noel wrote of salvation:

Men often account 'salvation' to be a mere deliverance from the penalties of the law—the shutting of the gate of hell; whereas salvation is a complex term, comprising deliverance from the *multiplied* effects of sin, of which

[25] Boulger, p. 176.

[26] A. R. Vidler, *F. D. Maurice and company*, 1966, p. 142.

[27] O. Pfleiderer, *The development of theology in Germany since Kant and its progress in Great Britain since 1825*, 1890, p. 382.

[28] Erskine found 'Christian intercourse' with Noel 'a great comfort', and commented on his excellent sermons. W. Hanna, *Letters of Thomas Erskine*, 1877, i, 49, 53. Letters of 1823.

the most disastrous are to be found in the sensual and earthly passions of the heart; and hence, the conversion *of the heart*, the return of the affections to God, is in very truth, *salvation*.[29]

Similarly, he claimed, the happiness of heaven was the conformity of the mind to God, not a reward conferred on the elect through the merits of Christ, and sanctification was, therefore, a necessary element in salvation.

Although the design of Christianity be general, though the door of mercy be so wide as to admit all who come to it, though the 'sin which is as scarlet may be made as white as snow', though 'the blood of Jesus Christ cleanseth from all sin', yet all these blessings are eternally connected with *the characters* to which they apply. These blessings are not forced upon man, are not the *necessary* and compulsive result of Christianity.[30]

Likewise, death made no mysterious difference to character: the principles of happiness and misery remained the same for this world and the next.[31]

Whether Erskine owed anything to Noel or not, it is certain that he was deeply influenced by the writings of William Law. In 1827 he wrote of Law's works, the *Spirit of Prayer* and the *Spirit of Love*, that, though their doctrine 'was not the gospel', they could profitably be read by those with a knowledge of the gospel, and he had already followed Law into universalism:

I trust that He who came to bruise the serpent's head will not cease from his work of compassion until He has expelled the fatal poison from every individual of our race. I humbly think that the promise bears this wide interpretation . . . in fact my soul refuses to believe in final ruin, when it contemplates the blood of Christ.[32]

The most succinct account of Erskine's theology, particularly its eschatological aspect, is to be found in a small work, *True and False Religion*, which originally appeared in 1830.[33] In this Erskine attacked those who made religion either an intellectual or a moralistic system, and who, whilst acknowledging the forgiveness of God, in practice restricted that forgiveness to those of a certain character. 'This idea

[29] G. T. Noel, 'The Return of the Affections to God', *Family Sermons*, 1827 ed. p. 9.
[30] 'Necessity for religious caution', ibid., pp. 102–3.
[31] 'Perception of Christ's love the source of moral obedience', ibid. pp. 244–6.
[32] *Letters of Erskine*, i, pp. 92–3 (1827); cf. pp. 114–15, 123, 343–4.
[33] Originally published in 1830 as the introduction to *Extracts of letters by a lady*. Republished separately as *True and False Religion*, Leicester, 1874.

runs through them all, that the object to be attained is a deliverance from penalties, and an assurance of safety—and that the way of attaining it is by believing or doing something.'[34] For Erskine, however, such men were not really concerned with God at all; they were merely anxious about what could be obtained through him, the escape from certain penalties. A man who fears that he may be damned cannot but wish that he was the master of his own fate, and is, therefore, unlikely to respond to exhortations to submit to the will of God. He may indeed acknowledge this to be a duty, but, if this is as far as his religion takes him, his religion, in Erskine's opinion, has not answered his real needs.

The religion which he needs, is one which contains a provision for converting the *knowledge of duty* into the *acting of the will* . . . A man cannot submit in his heart to God, until he knows himself to be safe in God's hands—and he cannot know himself to be safe in God's hands until he knows himself to be forgiven.[35]

Erskine strongly opposed all moralism in religion, and stood by his conviction that man was indeed *simul iustus et peccator*, as is clear from his comments on the gospel story of the woman with the alabaster box of ointment.

In Simon's case . . . we have the proof that unbelievers are forgiven, though they are not saved; and, in the woman's case, we have the proof, that forgiveness must precede belief, *for it is the very thing believed*, and that salvation must follow belief, for salvation is nothing else than love, which is produced by knowledge of God's forgiving love already bestowed.[36]

All men are already forgiven by God: this was basic to Erskine's theology, and he was alarmed by anything which might compromise it, or revive a religion of good works for a future reward. Thus, at the time when Maurice was deprived of his professorship, he was concerned at the possibility of the Church of England's committing itself to an uncompromising position on eternal punishment: the love in which perfection consisted could never be created by frightening men.[37] At the same time he was alarmed at the state of religious teaching in Scotland. Everywhere, he wrote, salvation from punishment was substituted for salvation from sin, and sin itself was conceived as a series of particular offences, rather than as the whole

---

[34] *True and False Religion*, p. 1.   [35] pp. 6–7.   [36] p. 27.
[37] *Letters*, ii, p. 81 (1853).

state of man's alienation from God. Men were being told to make themselves children of God, instead of being told that they were already that, and hence had the capacity to live up to their calling.[38] For Erskine the righteousness of God was not a righteousness external to men, the conscientious and scrupulous fairness of a judge, but it was a righteousness which desired to communicate itself. As long, however, as an external righteousness was preached, it was not surprising that men remained enslaved to law, and tried to make themselves righteous by good works.[39]

There can be no doubt of Erskine's universalist hope, which he first seems to have derived from William Law, and which he later expressed in the language of F. D. Maurice, whom he had first met in London in 1833, when he described him as 'a very metaphysical man', who mixed a good deal with Pusey and the other Oxford clergy, without being regarded as completely at one with them.[40] Like Maurice, Erskine insisted that αἰώνιος should be taken as referring to man's spiritual state, not to any infinite period of duration: 'eternal life is living in the love of God; eternal death is living in self; so that a man may be in eternal life or in eternal death for ten minutes, as he changes from the one state to the other'.[41] For all his hope of a universal restoration, however, Erskine was too sensitive to the realities of good and evil to turn that hope into an absolute certainty. The work of Christ was an actual putting away of sin, and a manifestation of the holy love of God. Those who believe in it receive this love, which is eternal life; but, if this love is rejected, eternal life is excluded also. Nevertheless, despite his caution, it was his universalist hope which dominated his eschatology. As he put it in a letter of 1864: 'He who waited so long for the formation of a piece of old red sandstone will surely wait with much long suffering for the perfecting of a human spirit'.[42] Or, more eloquently, at the end of *True and False Religion*:

The love of God which gave Christ, is the immense ocean of the water of life, and men's souls are as ponds dug upon the shore, connected each of them, in virtue of Christ's work, with that ocean by a sluice. Unbelief is

---

[38] pp. 88–9 (1854).

[39] p. 229 (1864). In 1865 he told Alexander Ewing, the Bishop of Argyll and the Isles, that false concepts of salvation were at the root of the substitutionary view of the Atonement. In Erskine's view the life and death of Christ were 'the acting of the root of the human tree, by which the sap is prepared for and propelled into the branches'. (ii, p. 223).

[40] i, p. 300 (1853).   [41] ii, p. 240. cf. p. 238.   [42] ii, p. 242.

the blocking up of that sluice; belief is the allowing the water to flow in, so that the pond becomes one with the ocean, and man becomes partaker of the divine nature, and has one life with the Father and the Son.[43]

Erskine's theology had a considerable influence in England. D. J. Vaughan believed that it was largely amongst those who welcomed a critical outlook and the scientific study of Scripture that his views were most favourably received, and this is not surprising.[44] Those who welcomed critical views did so on the grounds that an honest quest for truth could only clarify the message of the gospel, believing there to be no fundamental opposition between truth and the biblical revelation. Such an outlook was consonant with a *Logos* theology, which emphasized that Christ was already present wherever there was truth, and that, consequently, as Erskine also perceived, there was already a relationship between unbelievers and the truth revealed in the gospel. From the time of Origen onwards such a position had often been linked with a belief in the restoration of all things as the consummation of the divine purpose, and this universalism was, as we have seen, also characteristic of Erskine.[45] Evangelicals, on the whole, were suspicious of Erskine, as Newman noted in a letter of 1883, looking back on his Oxford period.

I knew, when young, Mr. Erskine's publications well. I thought them able and persuasive; but I found the more thoughtful Evangelicals of Oxford did not quite trust them. This was about the year 1823 or 1824. A dozen years later I wrote against them or one of them in the Tracts for the Times and certainly my impression still is that their tendency is anti-dogmatic, substituting for faith in mysteries the acceptance of a 'manifestation' of divine attributes, which was level to the reason.[46]

Erskine's theology centred on the point at which Christian doctrines were related to human experience, and consequently, for him, the doctrine of the future life became closely linked with, if not reduced to, man's participation in the life of God in the present. This was clearly far removed from those theologies which regarded eschatology as being primarily concerned with ethical sanctions, and

[43] *True and False Religion*, p. 46.

[44] 'Scottish influences upon English theology', *Contemporary Review*, xxxii, 1878, 472.

[45] Cf. C. E. Braaten's comments on Paul Tillich's use of Origen's *Logos* theology and universalism. P. Tillich, *Perspectives on 19th and 20th Century Protestant Theology*, 1967, pp. xix-xxi.

[46] Newman MSS., Birmingham Oratory, (Copied letters, 83:1), J. H. Newman to G. F. Edwards, 2 Jan. 1883.

it is not surprising that Erskine aroused considerable hostility. It is also apparent that Erskine stood in a definite tradition, having links with mystical writers like William Law, and demonstrating similar characteristics to 'Christus Victor' theologians, like Schleiermacher, who placed the change in man's spiritual life (salvation) before the reconciliation which followed as its completion (atonement).[47] Like Coleridge, his approach may be characterized as existential, and, also like Coleridge, he was in danger of divorcing Christian faith from the events of the gospel and relating it primarily to events within a man's soul.

F. W. ROBERTSON

The theological approach mapped out by Erskine found an English counterpart in the theology of F. W. Robertson, the minister of the Trinity Chapel at Brighton. Like Coleridge and Erskine, Robertson refused to separate justification and sanctification, and he criticized the Calvinists for their perpetual concern with election. For him the one thing needful was for a man 'to win the character of heaven' before he died.[48] Yet how was this character to be won? Robertson believed that men were saved 'by the Life of God without us, manifested in the Person of Christ, kindling into flame the Life of God within us'.[49] The holiness of Christ was not a holiness which repelled, but one which inspired men with hope, and drew them to live in the same way. Christian faith, Robertson believed, must change a man's character, and men must be drawn to Christ rather than threatened with punishment. To talk of eternal life was to talk of a life of a particular quality, not of a life of endless duration. Theology was not concerned with the forensic and external but with actual and inward change in the life of man. Faith was not assent to a credal formula, but 'the broad principle of saving trust in God, above all misgiving . . . a living for the invisible instead of the seen'.[50] As he put it in his confirmation class catechism:

Q. Why is a correct faith necessary to salvation?
A. Because what we believe becomes our character, forms part of us, and character is salvation or damnation; what we *are*, that is our *heaven* or our *hell*. Every sin bears its own punishment.

[47] Cf. G. Aulen, *Christus Victor*, E. T., 1931 p. 153.
[48] Stopford Brooke, *The Life and Letters of F. W. Robertson*, 1880 ed., i, p. 100.
[49] F. W. Robertson, *Sermons*, (2nd series), 1897 ed., p. 203. (preached 1853).
[50] *Sermons*, (4th series), 1886, p. 141 (preached, 1849).

And the consequence, for instance, of denying the doctrine of immortality, would be to 'narrow all our infinite desires to a span' so that, 'almost inevitably, the passion of temptation of the moment will conquer'.[51] Likewise the anguish of the lost consisted in their sense of having failed to fulfil their potentialities.[52]

One instance in which Robertson took exception to contemporary Evangelical orthodoxy is particularly interesting, and that concerns the pious death-bed scenes in which Evangelicals so often delighted. It was only too easy, he wrote, to paint pictures of dying Christians sinking into the grave full of hope and triumph, when the reality was far from it: 'either very few death-beds are Christian ones, or else triumph is a very different thing from what the word generally implies . . . Rapture is a rare thing, except in books and scenes'. The true Christian death, he argued, was marked by calm, not by an ecstatic confession of faith: 'true fearlessness makes not parade'.[53] Such an attack on stage-managed death-beds was rare at the time.

F. D. MAURICE

Although it is legitimate to see in Maurice's theology the influence of those who preceded him, it is misleading to categorize it too rigidly. As his son wrote,

his thoughts and character were not . . . built up like rows of neatly ordered bricks. Rather, as each new thread of thought was caught by the shuttle of his ever-working mind, it was dashed in and out through all the warp and woof of what had been laid on before, and one sees it disappearing and reappearing, continually affecting all else, having its colour modified by successive juxtapositions, and taking its own place in the ever-growing pattern.[54]

Maurice undoubtedly owed much to his father's Unitarianism, with its 'conviction of divine benignity and [God's] designing all for ultimate good',[55] but, as with many who moved away from Unitarianism, he came to find a religion, which represented 'good nature' as the highest perfection of God, unsatisfying. He agreed with the

---

[51] *Life and Letters*, ii, p. 295.
[52] *Sermons*, (2nd ser.), 1897, pp. 198–9.
[53] *Sermons*, (3rd ser.), 1874, pp. 224–5 (preached 1852).
[54] F. Maurice, *Life of F. D. Maurice*, 1884, i, p. 147.
[55] Lant Carpenter MSS., Manchester College, Oxford, Michael Maurice to Lant Carpenter, 15 Feb. 1820 (Misc. letters).

orthodox charge that Unitarians had in general an inadequate and unrealistic understanding of sin. As early as 1836 there is a reference in a letter of Maurice's declaring that a universal restoration would need a special revelation before it could be accepted as divine truth.[56] In the same year Maurice told R. C. Trench that he had been learning much of Erskine's teaching from one of Edward Irving's assistants. This was in a letter which also reveals one of the basic axions of Maurice's theology: that a covenant does not establish a relationship but presupposes it, even though 'every man practically denies the relationship who does not enter into the covenant'.

Without a covenant we are not members of a Body; the Spirit dwells in the Body and in each of its members *as such*, and not as individuals. The Spirit in an individual is a fearful contradiction. The difference as to preaching seems to be—You declare forgiveness of sins as belonging to mankind, and invite them to become (which they have not been hitherto) portions of the kind—the Church; to the others you say—You are forgiven, you have the spirit.[57]

Although this may be found in Erskine, Maurice may also have drawn something from Irving's insistence that the Incarnation was more than a means to the Atonement, it was the manifestation of God to men.

There is no doubt that Maurice had a Platonic cast of mind, but he was also aware of the danger of withdrawing into an ideal world. He took issue with those who disparaged the 'matter-of-fact men' of the eighteenth century, in order to exalt the Coleridgean approach, which he characterized as emphasizing 'the preciousness of truth as distinct from facts'. With all his sympathy for the Coleridgean position, Maurice believed that truth, by which he seems to have meant existential truth, was not to be divorced from a more factual, presumably empirical and evidential, approach. He wrote in 1838 that

we are come upon an age in which truth without facts will be as impossible as facts without truth; and that the attempt to set up either must be conducted in quite a different spirit from that which animated Coleridge or the good men of the preceding age, however much the results may correspond.[58]

---

[56] *Life of Maurice*, ii, p. 15. Letter to F. J. A. Hort.   [57] i, p. 208.
[58] i, p. 251. F. D. Maurice to Strachey, 20 Aug. 1838.

An important early work, which gives considerable insight into the development of Maurice's characteristic theology, and which has perhaps been unduly neglected in studies of Maurice, is the introduction which he wrote in 1844 to an edition of William Law's reply of 1723 to Bernard Mandeville's cynical poem, *The Fable of the Bees*.[59] Maurice's introduction was written at the request of the unhappy John Sterling, the friend of Carlyle and Julius Hare, who had first come across Law's work. Maurice was of the impression that Law's arguments were 'rather too clever', but his introduction shows clearly that on many points he was in agreement with Law.[60] Law's strength lay, Maurice believed, in his refusal to treat the evidence of human depravity as being the only significant fact about the moral world. Evil was, Maurice and Law agreed, always anomalous, and so to talk about sin without implying that there was a right state from which sin was a departure was to talk nonsense. 'All reproof and moral censure imply the existence of it; all restoration implies the existence of it. Deny that there is such a state belonging to any man, and you say in effect that as to him, the words *reproof*, *judgment*, and *restoration* are without meaning.'[61] Popular preaching, with its emphasis on reward, treated evil as something which would only become a burden in the future, when punishment was added to it, just as good would only become an experienced good in the future when a certain amount of pleasure was added to it. Such notions were tantamount, Maurice claimed, to a position of 'Religious Eudaemonism', in which the ideas of 'lost' and 'saved' had ceased to have any moral connotation, and preaching only appealed to selfish motives.[62] Where even such appeals to man's self-interest were of no avail, it was not surprising that attempts were made to frighten women by lurid hell-fire preaching: 'in the dialect of some popular

---

[59] Mandeville's poem, originally published in 1714, and expanded and annotated in 1723, had as its theme the story of a hive of bees, who prospered by fraud, but were ruined when they turned to honest practices. Law objected both to Mandeville's effectual reduction of man to the status of an animal, and to his doctrine that morality was to be ordered according to the consequences of actions rather than by Divine law. It's appeal to John Sterling (and Maurice) is shown in Sterling's comment, quoted in Maurice's introduction: 'I have never seen, in our language, the elementary grounds of a rational ideal philosophy, as opposed to empiricism, stated with nearly the same clearness, simplicity, and force.' (J. H. Overton: *The Life and Opinions of the Rev. William Law*, A.M., 1881, pp. 31–6.)

[60] Cf. T. Hughes, *Memoir of Daniel Macmillan*, 1882, pp. 218–19.

[61] F. D. Maurice, *Introduction to Law's 'Remarks on the Fable of the Bees'*, 1844, p. xix.

[62] pp. lxi–lxii, lxviii.

preachers the affections and the nerves seem to be convertible terms'.[63]

Maurice attacked both religious teachers whose preaching was in terms of laws which it was impossible for men to fulfil, and those who couched their sermons in more personal terms, which produced a self-centred concern with the benefits of religion instead of with God. The old sense of the moral law had to be linked to the newer desire to see everything embodied in personal terms if a 'sound and manly theology' was to be developed. Maurice concluded his introduction to Law with a strong attack on those who tried to drive a wedge between the ethical values known by men, and those same ethical values when predicated of God. As such it is a valuable statement of the position which Maurice was later to defend against H. L. Mansel. Moreover there is a hint that the position Law attacked was one which had once greatly appealed to Maurice himself.

In the notion which has formally received the sanction of some great names and which has secretly incorporated itself with much of our popular divinity, that the words which express characteristics of the Divine Being may possibly have an altogether different signification in that application from the one which they bear when they are used respecting human agents, he will discover a root out of which all uncertainties and contradictions in every region of thought may naturally develop themselves. How plausible the opinion is—how readily it commends itself to the heart which does not like to retain GOD in its knowledge, and is glad to have substituted for Him, even to its own bitter cost, a POWER, utterly arbitrary, imposing rules which have no counterpart in itself, making Right, not being Right— how hard it is to shake off the dreadful vision, when once it has been contemplated, and to rise into the confession of One whom we may call our Father, describing by that name a real, not an imaginary relation—he will know too well from his own history and from this history of the world . . . Once sanction the doctrine that there is, or can be, a diversity in kind between the mercy and justice of the perfectly Merciful and Just, and the mercy and justice which he begets in his creatures, and these words become mere counterfeits, upon which we may put any value, or traffic with in any way we please.[64]

Maurice worked this out in the field of eschatology by insisting that the end for which God had made the world and man, was not the apportionment of rewards and punishments, but the knowledge of himself, which was eternal life, a real knowledge with sanctifying

[63] p. lxiii.   [64] pp. lxxvii–lxxix.

power.[65] Those who rejected God would indeed suffer punishment, but the heaviest punishment the wicked man could expect was 'that the state should continue, that he should be alienated from goodness and truth', for to be in such a state was 'to be in the deepest pit of hell'.[66]

Maurice was not concerned to develop an elaborate eschatology. His task he conceived to be the setting out of the relationship between God and man as the basis from which all else must start; and that relationship he believed really existed even when it was ignored or denied by the majority of men. His own sense of reverence and acuteness of conscience gave him a sensitivity to evil, which led him to interpret punishment as leaving the wicked man where he was, alienated from God. He believed that this understanding corresponded to the deepest thoughts of men, and, as he wrote to Tennyson in the dedicatory letter at the beginning of his *Theological Essays*, a theology which did not correspond to such thoughts and feelings was not a true theology.[67] This was one motive in the writing of the *Essays*, but they had a special purpose in that they were addressed to those amongst whom he had been brought up, the Unitarians, and this dictated to a large extent the subjects treated.

Maurice's background and temperament meant that he was anxious not to misrepresent Unitarianism, but his caution in this respect meant that he was in danger of giving the impression that his own views were nearer to those of Unitarians than was in fact the case. It was not surprising that the Evangelical peers on the council of King's College, London, where he held his professorship, were suspicious, the more so since they had already been alarmed by his advocacy of Christian Socialism.[68] Maurice, however, had little use for counsels of prudence, and believed that he had a duty to use his special understanding of Unitarianism to present the doctrine to which they objected in a way which might overcome their difficulties.

In the section of the *Theological Essays* concerned with eternal life and eternal death, Maurice began by demonstrating the ambivalence of attitudes towards hell. On the one hand it was admitted that the doctrine furnished the most plausible arguments against Christianity,

[65] F. D. Maurice, *The New Statute and Mr. Ward*, 1845, pp. 19–21.
[66] F. D. Maurice, *The Church a family*, 1850, pp. 195–6.
[67] F. D. Maurice, *Theological Essays*, 1853, p. v.
[68] H. G. Wood, *Frederick Denison Maurice*, 1950, p. 95.

and scared many into unbelief; on the other there was a demand from those, like the Evangelical Alliance, worried about liberal tendencies, for a stricter definition of the doctrine and its use as part of a common confession of faith.[69] In view of this Maurice looked anew at the doctrine, refusing to endorse either a rigorist position, or an easy universalism, with its different understanding of the word 'eternal' when it was applied to life and when it was applied to death. He took his stand on the qualitative nature of eternal life and eternal death.

What, then, is Death Eternal, but to be without God? What is that infinite dread which rises upon my mind, which I cannot banish from me, when I think of my own godlessness and lovelessness,—that I may become wholly separated from Love; becomes wholly immersed in selfishness and hatred? What dread can I have—ought I to have—besides this? What other can equal this? Mix up with this, the consideration of days and years and milleniums, you add nothing either to my comfort or my fears. All you do is to withdraw from me the real cause of my misery, which is separation from the sources of life and peace; from the hope which must come to me in one place or another, if I can again believe in God's love and cast myself upon it.[70]

Although he objected to Evangelical preachers for magnifying the horrors of hell in quantitative terms, he commended them for their insistence that one of the essential pains of hell was being left alone. Maurice believed that one of the contributory causes of secessions to the Church of Rome was the quest for a more merciful understanding of God's dealings with men which seemed to be offered by the doctrine of purgatory, but Maurice himself rejected the doctrine. For him it was too connected with mercenary ideas of payments to God to release souls, prayers for the dead, and 'idle fancies about places where spirits may be dwelling' to be an adequate answer. His own conclusion is to affirm that man must not attempt to set limits to what God may do, but must acknowledge that Christ has already broken down the barriers of space and time. He is the true judge, and, whenever man attempts to usurp that position, he proceeds on the principle that 'there is no living relation between Him and the creatures whose nature He took and for whom He died', a position which, for Maurice, was a denial of the heart of the gospel.[71]

---

[69] *Theological Essays*, p. 433.   [70] p. 437.

[71] p. 442. Maurice hoped that narrow interpretations of the text, 'where the tree falleth it shall lie', would be avoided. This was a favourite quotation of the supporters of

Maurice was fully aware that the essay on eschatology would bring a storm about his head. In the July of 1853 he told Charles Kingsley that he knew when he wrote it that he was writing his own sentence at King's College. He was fearful too of the reaction to his essay, knowing that it might lead to a restriction on the theological liberty of the English clergy.[72]

As might be expected, the reception of the *Essays* was mixed. The Unitarians welcomed them for their charitable treatment of the Unitarian position, but criticized them for much of their content. Their journal, the *Prospective Review*, regretted that it could not be persuaded by Maurice's arguments.

His lofty tone, the realism of his faith, and his large charity, never (but in the final note) lose their fascination for our mind, or cease to make us deeply regret that we are separated from him by those spectral chasms of theology, which we may not cross because we dare not treat shadows as if they were realities, nor he, because he dare not treat realities as if they were but shadows.[73]

James Martineau, the keenest intellect amongst the Unitarians and a man with many similarities to Maurice, thought the *Essays* 'shadowy and unimpressive', and needing to be brought into 'distincter shapes and better defined relations'.[74] Other estimates were in the same vein. The qualitative use of the word 'eternal' was castigated as 'a marvellous infirmity';[75] the *Essays* were condemned as 'Nebular';[76]

---

everlasting punishment, and almost the entire history of changing theological attitudes to hell could be written on the basis of the mutations of the verse of Edward Caswall's hymn, 'Days and moments quickly flying', which was based on it. The original, and strictest, version runs:

> As the tree falls,   As the man dies,
> So must it lie;   Such must he be,
> As the man lives,   All through the days
> So will he die,   Of Eternity.

(E. Caswall, *The Masque of Mary and other poems*, 1858, p. 220.)

[72] *Life of Maurice*, ii, 168–9.

[73] *Prospective Review*, ix, 1853, 599.

[74] J. Drummond and C. B. Upton, *Life and Letters of James Martineau*, 1902, i, p. 258. Letter of 1853 to R. H. Hutton. Martineau later revised his estimate of Maurice, and wrote in 1876: 'He has been the cause of a radical and permanent change in "orthodox" theology—viz., a shifting of its centre of gravity from the *Atonement* to the *Incarnation*.' (ii, p. 87.)

[75] *British Quarterly Review*, xviii, 1853, 459.

[76] *Eclectic Review*, 1854, i, 104. This also mentions a report that Cambridge students had been forbidden to buy the *Essays*.

James Anthony Froude wrote to A. H. Clough, that 'as thinkers Maurice, and still more the Mauriceans, appear to me the most hopelessly imbecile that any section of the world has been driven to believe in'.[77] George Eliot thought Maurice 'muddy rather than profound', and believed the *Essays* to be 'dim and foggy'.[78] The official journal of the Wesleyans warned its readers to steer clear of 'this new, complex and deadly heresy, which is little better than a modern Gnosticism of a refined character', and the reviewer bitterly attacked Maurice's statement that 'there is nothing which (man's) Lord and Master has not redeemed, of which He is not the King'.

> If this is the true doctrine, not only the peasant and the beggar, but the cold-blooded murderer, the brutal ravisher, the most fiendish of slave-drivers of all the children of the devil on earth, and all the demons of hell, may 'rejoice and sing merry songs' together. Hell may hold carnival on earth to the glory of the God of heaven. This does not seem to be the way in which our Loving Saviour and His Apostles preached to sinners; nor from the general proclamation of such a gospel as this could we expect anything but a fearful increase in wickedness.[79]

There can be no doubting the use of hell as a sanction for maintaining the moral and social order implicit in this criticism.

Others were less condemnatory. F. J. A. Hort, who had earlier corresponded with Maurice on the topic of eternal punishment, regretted Maurice's unequivocal rejection of purgatory, but agreed with Maurice on the three points at the heart of the controversy: that eternity was independent of duration; that the power of repentance is not limited to this life; and that it is not revealed whether or not all will ultimately be saved. Maurice's doctrine of eternity was, he believed, no different from that put forward by St. Augustine in the great discussion of the nature of time in the eleventh book of the *Confessions*, and his expression of a hope of universal salvation did not go beyond what was implied in traditional prayer for the

---

[77] F. L. Mulhauser: *Correspondence of A. H. Clough*, 1957, i, 466–7.

[78] G. Haight (ed.): *The George Eliot Letters*, 1954–6, ii, 125.

[79] *London Quarterly Review*, 1854–5, pp. 433, 436. For earlier expressions of horror at the consequences of universalism, and the assertion of a link between hell and the moral order, cf. D. P. Walker, *The Decline of Hell*, 1964. pp. 4, 15. An anonymous writer in 1878 made the same point against F. W. Farrar, 'Once remove the restraints of religion, teach the poor that future punishment is a fable, and what will be left to hinder the bursting forth with savage yells of millions of ravening wolves, before whom the salt of the earth will be trodden underfoot, Church establishments dissolved, and baronial halls become piles of blackened ruin?' (*Eternal Punishment: a critique of Canon Farrar's 'Eternal Hope'*, 1878, pp. 30–1).

departed. He hoped a number of High Churchmen would rally to Maurice's support. In a letter to Westcott he expressed his astonishment at how few had considered Maurice's doctrine to be other than novel and heretical. 'The prevalent idea seems to be that, right or wrong, Maurice had invented it to meet a particular case. No one seemed to enter into the impossibility of a theology, or the existence of a spiritual world, without it. Thompson was the only one I met who knew it was to be found in Plato.'[80] R. C. Trench told Samuel Wilberforce how pleased he was that Maurice had distinguished himself from modern universalists.[81]

Maurice's conflict with the council of King's College occasioned a number of pamphlets, but little theological argument. His dismissal from his chair was preceded by a long and tedious correspondence with R. W. Jelf, the Principal of the College, an old-fashioned High Churchman. The issues of reward and punishment, and the relation of time and eternity were both discussed, but to little purpose, and it became clear that both Maurice and Jelf were primarily motivated by a concern over the practical effects of their different doctrines. On 11 November 1853 the council of King's College declared Maurice's offices vacant.

The following year Maurice published a second edition of the *Theological Essays* with a new preface and much expanded essay on eternal life and eternal death, in which he attempted to explain why his views on eternity had met with such marked opposition. It was, he suggested, the influence of Locke on English thought which was to blame.

When anyone ventures to say to an English audience, that Eternity is not a mere negation of time, that it denotes something real, substantial, before all time, he is told at once that he is departing from the simple, intelligible meaning of words, that he is introducing novelties: that he is talking abstractions. This language is perfectly honest in the mouths of those who use it. But they do not know where they learnt it. They did not get it from peasants, or women, or children; they did not get it from the Bible. They got it from Locke.[82]

[80] A. F. Hort, *Life and Letters of F. J. A. Hort*, 1896, ii, 266; cf. 261, 275; and, for Hort's understanding of purgatory, ii, 336. Plato: *Timaeus*, 37C–38A.

[81] [M. Trench ed.], *Richard Chenevix Trench, Archbishop. Letters and Memorials*, i, 1888, 302–3.

[82] *The concluding essay and preface to the second edition of Mr. Maurice's Theological Essays*, 1854, p. 50.

Maurice was, of course, referring to Locke's *Essay on Human Under-standing*, in which Locke argues that infinity is a negative idea, arrived at by extrapolation from man's experience of duration, and that eternity can only be conceived quantitatively.[83] Eternal death, Maurice insisted, was just as frightening a concept to him as it was to the supporters of the Evangelical Alliance with their dogma of everlasting punishment. The difference between them was that the Alliance thought it was possible to overcome the dissemination of a vague universalism by leaving no loop-hole for doubt about the punishment of the wicked; Maurice, on the other hand, thought it more important to transform the understanding of eternal death, so that its real nature, man's alienation from God and from his own true nature was apparent.[84]

The most important criticism of Maurice's position came not from Jelf, nor from the Evangelicals, but from H. L. Mansel of St. John's College, Oxford. In his criticism of Maurice, Mansel argued that time could be considered in two ways, either as a 'portion of duration separated from that which succeeds it by some difference in the states of consciousness of which it is the condition', and he gives as an example 'the time when I was a boy' contrasted with 'the subsequent time when I became a man', or time could be considered as the condition of man's consciousness. According to the first view eternity differed from time in that it referred to a state of being without an end, as opposed to a terminable one, an indefinite rather than infinite duration. On the second view, if eternity is regarded as the opposite of time, it can only denote a form of consciousness not subject to succession, and therefore a form of consciousness of which, by Mansel's epistemology, we can have no knowledge.

We have thus two distinct senses of Eternity, the one that of unlimited duration, approximately and partially conceivable as indefinite duration; the other, that of a consciousness out of duration, absolutely and totally inconceivable. An idea of this latter kind, which has never been present in intuitition, and consequently cannot be represented in thought, is what I mean by a *negative* idea, and our admission or rejection of Mr. Maurice's teaching depends, if I understand him rightly, on the question of how far such negative ideas are admissible in theology.[85]

---

[83] John Locke: *Essay on Human Understanding*, II. xiv. 27 and II. xviii. Cf. R. I. Aaron: *John Locke*, 1937, pp. 160–4.

[84] Maurice: *Concluding Essay etc.*, p. 57.

[85] H. L. Mansel: *Man's conception of eternity: an examination of Mr. Maurice's theory of a fixed state out of time*, 1854, p. 8; cf. pp. 4–6.

Mansel's objection to Maurice's conception of eternity is that it is a state, of which, because of the nature of human knowledge, we can know nothing. Moreover, he argued, one of the essential conditions for personality to exist would appear to be memory. Since this is linked with temporal notions of succession it was very improbable that, even if the state for which Maurice argued, existed, man would be able to participate in it. Mansel took Maurice to task for applying Patristic language concerning the eternity of God to man, and questioned the validity of Maurice's assertion that the Divine Consciousness had no relation to time. Man was a creature of time, and this was, therefore, something of which he could have no knowledge.[86] Mansel concluded his attack by a résumé of his epistemological criticisms and by suggesting that Maurice's position was 'incompatible with the conception of the next life as a continuation and development of the present' and with 'a state of progress and increasing knowledge'.

It seems to substitute a negative notion for a positive one; to exchange the vivid anticipation of a living futurity for the vague and meaningless intimation of some possible state of existence under no conditions which we can figure to ourselves of human consciousness, or human personality.[87]

Mansel thus reflected the common nineteenth-century idea of the future life as progressive, whilst Maurice was asserting another nineteenth-century characteristic, that the future life was personal. Temporality for Maurice was connected with mechanistic doctrines of the relation of God to the world, and with a quantitative as opposed to a qualitative understanding of the future life. But since, for Mansel, the debate was an epistemological one, he was able to accuse Maurice of teaching the 'vague and meaningless intimation of some possible state of existence', which was the very opposite of Maurice's intention. For Maurice, Mansel's insistence on regulative truths supplied by revelation as comprising the only possible religion was a return to a religious system in which the highest value was the living out of certain laws, and which had no place for the growth of a loving relationship between man and God. It was a system which was too open to the mechanistic understanding that to Maurice was the negation of Christianity. For Maurice it was the only religion worth having which was at stake. For Mansel such a religion could not be worth having for the simple reason that it was impossible in terms of man's nature.

[86] p. 21.   [87] pp. 22–3.

The issues which were at stake in 1853 received further attention
in Maurice's later theological writing, and the *Theological Essays*
themselves included some interesting reflections on other aspects of
eschatology, which did not become matters of controversy to the
same extent as the doctrine of eternal punishment. *The Church of
England Review* had attacked Maurice for describing the popular
understanding of the resurrection of the body as 'a resurrection of
relics', and Maurice replied to this charge in the second edition of the
Essays.[88] His purpose had been, he wrote, to present the doctrine
in a credible way so that it might again be taken seriously. He did
this by a discussion of death, pointing to the isolation of man in
death, and the sense of dread which this engenders, and arguing that,
for the Christian, this isolation has been overcome by the death of
Christ. The death of Christ was for him, the way to a true understanding of death, as the voluntary surrender of both body and soul,
the whole man, into the hands of God.

Christ gave up all that was His own—He gave Himself to His Father. He
disclaimed any life which did not belong to Him in virtue of His union
with the Eternal God. It is our privilege to disclaim any life which does not
belong to us in virtue of our union with Him. This would be an obvious
truth, if we are indeed created and constituted in Him,—if He was the root
of our humanity. We should not then have any occasion to ask how much
perishes or survives in the hour of death. We should assume that all must
perish to the end that it all may survive.[89]

Failure to appreciate the fact that it was the whole man which died,
had led, Maurice argued, to a clinging to the corpse in an attempt to
understand death, whether by the Roman Church's cult of relics, or
by a literal interpretation of the resurrection of the body in Protestantism, the belief that 'at a certain day (the relics of a man) will all be
gathered together and ... the very body to which they once
belonged will be constructed out of them'.[90] One of the sources of
this literal interpretation Maurice believed to be the first chapter of
Butler's *Analogy*, which had been misused as a handbook of Christian
evidences. But for Maurice what the resurrection of the body represented was the fact that the Christian's redemption was a redemp-

---

[88] *Theological Essays*, 1854[2], p. xxi. Cf. 'The future parties in religion', *Church of
England Review*, N. S., iii, 1854 pp. 158–83.

[89] pp. 155–8, 167.

[90] p. 167. Maurice anticipates some twentieth-century writing on the theology of
death, cf. L. Boros, *The Moment of Truth*, 1965; K. Rahner, *On the Theology of Death*,
1961.

tion out of the corruption which was the concomitant of earthly life. Resurrection is the manifestation of redemption.

The strong existential reference of Maurice's theology is also apparent in his treatment of God's judgment. This was to be seen as operating in man's present life, and references to a future judgment were to be interpreted as the revelation of the true relationship between man and God. This was the true judgment, not a supposed 'gathering together, in some certain space, of multitudes that never could be gathered together in any space', a view which he considered reproduced 'all the pomp and solemnities of earthly courts of justice' and reduced Christ to 'the mere image and pattern of an earthly magistrate'.[91] It was an all too common error, he wrote in his *Lectures on the Apocalypse*, to make earthly events the pattern of God's activity, instead of seeing them as reflections of that activity.[92] At the end of the same *Lectures* he stated his conviction that God was the god of hope, and to be alienated from him was to be shut up in despair: hell has an existential quality.

All blessedness—oh! when shall we understand this?—consists in the acknowledgment of that which is; all misery and damnation in the denial of it. That men disbelieve the good and gracious God to be their Father—that they count Him not their Father but their enemy . . . this is the lie of which all other lies are the offspring. Those spirits which reject truth, which feed on a lie and live in a lie, are in the lake of fire. There is no other way of describing their condition but that. A fire is burning in them which nothing can quench . . . If we look at this fire merely as reason, without Revelation, looks at it, we could find in it only despair. When God enters, despair ceases. He is called in Scripture the God of Hope. That which we think of as His must give us hope.[93]

It would be wrong to describe Maurice as a universalist, for universalism states as a dogmatic certainty that all men will be eventually saved, and Maurice suspected the certainty of system. There is no doubt, however, that his understanding of God led him to hope that all men would eventually be saved. His struggle against the harshness of the contemporary belief in an everlasting hell, and his attempt to express Christian doctrine in more personal terms, won him much sympathy. Tennyson, a firm believer in the 'wider

[91] F. D. Maurice, *The Gospel of St. John*, 1857, p. 487.

[92] F. D. Maurice, *Lectures on the Apocalypse*, 1861, pp. 71–2.

[93] pp. 414–15. Maurice finds grounds for hope in that the Apocalypse speaks not only of those who are in a state of alienation from God, but also of the things which alienate them being cast into the 'lake of fire'. pp. 404–7.

hope', dedicated a poem to him shortly after his dismissal from King's, and his fellow Christian Socialist, J. M. Ludlow, told him in 1859 of a conversation in which a friend had said to him, that he was not afraid of Maurice's views gaining ground, but that '20 years hence they will form a new orthodoxy, and that men will not be allowed to speak against them'.[94] Maurice's theology was not, however, conducive to the establishment of a new system of orthodoxy, although his influence remained powerful. Self-conscious Mauriceans, like the Congregationalist, James Baldwin Brown, were few, but many welcomed a theology in which salvation was seen in the context of the relationship between men and God which had already been established. Maurice's eschatology was never the final chapter of a doctrinal system. For Maurice, as for Newman, the significance of eschatology was that it spoke of the final consummation of the relationship with God, in which man existed in his present life. Heaven was the acknowledgement of, and growth into, that relationship. Hell was the failure to recognize and live in terms of it; it was the failure to recognize where the true fulfilment of human nature was to be found.

[94] Ludlow MSS., Cambridge University Library Add. Mss. 7348/17/30. Tennyson's poem 'To the Rev. F. D. Maurice'.

V   Holiness Necessary for
Future Blessedness

The eschatology of the early Tractarians may best be understood as the extension to the future life of the emphasis which they placed on the doctrine of the Church and the necessity of sanctification. In an eschatological context the doctrine of the Church was developed in a stress on the communion of saints, and the call to sanctification led to a gradual acceptance of some kind of purgatory. The revival of prayers for the departed was associated with both these themes.

The early Tractarian understanding of the communion of saints was drawn both from the older High Church tradition, and from the Fathers, but it was set within the framework of a seriousness shared with Evangelicalism and a sharp awareness that the drama of salvation was set against the ultimate choices of heaven and hell. Although the Tractarians differed from the Evangelicals about the means by which men were brought to salvation, they were at one with them in stressing the seriousness of the quest and the holiness which was its precondition. Like F. D. Maurice, however, they reacted from a system whose language of rewards and punishments made it appear mechanical and impersonal, and by placing ideas of reward in the context of the communion of saints, which was grounded in the holiness of God himself, they attempted to convey a more personalized eschatology.

A preliminary glance at some of the characteristics of Evangelical eschatology will illustrate some of the similarities and contrasts with Tractarian teaching, and we may turn to the sermons of J. W. Cunningham, the Evangelical vicar of Harrow who profoundly influenced the young Frederick Faber, for examples of common Evangelical teaching.[1] Cunningham's theology was Arminian and therefore, when he divides men into two classes, it is not into the elect and the damned but into the committed and the undecided

---

[1] H. N. Oxenham observed that Faber's early Evangelicalism was more pronounced than that of many of the Tractarians and exercised a more perceptible influence on his religious writing. (*Studies in Ecclesiastical History and Biography*, 1884, p. 260.)

waverers. Whilst all men may be saved, it is far from certain that all will in fact be saved, and the evidence suggests that the great majority of men are waverers, who teeter all their lives on the edge of destruction and ruin, enjoying the delights of profligacy, 'till perhaps death surprises them, and dismisses them to the region of everlasting and unspeakable misery'.[2] The appeal which Cunningham makes to those in this condition is typical of much Evangelical preaching:

But, Oh the horror of such a state! of standing from hour to hour on so fine an edge, with the pit 'whose smoke ascendeth for ever and ever' enlarging its mouth beneath you! *Awake, awake*, poor lost creature, to a sense of your miserable condition! . . . 'Escape for your life! Look not behind you!'[3]

For believers also Cunningham has his warnings. They must not rashly lay claim to the promises of God, nor must they forget that there can be no salvation in heaven without preparation on earth. 'The future inhabitant of heaven is not to be merely a corrupt man lifted to heaven, and forcibly introduced into the house of many mansions; but a man purged of his corruptions and fitted for the world of glory before he enters it.'[4]

If heaven is the world where these promises are to be enjoyed, this is the world where the title to them is to be obtained. If that is the region of triumph, this is the field of conflict . . . If the heart is to be transformed, the temper to be subdued, and the whole of man to be subjugated to the will of God, the change must be accomplished *here*. There is no intermediate world, no border country, measured by the hand of the great Judge, in which you may shake off the corruption of the flesh, and cloth yourself in the vesture of righteousness. *Here* it is that you must . . . acquire the tastes, the habits, the qualifications which are to fit you for the kingdom of God.[5]

After death the soul will be brought face to face with God, and to one who died penitently and believing this will be an admission into the bliss of heaven. The impenitent, on the other hand, will experience only the naked justice of God, untempered with mercy, and Christ himself will tread the winepress of God's wrath.[6] In his sermon on 'The Invisible World' in which he develops these themes, there are a number of passages reminiscent of both *The Dream of Gerontius* and

---

[2] J. W. Cunningham, *Sermons*, i, 1822, 1.   [3] pp. 241–2.
[4] ii, 433.   [5] i, 430.   [6] ii, 55–6.

the eschatology of Faber's later devotional writings.[7] Similarly Cunningham's insistence on sanctification and his warnings against presuming on God's mercy clearly anticipate Tractarian themes.

In his eschatology Newman retained many of these characteristic Evangelical emphases, though the Evangelicalism he had known was Calvinist rather than Arminian. From the time of his first conversion, as he acknowledged in the *Apologia*, he had held 'with a full inward assent and belief the doctrine of eternal punishment, as delivered by our Lord Himself, in as true a sense . . . as that of eternal happiness', though he had always looked for ways of making the idea less terrible to his imagination.[8] In 1819, when he had been troubled by the damnatory clauses of the Athanasian Creed, he listed in his journal his reasons for accepting them: the piety of the Reformers who had approved them; the fact that it would not be uncharitable to hold that drunkards and extortioners were in a state of perdition since a man's faith and practice were intimately related; and the lessening of the significance of the Incarnation which a denial of eternal punishment would seem to entail.[9] This last reflection weighed powerfully with Newman, who had an acute sense of what the Evangelicals like to call 'the sinfulness of sin'. When sin first marred God's good and holy creation, he wrote in his journal in 1823,

How must have all nature shrunk in horror and awe at the unnatural event! To perceive one little spot in the eternal atmosphere infected and fevered with sin! and what can be more exquisite presumption than for that guilty being himself to pretend to measure his own transgression, to call it mere imperfection, to assign it its due punishment, to treat with anger the idea of its meriting eternal punishment, and to scoff at the doctrine which teaches the necessity of a Saviour, and Him, the Eternal Son of God.[10]

Holiness, not comfort, must, therefore, be the end of all preaching, and Newman's early sermons show how closely he stuck to this rule.[11]

In 1824 we again have a record of him disputing about hell, this time whilst walking with a friend from Turnham Green to Knights-

[7] A remark of Cunningham's, 'Coldness in your case is treason' (i, 185), could almost be taken as a text for Faber's writings.

[8] J. H. Newman, *Apologia pro vita sua*, World's Classics ed., 1964, p. 6.

[9] J. H. Newman, *Autobiographical Writings*, (ed. H. Tristram), 1956, p. 162.

[10] p. 170.

[11] p. 172. Cf. John E. Linnan, 'The search for absolute holiness: a study of Newman's Evangelical period', *The Ampleforth Journal*, 73, ii, 1968, 161–74.

bridge. His friend was vehemently opposed to the idea of eternal punishment, and Newman noted the arguments he put forward in his journal:

The antecedent improbability of eternal punishment is so great that it is absurd to believe in it. The argument about the word *aionios* is an absurdity; to be so nice as to make a doctrine depend upon the meaning of a word!... A woman murdered her four infants that they might not go to hell—now, if punishment were eternal, she was very wise... Many presume on the aid of supernatural assistance, who have no such assistance. They weaken and soften their minds. All those arguments you produce about our being prisoners, and thus bad judges of our guilt, and that we ought to feel love etc. to God etc., etc., seem to be absurd. People are not in earnest when they call themselves the vilest of sinners.[12]

To these standard objections Newman replied, that nobody could understand Scripture properly without Divine illumination; that in his view salvation was not confined to one sect; and that all who sincerely sought the truth would not be excluded from heaven.

Pusey's early views, which were little affected by Evangelicalism, nevertheless show the same seriousness as Newman's. In 1828, after his father died, he wrote to Maria Barker, his future wife, that he was convinced that his father was in heaven, though he regretted that he had not spoken any last words.[13] The previous year he had discussed with her eternal salvation and the number of the saved, in which he had stressed that it was far more important for men to be concerned with the primary task of the salvation of their own souls than with fruitless speculation about the population of heaven. He himself at this time had no doubts about the heathen being saved, and even the Jews—popularly held to be condemned for wilfully rejecting the Gospel—would, he believed, 'be tried by the degree of spirituality to which under their darkness' they attained.[14] 'God will, one may safely be convinced, pardon all whom He *can* pardon, admit to Heaven all to whom it would be a Heaven.' At this early period he can even sound Mauricean, maintaining that the controversies with the Unitarians had led to a debasement of the idea of God, with the Divine justice being opposed to the Divine mercy.

It is nowhere in Scripture said 'God is Justice' but it is said 'God is Love'; not of course a cold human love, but one which we may hope that our own may partake in a purer state . . . I dwell on this . . . because . . . far too much stress is laid on the terrors of the Lord; and looking upon Him as an object of dread, we cannot make any approaches to that 'perfect love which casteth out fear'.[15]

Pusey was never, however, a universalist. If men knew themselves to be certain of salvation it would infallibly diminish their desire for holiness, and, as a preacher, Pusey felt himself unable to hold out any hope where Scripture did not give positive grounds for it, though privately he hoped for 'the extension of mercy to thousands, whose case, to our limited view, would seem desperate'.[16]

Pusey later came to hold much narrower views, almost certainly because of the deaths of his wife and daughter, which he took to be a judgment upon him. He became increasingly worried about the laxity of Christians, and the apparent betrayal of the Church by those who ought to be devoted to its welfare. The sterner notes are apparent in a sermon on the Day of Judgment (1839). God, Pusey maintains, always reveals Himself to men under a twofold aspect— as an object of awe and fear, and of faith and love—but it is usually the terror which comes first, the knowledge that 'we are living in the ruins of a lost world' and 'they who escape, escape like Lot out of the midst of the overthrow, out of the flames of God's wrath'. He who lives in such a world is bound to keep the thought of judgment perpetually before his mind:

Be this then ever before us; be our first thought morning by morning to think of the morning of the resurrection; be our last night by night, the sleep of death, after which cometh the judgment . . . remember the parching flame, the never-dying worm, the everlasting fire, the gnashing of teeth, 'the smoke of torment' which 'goeth up for ever and ever'; where they have no rest day nor night. Set heaven and hell before your eyes, so you may escape hell, and by God's mercy attain heaven.[17]

The note of *memento inferni* was from this time a constant one in Pusey's preaching; if anything the gloom descended even more later on, as can be seen from his 1856 sermon on hell and his reply to *Essays and Reviews* in 1864.

Although Newman's eschatology was strict, compared with Pusey he had a certain flexibility in his handling of ideas. For Newman holiness was the pre-eminent qualification for heaven, and this

---

[15] Ibid., 21 Oct. 1827.   [16] Ibid.
[17] E. B. Pusey, *The Day of Judgment*, 1839, pp. 11–12, 29.

stress runs through all his sermons. It was not that holiness was a kind of arbitrary qualification laid down by God for those who wished to enjoy his blessings, the sober truth was that an unholy man could not bear to see the face of God: 'heaven is *not* heaven, is not a place of happiness, except to the holy'. Consequently for an 'irreligious man' heaven would be nothing less than hell.[18] The converse of this demand for holiness was the sensitivity to the magnitude of sin, which we have already noted in Newman, and it was a characteristic of Newman's preaching which made its mark on his hearers. As James Anthony Froude put it, 'sin with Newman was real':

... not a misfortune to be pitied and allowed for; to be talked of gravely in the pulpit and forgotten when out of it; not a thing to be sentimentally signed over at the evening tea-party, with a complacent feeling that we were pleasing Heaven by calling ourselves children of hell, but in very truth a dreadful monster, a real child of a real devil, so dreadful that at its first appearance amongst mankind it had convulsed the infinite universe, and that nothing less than a sacrifice, so tremendous that the mind sinks crushed before it, could restore the balance ... Sin is of faith, not of mathematics.[19]

This characteristic of Newman is basic to any understanding of his eschatology or his conviction of the need for sanctification. Newman was aware that sin most frequently showed itself in small short-comings rather than in great acts of rebellion against God, yet for him, however small such faults might appear, they must be regarded with the utmost seriousness. 'A slight deviation at setting out may be the measure of the difference between tending to hell and tending to heaven.'[20] No *via media* between good and evil existed. As Augustine taught, only two states are to be found, one subject to God's favour, the other to his wrath.

Though as far as the sight of the external world goes, all men seem to be in a middle state common to one and all. Yet, much as men look the same, and impossible as it is for us to say where each man stands in God's sight, there are two and but two classes of men, and they have characters and destinies as far apart in their tendencies as light and darkness: this is the case even of those who are in the body, and it is much more true of those who have passed into the unseen state.[21]

[18] J. H. Newman, *Parochial and Plain Sermons*, i, 1868, 7.
[19] J. A. Froude, *The Nemesis of Faith*, 1849, pp. 160-1.
[20] *Parochial and Plain Sermons*, iv, 39.   [21] p. 87.

Yet, as Newman recognizes, men are, for the most part, unaware that a great gulf divides them, and that salvation is not easily won, and that they possess eternal souls.[22] The way to hell is indeed broad, and there are many grounds for the opinion that more men are lost than are saved. It is only too easy mistakenly to suppose that because a person is baptised, or because a notorious sinner is a friend, that he is saved.[23] Only in the eternal world will the realities of a man's situation stand out clearly.

There will be no need of shutting your eyes to this world, when this world has vanished from you, and you have nothing before you but the throne of God and the slow continual movements about it in preparation of the judgment. In that interval, when you are in that vast receptacle of dis-embodied souls, what will be your thoughts about the world which you have left! How poor will seem its aims, how faint, its keenest pleasures, compared with the eternal aims, the infinite pleasures.[24]

In his presentation of this Augustinian picture of the two realities of light and darkness Newman strives to avoid depersonalizing the relations between God and man, even when he attempts to speak of the wrath of God. For instance, in talking of the death of Judas, Newman says that his death was not the result of 'some unfeeling fate, which sentences the wicked to hell—but [of] a Judge who surveys him from head to foot, who searches him through and through, to see if there is any ray of hope, any latent spark of faith'. And he holds that this also will be true of God's treatment of the wicked at the Day of Judgment, who will be condemned 'not in a mass, but one by one', each in turn being dealt with firmly and justly, yet 'with all the circumstantial solicitude and awful care of one who would fain make, if He could, the fruit of His Passion more numerous than it is'.[25]

We also find in Newman's early sermons a discussion of the resurrection of the body. His sermon on this begins with a warning to his hearers against deciding too easily that the distinction between soul and body is an easy one to make, and he asks them to recognize that 'we have no direct cognizance of what may be called the substantive existence of the body, only of its accidents'.[26] A false 'spiritualism' must at all costs be avoided. The body is not ex-cluded from man's redemption, and through the sacraments, 'the medicine of immortality', the body is brought within the range of

[22] i, 25; iv, 87.   [23] iv, 88–91.   [24] iv, 92.   [25] iii, 122.   [26] i, 273.

God's redeeming activity, though Newman allows that God may sustain immortal life apart from the sacraments.

We eat the sacred bread and our bodies become sacred; they are not ours; they are Christ's; they are instinct with that flesh which saw not corruption; they are inhabited by His Spirit; they become immortal; they die but to appearance and for a time; they spring up when their sleep is ended and reign with Him for ever.[27]

But if the sacraments provide the principle of the resurrection, there is no easy explanation of its mode, nor of the way in which bodily identity is maintained between the earthly and the resurrection body: for Newman it suffices that God's declaration is accepted and acted upon.[28]

Henry Manning's Anglican sermons reveal a similar eschatology to that of Newman. Here again we find the same stress on sanctification, with its correlate, the horror of sin, though there is a lack of the almost frightening intensity which marks Newman's preaching. For Manning men perpetually fail to realize their need of salvation and shrink from 'the severe holiness' which God demands of them, yet they know that 'salvation is being saved from sin, from its guilt and from its soil, from the power with which it rules over us, from the love with which we cling to it;—in a word, it is the health of the soul cleansed of its deadly sickness; the making of the sinful creature a holy being'.[29] Maurice himself could not have underlined so firmly that salvation is from sin and not from punishment. Like Newman, Manning protests against the generality of Christians who follow a moderate, middle way, forgetting that the judgments of eternity know of no such course. Such Christians lack the print of the Cross, without which sin cannot be removed, and if sin is not removed a man's life remains like a biased wheel: 'if it runs a thousand years [it] will never run true'. As long as a man remains in sin he is unable to realize his condition, only when he has stepped outside it can he see it in its true horror as a rebellion against God.

It is a change in *us*, which is needed to reveal us to ourselves. What we were and what we are is as objectively real as the firmament of heaven. But the blind cannot behold it and dim eyes see but little of it . . . If we would but slowly say to ourselves, 'I was made to love God and to be happy in

---

[27] i, 275. Härdelin points out that Newman stressed the link between sacramental theology and soteriology, whereas R. I. Wilberforce emphasized its connection with Christology. (*The Tractarian Understanding of the Eucharist*, Uppsala, 1965, p. 155.)

[28] i, 277.   [29] H. E. Manning, *Sermons*, 1842, i, 79.

Him'; and then remember not our rebellions, but the great gulf of coldness and distance which stands open between Him and us; we should feel that to love God is itself life everlasting, and not to love God is itself eternal death.[30]

On the details of the future life Manning is in some cases more definite than Newman. The resurrection body will be, he declares, 'the very same body which we now dwell in', but reorganized and raised to the conditions of the spiritual life. To believe in the resurrection of the body, is to believe in the restoration of the whole man, 'of all in which consists the integrity of our nature and the identity of our person'. This will be true for both the saved and the damned, though the latter will have that flesh and blood in which they sinned changed by its being endowed with 'a capacity for suffering and a sense of agony which surpass the imagination of our hearts', and in hell 'being itself shall become an intolerable anguish'. But neither suffering nor glory is an individual possession in the future life. Both are corporate, and there will be a consequent recognition of each other amongst both good and evil, and in hell each will reflect another's agony and make the suffering more intense.[31]

The understanding of the future life shown by both Manning and Newman is but an extension of their general teaching. The insistent note that sin is an offence against the infinite holiness of God sounds clearer for both of them beyond the grave, where it is no longer blurred by the medley of other sounds. Without repentance there can be no admission to heaven, for heaven is essentially communion with a holy God, and Newman was not alone in his awareness of 'two and two only absolutely and luminously self-evident beings, myself and my Creator',[32] between whom all that was of any importance took place. It was because God was holy that hell was a reality to them, which cannot be doubted, even though they do not care to enumerate its pains beyond the traditional *poena damni*, the pain of the loss of God. There is indeed a Christian joy to look forward to in the fullness of the presence of God, but this is always on earth tempered by an astringent awareness of the frailty of human nature. The perspective remains clear, that the issues of life are momentous, that the choices are serious, and that the result is heaven or hell.[33]

[30] iii, 1847, 83, 90–1, 93, 302–3.   [31] i, 366, 367, 371–3.
[32] *Apologia*, p. 4.
[33] David Newsome has suggested that the sternness of much of Newman's and

PURGATORY AND PRAYERS FOR THE DEAD

The Tractarian emphasis on God's holiness, coupled with their Patristic studies, led to a re-examination of prayers for the dead and the theory of a purificatory state after death. As early as 1826 the death of Pusey's younger brother, Henry, had led Pusey to ask Newman if one should dare to pray for the dead: 'Nothing, I am sure, can be found in Scripture against praying for the dead.'[34] But it was the proposed publication of Archbishop Ussher's work on prayers for the dead as one of the *Tracts for the Times* in 1835, which was the first occasion of serious discussion of the question. Pusey was doubtful about the wisdom of the publication. He argued that there was not the same need to bring prayers for the dead before the notice of the public as there was with other neglected doctrines, and to do so might be to risk arousing ultra-Protestant feeling against the tracts and prevent more important doctrines being given proper attention. Moreover it seemed likely to him that the doctrine could be used to give support to lax ideas about sin and salvation, and therefore any publication of Ussher's work ought to be accompanied with a note of protest against 'the laxity of the present day, which seems to think it scarcely possible that any can miss of heaven'.[35] Newman was, however, determined on publication and finally won Pusey's nervous agreement, Pusey hoping that a clearer distinction might be drawn 'between Romish abuses and the primitive use'.[36]

In 1836 Dr. Dickinson, one of Archbishop Whateley's chaplains, published an attack on the tract writers in the form of a fictitious letter from the Pope, and included amongst his targets the Tractarian teaching on prayers for the dead. Pusey undertook to reply, carefully contrasting 'the early practice of commemorating God's departed servants at the holy communion, and praying for their increased bliss and fuller admission to the beatific vision' with 'the modern abuse of masses for the dead and the doctrine of purgatory'.[37] Whilst he conceded that the reason for the omission of the prayers for the dead

---

Manning's preaching was the result of their combination of the severer aspects of Calvinism and Catholicism, election and the necessity of attaining sanctification, whilst rejecting the comforting side, the assurance of the grace of final perseverance, and the ascription of merit to good works. (*The Parting of Friends*, 1966, p. 209.)

[34] Liddon, *Life of Pusey*, i, 112.   [35] ii, 6.   [36] pp. 6–7.

[37] *Pastoral Epistle from His Holiness the Pope to some Members of the University of Oxford*, 1836, p. 25; E. B. Pusey, *An earnest remonstrance to the author of the 'Pope's Pastoral Letter'*, 1836, p. 21.

found in the 1549 Prayer Book in that of 1552 was their association with the doctrine of purgatory in the popular mind, he believed that there was no necessary connection between the two, and warned of the consequences which had followed from the neglect of prayers for the dead. 'We who so lose out of mind God's departed servants, have also lost the notion of the intermediate state.'[38] Pusey at this time stood strongly opposed to purgatory, and when Newman showed him a tract he had written comparing the Roman doctrine with the scriptural and Patristic texts cited in support of it, told Newman that he thought it treated Roman errors too lightly. A stronger line against the practical effects of purgatory was needed. Liddon comments that Pusey's letter about this tract was 'the first indication of a divergence between Pusey and Newman'.[39]

Newman's own attitude to purgatory at this time is made clear in his sermon on 'The Intermediate State'. The idea of purgatory as a prison, where men's sins are burned away, he considers a depressing notion, though he allows that God could with perfect justice adopt this way of acting towards men, for, in reality, all deserve eternal punishment. Yet, Newman claims, there are no grounds for supposing that such a state has been revealed: 'everyone must admit it to be a very frightful notion at least that [the souls of the righteous] should be kept from their rest and confined in a prison beneath the earth.' But, being aware that the New Testament emphasis on the Second Coming of Christ did not quite tally with accepted ideas that death was the moment of triumph for the righteous, Newman maintains that there is an intermediate state in which the faithful departed are preserved free from further trials and the possibility of sinning. It is a necessary time of preparation for heaven, a period of maturation, and 'a school-time of contemplation' in comparison with the 'discipline of active service' in this world.[40]

In Tract XC Newman's attempted distinction between the primitive and the Roman doctrine of purgatory brought the subject into discussion again. Keble doubted whether Newman's distinction could be made, though, for historical reasons, he was clear that Article XXII could not be taken as referring to the Tridentine doctrine. Nevertheless he thought it almost certain that Trent had, implicitly at least, meant to establish the doctrine referred to in the

[38] *An earnest remonstrance . . . ,* p. 26.
[39] Liddon, ii, p. 8. The tract was published as No. LXXIX.
[40] *Parochial and Plain Sermons,* iii, 371–2, 377–8.

article.[41] Further discussion of purgatory is also found in a section of William Palmer's reply to Wiseman's attack on Newman.

Palmer believed that the corner-stone of Roman teaching about 'satisfactions, indulgences and suffrages for the dead' was the idea that a temporal penalty for sin could still be exacted after the eternal penalty had been remitted. Once this basic principle had been conceded it was, he claimed, but a short step to teaching the remission of such temporal punishment by works of penance in this life and suffering in purgatory in the future life. Palmer was not content with providing an explanation of how the doctrine of purgatory arose, but attempted to set out a positive doctrine which would take account of the areas of experience on which the doctrine of purgatory had been based. Suffering, he suggested, should not be regarded as punishment but as an education for a higher glory. If evil is inflicted on a pardoned sinner it can only be for the sinner's good and consequently any prayers to avert the evil would be wrong. He refused to accept Bellarmine's argument that, since death was the unremitted penalty for original sin, all individual sins must have similar penalties attached to them. The two cases were not parallel. If God did require further satisfaction after the remission of sins, it could only be in terms of eternal punishment, which remained the proper penalty for sin.[42] In the sixth letter of his reply to Wiseman Palmer gave more particular consideration to purgatory. The doctrine stated that those who suffered in purgatory were the righteous and the justified, yet, Palmer maintained, God gave sanctifying grace when he justified sinners. If this was the case, it was intolerable to claim that the justice and mercy of God were glorified by the infliction of torments akin to those of hell, and, what is more, it subverted the Christian's hope of salvation.

It leaves the justified without any shield against the demands of infinite and awful justice. Let it not be alleged in reply that the justice of God is *partially* appeased by the merits of Christ applied in justification, but that it has further demands on us; for this still subverts our belief in the *infinite* value of Christ's atonement: it assumes most unwarrantably that the demands of *infinite* justice are capable of *division*: it leaves us in total uncertainty as to the amount of demands which Divine justice may have upon us: *in fine* in admitting that it has any demands on us at all, it

[41] Liddon, ii, p. 181.
[42] W. Palmer, *Letters to N. Wiseman, D.D., on the errors of Romanism*, 1842, (Letter II, 1841), pp. 7–8, 13–14, 21, 32, 34, 37.

shakes our confidence in the atonement of our Lord: it teaches us to look away from that atonement, and to place our confidence in other things which still remain, to save us from the tremendous inflictions of a justice and a wrath which not even the death of the incarnate Deity could appease![43]

It is clear that Palmer's attack on the doctrine of purgatory presupposes a doctrine of the Atonement seen primarily as a legal transaction, and it consequently remains remote from the more personal understanding of Newman and Manning, and to some extent of Pusey. Newman's 'school-time of contemplation' has little in common with the doctrine which Palmer so vigorously attacked.

The distinction between the belief and practice of the ancient Church, which they claimed to be following, and the modern Roman doctrine remained characteristic of Tractarian discussions of purgatory for some time. In 1852 Pusey wrote to Samuel Wilberforce that his studies had led him to the conclusion that in Patristic theology the element of satisfaction was seen as part of true repentance, and the language that the Fathers used in this connection was not to be interpreted in terms of the modern Roman doctrines of purgatory, indulgences, 'the celestial treasury of merits', and temporal punishment owing for sin.[44] Pusey had reached these conclusions seven or eight years earlier. In 1844, when his daughter died, he had still been uncertain about prayer for the dead and had written to Keble to say that she no longer needed his prayers as she was in paradise. The following year, when he was engaged in preparing an edition of the *Paradisus Animae* for Anglican use, he consulted Keble about several of the devotions which included references to purgatory.[45] Not only were they too frequent in a book which might be widely used, many of the expressions were so 'transcendent and awful' that they seemed impossible for ordinary people to use. They might, he thought, be retained as a reminder of zeal for God's glory, providing that a note was added warning that they would be unreal on the lips of most people, and therefore should not be used generally: 'it seems very awful, hypothetically, to offer and invoke upon oneself all the pains of hell'.[46] Keble replied that all the prayers appeared to him to be 'aspirations after the highest saintliness', and it might therefore be possible to retain them with a suitable explanation, but references

[43] Letter VI, p. 19.   [44] Liddon, iii, p. 338. (18 Apr. 1852).
[45] Pusey MSS., Pusey to John Keble, 25 Apr. 1844; 1 Mar. 1845.
[46] Ibid., 27 Apr. 1845.

to purgatory and the flames of hell ought to be excised and only the expression 'what men had suffered and shall suffer' should be allowed as a prayer for increased suffering to aid humanity.[47]

It was Pusey's work on the Fathers, in particular his study of the *Acts of Perpetua and Felicitas*, which led to the change in his views, a change which he described as very painful. What weighed with him particularly was that Perpetua's witness to the power of prayer to redeem the dead had been given in the context of martyrdom, and therefore had acquired a special significance. 'Solemn as it was,' he told Samuel Wilberforce, 'I could not, taking all together, refuse my belief to an intermediate state of cleansing, in some cases through pain.' He concluded that the intention of Article XXII was only to condemn 'a certain practical system'.[48]

Once Newman had elaborated his theory of development the Roman doctrine of purgatory was no longer a problem to him, indeed it was a signal instance of the development of doctrine. In his *Essay on Development* he maintained that the doctrine of purgatory had developed along two lines, the Greek concept of the fire through which all would pass at the last day, and the more legalist Latin tradition, which had been particularly developed in the African Church.[49] It was only natural, he argued, that the doctrine should not have received its fullest expression in either tradition until the influx of large numbers of nominal Christians into the Church.[50] Whereas Scripture had considered Christians as saints rather than as backsliders, and had spoken of an immediate day of judgment, with the changed external circumstances which had made the Church both a temporal establishment and a remedial system, penance naturally developed as the complement of baptism and purgatory as the explanation of the intermediate state.[51]

After Newman's reception into the Church of Rome Pusey's correspondence with him on the doctrines which divided them occasionally refers to purgatory. These inquiries frequently resulted from Pusey's discovery of highly colourful doctrines in Roman books, such as Faber's description of the Virgin as 'Queen of Purgatory'. Pusey questioned Newman on this in 1865 as he thought that it conflicted with the views of other Roman theologians, who

---

[47] Ibid., John Keble to Pusey, 27 Apr. 1845.
[48] Liddon, iii, p. 44. (27 Nov. 1845).
[49] J. H. Newman, *An essay on the development of Christian doctrine*, 1845, pp. 18–19.
[50] p. 145.   [51] pp. 100–1.

maintained that the Virgin was no longer able to make satisfaction.[52] Newman replied judiciously. He had never read Faber's writings— an interesting admission—and, although they had a wide circulation in England and America, responsible people thought them 'crude and young, perhaps extravagant; he was a poet'.[53] He was prepared to see the Virgin as the great intercessor, and therefore supreme as regards purgatory, but anything else he considered to be a mere matter of devotion. Pusey was surprised at Newman's disparagement of Faber, and at the discovery that Faber's statements could be regarded merely as private opinions.[54]

In 1867, when Pusey was assisting Bishop Forbes of Brechin with an essay on Article XXII for his book on the Thirty-nine Articles, he again wrote to Newman, this time to ask him if the lines from the *Dream of Gerontius*,

> The longing for Him, when thou seest Him not;
> The shame of self at thought of seeing Him—
> Will be thy veriest, sharpest purgatory,[55]

were an adequate description of purgatory.[56] He himself considered that it was inconceivable that men who had shown little love to God on earth would be brought immediately to the Beatific Vision, and he was prepared to characterize the pain of judgment and the suffering of the time of waiting as purgatory, for even without fire they would be the most tremendous pains known to man.[57] Newman replied that the purgatorial pains, like those of hell, were comprised of the *poena sensus*, traditionally, though not necessarily, thought to be fire, and the *poena damni*. From the writings of Bellarmine and St. Francis de Sales, and especially St. Catherine of Genoa, it was possible to find grounds for the alleviation of those pains. Pusey was particularly impressed by the teaching of St. Catherine, and went so far as to suggest that, had it been the popular teaching at the time of the Reformation, it was very unlikely that Article XXII would have ever been included in the Anglican formularies. In 1869 he asked for further information about St. Catherine's teaching for use in his second *Eirenicon*, and told Newman that it appeared to him that Anglicans had been seeing the intermediate state too much in terms

[52] Pusey MSS., Pusey to Newman, [1 Feb.] 1865, (Copy).
[53] Ibid., Newman to Pusey, 31 Oct. 1865, (Copy).
[54] Ibid., 3 Feb. 1865, (Copy); Liddon, iv, p. 122.
[55] J. H. Newman, *Verses on various occasions*, 1868, p. 330.
[56] Pusey MSS., Pusey to Newman, 13 June 1867.   [57] Ibid., 16 June 1867(?).

of joy and the Romans too much in terms of suffering, but, rightly regarded, they were but two sides of the same thing.[58]

Throughout these discussions there is a constant emphasis on the distinction between the Patristic, and basically purificatory, and the Roman, and basically penal, concepts of purgatory. The interest in the purificatory aspect reflects a move away from a legalist interpretation towards a more personal one, though it may also owe something to contemporary appreciation of punishment as remedial rather than retributive. But behind the shifting doctrinal expressions lies a powerful sense of the holiness of God and the belief that man's true beatitude and fulfilment consists in union with him. The theology of Catherine of Genoa, with its positive emphasis, stressing the soul's willing participation in purifying suffering in order that its joy may be complete in God, was far more congenial than computations of the amount of satisfaction God required.

Later in the century expositions of Tractarian eschatology can be found in the works of F. G. Lee and H. M. Luckock. Lee's work, *The Christian Doctrine of Prayer for the Departed*, was published in 1872. Its author was an idiosyncratic figure, much involved with clandestine schemes for reuniting the Roman and Anglican churches, and his book was an attempt to show that Archbishop Tait had been in error when he had informed an Orthodox Patriarch that the Church of England did not sanction prayer for the dead. But, despite Lee's personal eccentricity, his work was in line with traditional High Anglican argument on the subject of prayers for the dead.

Lee was quite clear that to talk of an intermediate state was not to talk of a fresh period of probation for the impenitent, although many theologians, attempting to alleviate the problem of the salvation of the heathen, treated it in just this way. Lee, however, insisted that the intermediate state was the place where the elect are purified; for them alone was it appropriate to pray. He disliked the lurid pictures of purgatory found in Roman books and the toleration of indulgence societies by the Roman hierarchy, and appealed to antiquity and to the practice of prayer for the dead in the Anglican tradition to establish his own position.[59] At the end of his work he set out seven propositions in support of prayer for the dead. His most important

[58] Ibid., Newman to Pusey, 19 June 1867; Pusey to Newman, 24 July 1867; 31 Mar. 1869.
[59] F. G. Lee, *The Christian doctrine of Prayer for the departed*, 1872, pp. 15–16, 124n., 130n.

point was that there were no grounds for supposing that death brings men to their final state. In the intermediate state all the effects of sin must be removed from those who are to enter heaven, and he cites the text concerning the unforgivableness of sin against the Holy Ghost in the life to come as evidence that there are punishments and forgiveness of sins after death. Likewise he interprets Paul's language concerning the preservation of Christians until the Second Coming (Phil. 1:6; I Thess. 5:23) with reference to an intermediate state. The fact that prayer would not be refused to a dying man, even if he was considered incapable of relief, and that men do not hesitate to pray for absent friends, Lee also regarded as justifying prayer for the dead.[60]

Lee's argument is detailed, but rests heavily on an exposition of authorities, though the lack of quotation from Roman theologians is remarkable for one who was so much involved with reunion organizations, and was widely suspected of 'romanizing'. It demonstrates again the Tractarian insistence that their doctrine was only a revival of Patristic teaching. But the key point in his argument is the insistence that death as such cannot be considered as bringing a man to a final state of perfect sanctity; death was not a purgatory. But although he objected to the emphasis on death he did not follow Newman, who emphasized that the Last Day was the proper point of Christian hope, so maintaining a theological perspective which was much closer to that of the early Church.[61]

H. M. Luckock, a canon of Ely and subsequently dean of Lichfield, was the author of two major works on eschatology, *After Death* (1879) and *The Intermediate State* (1890). He believed that the recovery of a fuller appreciation of man's state after death was to be the final task of the Catholic revival in the field of doctrine, and his works were written to forward this.[62] He considered that, were the Vincentian canon, that the criterion of Christian doctrine was that which had been held 'always, everywhere and by all', to be strictly applied, prayer for the dead would have to be accepted, though in 1879 he thought it inopportune to encourage its public use. Like

---

[60] pp. 185-7.

[61] Cf. Newman, *Parochial and Plain Sermons*, iii, p. 378. At the 1874 conference with the Old Catholics in Bonn prayer for the departed was accepted by the Anglicans, only Dean Howson of Chester abstaining from voting. (Cf. C. B. Moss, *The Old Catholic Movement*, 1948, p. 264; E. T. d'E. Jesse, *Purgatory, Pardons, Invocations of Saints, Relics, Images, etc.*, 1900. pp. 79-81.)

[62] *Church Congress Report*, 1888, pp. 599-604.

many Tractarian writers he wished to emphasize the need for a purification after death without sacrificing the comfort to the bereaved which was to be found in the Evangelical teaching that the righteous went immediately to heaven, and he attempted to do this by speaking of a purgatory which was a state of both peace and purification. Not surprisingly he quoted *The Dream of Gerontius* in support of this concept. Although he held the popular nineteenth-century belief that man's mental powers would be amplified after death, for him this did not involve an increased knowledge of subjects like science and philosophy; the main activity of the future would be a spiritual ministry to others as Christ preached to the departed in Hades. Whereas earlier writers had insisted that there was no question of an extended probation after death, and that the heathen, if God's mercy was to be shown to them at all, would be judged by whether they had lived according to the highest standards known to them, Luckock was prepared to admit that there must be an adequate probation for them in the intermediate state, as their standards all too often fell far short of God's requirements.

This, then, is the conclusion of the whole matter; a righteous judgment presupposes of necessity an adequate probation; if this has been withheld from any man in this life, through circumstances over which he had not control, an extension of time may be granted after death; but wherever the choice of good has been fully offered and with such force and persuasion that a man might reasonably be expected to take it, if he should resist the grace of God, and trampling his offer under foot, accept the evil, the consequences are eternal. No new test, no opportunity of retrieving the past, no second probation is possible; the door of repentance has been closed against him.[63]

A purificatory intermediate state and an insistence on an 'adequate probation' for each man, undoubtedly mitigated the harshness of earlier eschatology. Some later writers in the Tractarian tradition even came to adopt universalism: if a man was allowed an 'adequate probation' after death, was it conceivable that any should in the end reject God? Moreover it could be shown that there was a strong universalist tradition in the primitive Church, particularly in the writings of the Greek Fathers.[64] But whether or not this universalist

[63] H. M. Luckock, *After Death*, 1879, pp. 236–54, *passim*; *The Intermediate State between death and judgment*, 1890, pp. 207–8.
[64] Cf. A. Gurney, *Our Catholic inheritance in the larger hope*, 1888; F. N. Oxenham, *What is the truth as to everlasting punishment?*, 1881.

tradition was followed, the theology of the Fathers provided all writers in the Tractarian tradition with a broad context in which to reflect on the themes of death and the future life.

THE TORMENTS OF HELL AND THE SHADOW OF DEATH

In 1871 Pusey mentioned in a letter to Newman that he was beginning to doubt the wisdom of stressing the 'terrors of the Lord' in preaching, particularly the bodily sufferings of the damned. His uncertainty was such that when, sometime previously, he had considered publishing a volume of sermons, he had refrained, as the first one dealt with the subject of hell.[65] The sermon in question was one he had preached in 1856. In 1881 he again thought of publishing it as the first sermon in the collection, *Parochial and Cathedral Sermons*, but, even though it was actually printed, he eventually decided that it would be impolitic to include it.[66] The sermon is a good illustration of the language which a preacher like Pusey, who cannot be classified as a traditional 'hell-fire' preacher, could use in preaching about hell.

It begins with a clear assertion of belief in hell, a belief which was so cardinal a part of the Christian faith that, were it denied, there would be nothing left to believe in: salvation from hell was the object of the Incarnation, and the Christ who won that salvation for man is also the revealer of that endless hell. Pusey does not spare his hearers in his description of the horrors of hell. Just as everything beautiful in the world is an analogue of paradise, so all that is loathsome is to be considered as 'some faint picture of the suffering of the damned'. Hell itself is a place of almost indescribable torment.

This, then, is the first outward suffering of the damned, that they are purged, steeped in a lake of fire. O woe, woe, woe! Woe unutterable, woe unimaginable, woe interminable! . . . You know the fierce, intense, burning, heat of a furnace, how it consumes in a moment anything cast into it. Its misery to the damned shall be that they feel it, but cannot be consumed by it. The fire shall pierce them, penetrate them: it shall be, Scripture says, like a molten 'lake of fire', rolling, tossing, immersing, but not destroying.

All hell is paroxysm without rest, with pains worse than the tortures of red-hot plates against the body, racks, flaying, or being torn with iron hooks. Yet the worst pain of all is the pain of the loss of God, and whenever Christians give way to temptation it is this agonising loss

---

[65] Pusey MSS., Pusey to Newman, 23–25? Feb. 1871.
[66] MS. note on the printed version of the sermon preserved at Pusey House.

that they risk. 'Hell, my brethren, is full of Christians, who, when on earth never thought of it.'[67]

After such a concatenation of agony one may well think that it was Pusey's better judgment which prevailed in his decision not to publish. Moreover his insistence that the pain of the loss of God would be so much worse than the physical horrors he has described leads one to suspect that for him the main point of dwelling on the physical torture is to bring home to his hearers the agony of the loss of God, which otherwise they might be inclined to treat cavalierly. Yet we may legitimately ask, to what extent the preacher really believed in the reality of the torments he was describing, and how far he was merely making use of what, to him, were legitimate, homiletic methods. D. P. Walker has cited a number of examples from an earlier period of men who believed hell to be doubtful, or even untrue, and yet maintained that it was necessary for it to be preached to the mass of men.[68] Was this the case with Pusey? From his correspondence at the time of the *Essays and Reviews* controversy it was almost certainly not, though this sheds little light on how much of the detail in his preaching he regarded as mere imagery. With Pusey's disciple, H. P. Liddon, however, we can see quite clearly how a scholarly, Tractarian theologian warned himself in his private devotions of the future torments which he preached to his congregations. The source of our information is a volume of private meditations, compiled when Liddon was Vice-Principal of Cuddesdon Theological College in 1858, entitled *The End of Life*, which consists of a series of reflections on sin, death, and punishment.

In Meditation 11, after a reflection on the character of God, Liddon considers both the nature of punishment and its consequences for himself in the context of the punishment of the rebel angels. He notes that God's wrath was not stayed by considerations of the number or rank of those who had sinned against him, nor by the possibility of his glory being advanced if he allowed them to repent, and he reminds himself that God punished the rebel angels for only a single sin and did not consider his former relationship of love with them. All this Liddon takes as a sign of the severity with which his own sins will be treated. This severity appears in many of the other meditations. In hell, Liddon reflects, there are probably souls condemned for single, unrepented sins, and there may well be

[67] *Hell*, 1856, pp. 3, 6, 7, 10–11, 19, 21.
[68] D. P. Walker, *The Decline of Hell*, 1964, p. 6.

thousands.[69] Better to be over-scrupulous than to offend God with a single lie, for Ananias and Sapphira were struck down for such.[70] Priests are in greater danger than other Christians, for they risk becoming over-familiar with holy things, and their punishment is likely to be of the severest kind. 'Picture his misery', Liddon warns himself, 'as the evil Spirits, who of old had mocked him in the Ranks of Christ welcome him as their associate for ever.'[71]

The theme of Meditation 28 is the 'Last Wages of Sin' and in it Liddon considers the problem of the meaning of αἰώνιος in the context of future punishment.

That wh. is most terrible in connection with the future punishment of the wicked is that it will last for ever. I am tempted perhaps to play with the words αἰώνιος and עֹלָם when Scripture says that some shall awake to Everlasting Contempt . . . But I must remember (i) that the same word is used of the life of the blessed, so that I can only imagine an end to the pains of hell if I can consent to disbelieve in the immortality of the Life of Heaven (ii) That the sense attached to αἰώνιος by Catholic theologians is supported by (a) the word, ἄσβεστος, . . . (b) The statement . . . their worm shall not die . . . (c) Our Lord's words . . . (Mk. x. 43, 44)—These passages all deny there being an end of punishment and so support the sense of αἰώνιος (iii) That this sense is further illustrated by all the passages which speak of their being no *locus paenitentiae* after death, and consequently no change in the condition of the lost, e.g. Ecclus. xi. 13.[72]

To interpret αἰώνιος as other than endless duration is for Liddon a moral temptation not an academic argument. The reality of hell is too awful a reality with which to trifle.

Reflect then, my soul, that those who are cast into the Lake of Fire and Brimstone shall be tormented day and night for ever and ever. The penalty is eternal. The lost soul asks How many years of ages it must spend in this terrible prison. It is there for ever. How long in the society of Satan? For ever. How long burn in the flame of God's indignation? For ever. But will God never turn and pity? Never. Will there be no temporary alleviation of these unendurable pains? None whatever. Sin is infinite because its object is Infinite; therefore the punishment of sin is infinite. i.e. it is eternal. Add years to years, ages to ages, count the leaves of the forest or the sand on the shore of the ocean—and you are as far as ever from achieving the idea of eternity.[73]

[69] Liddon MSS. (Cuddesdon), 'The End of Life', Med. 11; Med. 14.
[70] Med. 25.   [71] Med. 23; 29.   [72] Med. 29.   [73] Ibid.

It is a conception of eternity that stands in sharp contrast to that of F. D. Maurice.

The End of Life also contains seven meditations on death, which, to modern taste, seem morbid and repulsive. The first is a consideration of death in general, beginning with the picture of the churchyard and the death-bed, in which death is seen as a farewell to the things of this world and an obliteration from the memory of the living.

It is to leave my bedroom for the last time, to be laid in a deep, narrow trench—to await the day of Judgment six feet under ground with no other covering than that of a linen shroud—with no other society than that of the worms and insects—with no other titles beyond an inscription which few people will ever read, and which time will soon obliterate.

It is to hand over this body in which I have so long thought, loved, walked, slept, prayed, and which I have so often indulged—to humiliations, which must seem painful and degrading, to an utter solitude where I shall see nothing, not even the labours of the worms which will have taken possession of my entire person, where I shall become the food of creatures from which I should have shrunk with loathing, and shall gradually lose form and feature and subside into a mess of corrupt infection—which in time will resolve itself into my native dust.[74]

Other meditations deal with the inevitability of death; the uncertainty of when it will occur; and the need for preparation. It is vital, Liddon argues, that a man should die a good death, for, whilst a bad life may be repented of, this is not true of a bad death. At the moment a man may fall from grace and be lost for ever, no matter how excellent his life has been up to that point. In illustration of this Liddon anticipates his own death-bed, picturing the room full of people and death drawing on, marked by the ticking of the clock in the physical world and the onslaught of diabolical temptation in the spiritual. In much of this description he draws on Dean Sherlock's *Practical discourse concerning death* (1689) and, like Sherlock, holds that the particular judgment takes place at the very moment when the last breath is drawn.

He the Omnipotent may erect His Tribunal in that very bedroom where I have just left my corpse; close to the very bed on which it lies, close to those friends who are surrounding it with their affectionate and sorrowing care—but who little think of the more awful scene which is enacting in the Unseen world around them.[75]

[74] Med. 32.   [75] Med. 37.

His accusers will be both the devil and the guardian angels, both his own and those of men whom he has led into sin. Christ will be seen only as the Judge: 'Shall I take refuge in the mercy of Jesus? He will tell me that His Eye shall not spare. That the Day of Mercy is over and that it is the time of vengeance.'[76]

Liddon's meditations show the Tractarian sterness passing into an almost unmitigated gloom in a manner reminiscent of the macabre speculations of the fifteenth century. Death is treated by Liddon in an almost entirely negative way, and we find little hint of that sacramental understanding which appears in the theology of both Pusey and John Mason Neale. Pusey speaks of death as a means of grace, whereby God offers each man the chance of communion with him. As such he can write of it as 'that almost sacrament', and he is able to make use of this understanding of death to mitigate somewhat the popular doctrine of hell with its implication of the fewness of the saved.[77] By contrast Liddon, with his conception of death as a time of special temptation, offers little comfort. Neale is more specific than Pusey in his description of death as a sacrament. Preaching a sermon to his community at East Grinstead in 1865, when one of his nuns was on her death-bed, he maintained that the sacramental character of death was too frequently overlooked.

Take the definition of a sacrament as laid down in our Catechism . . . It is an outward and visible sign of an inward and spiritual grace. What grace? The grace won for us by the Death of Calvary; and this, speaking technically, is the only reason why death should be accounted a sacrament. It is not the outward and visible sign of an inward and spiritual *grace*, but of the *source* of that grace.[78]

Neale's eschatology differs in other ways from that of Liddon, who knew little of Neale's 'Ecclesiology', interest in the paranormal, and delight in hymns of glory. It was as early as 1839 that Neale, on his way to an uncle's funeral at the new Kensal Green cemetery, wrote a poem which in many ways summarized all that he was to attempt to restore in the contemporary understanding of death, and marked his first known break with the narrow Evangelicalism of his home. It is such a remarkable poem for one from Neale's background that it is worth quoting in full.

[76] Med. 38.
[77] E. B. Pusey, *What is of faith as to Everlasting Punishment?* 1880, p. 113.
[78] Neale MSS. (East Grinstead), Volume of sermons, pp. 104ff.

Oh, give us back the days of old! oh! give me back an hour!
To make us feel that Holy Church o'er death hath might and power.
Take hence the heathen trappings, take hence the Pagan show,
The misery, the heartlessness, the unbelief of woe:
The nodding plumes, the painted staves, the mutes in black array,
That get their hard-won earnings by so much grief per day:
The steeds and scarves and crowds that gaze with half-suspended breath
As if, of all things terrible, most terrible was death:
And let us know to what we go, and wherefore we must weep,
Or o'er the Christian's hopeful rest, or everlasting sleep.
Lay in the dead man's hand the Cross—the Cross upon his breast
Because beneath the shadow of the Cross he went to rest:
And let the Cross go on before—the Crucified was first
To go before the people and their chains of death to burst;
And be the widow's heart made glad with charitable dole,
And pray with calm, yet earnest, faith for the departed soul.
And be the *De Profundis* said for one of Christ's own fold,
And—for a prisoner is set free—the bells be rung not tolled.
When face to face we stand with death, thus Holy Church records,
He is our slave, and we, through Her, his masters and his lords.
Deck the High Altar for the Mass! Let tapers guard the hearse!
For Christ, the Light that lighteneth all, to blessing turns our curse,
And be Nicea's Creed intoned and be the Gospel read,
In calm, low voice, for preaching can profit not the dead.
Then forth with banner, cross, and psalm, and chant, and hymn and prayer,
And look not on the coffin—for our brother is not there;
His soul, we trust assuredly, is safe in Abraham's breast,
And mid Christ's many faithful, his body shall have rest.
When earth its cares and turmoils, and many sorrows cease—
By all Thy woes, by all Thy joys, Lord Jesus grant them peace.[79]

The same year (1839) Neale confessed in his journal to a 'panting
after immortality'.[80] This was to remain with him throughout his
life, and influenced both his eschatology and his understanding of
the Church, and was apparent in many of his hymns, both his own
compositions and his translations of early Greek and Latin ones.
Together with his fellow ecclesiologists he did much to change the
character of Victorian funeral monuments and services, and his
hymns had a wide influence.[81] Although the characteristic note of

[79] Gordon Phillips, MS. on early life of Neale, preserved at E. Grinstead, pp. 32–3.
[80] Ibid., p. 46.
[81] The Cambridge Camden Society offered much advice on funeral reform in the
pages of the *Ecclesiologist*. For a summary of their main proposals cf. Geoffrey Rowell,

Neale's eschatology is the joy of heaven the Tractarian strictness is also there. God's free forgiveness, he wrote, was only offered to men inasmuch as they were tainted by original sin, for those sins which they had themselves committed, it was necessary that they should work out their own salvation. To fail to do so would be to discover that the joys of heaven were but weariness. Struggle is a necessary part of life, and even after death it is only the martyrs and the great saints who enjoy the Beatific Vision, the rest of the faithful require the prayers of men in order that they may be made perfect, even though their particular needs remain unknown.[82]

'LUX MUNDI'

The publication of *Lux Mundi* in 1889 has long been considered a turning-point of Anglican, and in particular Tractarian, theology, because of its contributors' acceptance of many of the conclusions of biblical criticism. Yet the essays contain very little discussion of eschatology, and such as there is is to be found in R. L. Ottley's discussion of Christian ethics. Here it is placed clearly in the context of the Tractarian concern for sanctification and is related to the incarnational emphasis of *Lux Mundi* as a whole. Ottley maintains that the last stage of the kingdom of God is the revelation of the glory of God 'in the perfection of moral community' brought about by God exercising his judgment on all that is less than this, and putting an end 'to that mixed condition of human things, which it is our tendency to accept and assume as necessary and perpetual'. The extent of this community and of Christ's final triumph is, Ottley maintains, limited by the character of God and the analogies afforded to us by the present order, and in the last resort it is impossible to construct a coherent picture.

We read of a gathering into the kingdom of all that is in true harmony with its purpose. We find warrant for the belief in an intermediate state in which imperfect character may be developed, ignorance enlightened, sin chastened, desire purified. And yet we are assured the consequences of action and choice abide, and are eternal in their issue; and we know that impenitence must finally and under awful conditions separate the soul

---

'Nineteenth-century attitudes and practices' in G. Cope (ed.), *Dying, Death and Disposal*, 1970.

[82] J. M. Neale: *Readings for the Aged*, 1850, pp. 64-6, 78, 206; *Sermons for the Church's Year*, ii, 1898, 225.

from God. But we have not enough for a coherent system. All that we can affirm is that the victory of Good seems to demand the preservation of all that has not wilfully set itself in antagonism to Divine Love, Holiness and Power. We cannot think that helpless ignorance, or inevitable poverty of character will finally sever a human soul from God.[83]

Universalism, in Ottley's opinion, not only lacks any basis in Scripture, it also denies the facts of experience, that those who become habituated to evil become incapable of choosing the good. But whilst he accepts a final separation of good and evil, he does not consider that the damned will be in a perpetual state of defiance and rebellion, they will, on the contrary, accept the justice of their state. Those who through the circumstances of their earthly life have not had the opportunity of knowing the salvation offered to them will be ministered to by the righteous. The righteous themselves will be possessed of a harmony between their soul and their body, and between the demands of the moral law and the claims of freedom, and the blessedness they enjoy will be that of a moral community. It is this 'community of free and perfected beings, with God as its Centre', which is 'the revealed ethical consummation' of humanity, and it is this which is the vision which must be given concrete expression on earth.[84]

By the time of *Lux Mundi* the Tractarian emphasis on sanctification of the individual as the prerequisite for the life of heaven has broadened to a social vision of heaven, with definite consequences for life on earth. Human life moves towards the communion of saints, and that communion is already proleptically present in the Church, which is the social context of God's grace, and it is through the Church that this community is brought into being.

[83] *Lux Mundi*, 1913 ed., p. 377.
[84] Ibid., p. 379.

One of the most celebrated of the nineteenth-century controversies concerning eternal punishment was the lawsuit brought against the Reverend H. B. Wilson for passages in his essay on the national Church in the volume *Essays and Reviews*. The course of events in the *Essays and Reviews* controversy has often been described. The book was published in the February of 1860, and it was not long before what was generally considered to be the dangerously liberal theology of its contributors attracted attention. In June 1861 the Lower House of clergy of the convocation of Canterbury found that there were grounds for proceeding to a synodical judgment on the book, but the bishops of the Upper House, aware that some of their number were liable to be called upon to sit as members of the judicial committee of the Privy Council if there was an appeal from any lawsuit brought against the book in the ecclesiastical courts, refused to act. Convocation being thus unwilling to make any move, efforts were made to initiate legal proceedings against some of the contributors. Two lawsuits were eventually brought, one against Dr. Rowland Williams, on the issue of the authority and inspiration of Scripture, the other against H. B. Wilson, on the issue of eternal punishment.

In his essay Wilson had pleaded for a greater comprehensiveness in the national Church, and had tended to discount doctrinal orthodoxy in comparison with the moral quality of a man's life. In his conclusion he had stated, that, whilst Calvin and Augustine had rightly recognized that only a few men ever attained Christian perfection, they had drawn the wrong conclusions from this insight. Those who did not attain this perfection were not doomed, but 'germinal souls'. Unlike Newman, when Wilson considered the apparently 'neutral' position of the majority of mankind, he concluded that it would be inappropriate to apply to them 'either the promises or the denunciations of revelation'. Consequently, he wrote:

... we must rather entertain a hope that there shall be found, after the great adjudication, receptacles suitable for those who shall be infants, not as to years of terrestial life, but as to spiritual development—nurseries as it were and seed-grounds, where the undeveloped may grow up under new conditions—the stunted may become strong, and the perverted restored. And when the Christian Church, in all its branches, shall have fulfilled its sublunary office, and its Founder shall have surrendered His kingdom to the Great Father—all, both small and great, shall find a refuge in the bosom of the Universal Parent, to repose, or be quickened into higher life, in the ages to come, according to His Will.[1]

Wilson appears to have held his views on eternal punishment for some time previously to *Essays and Reviews*, and he was already under suspicion in Tractarian circles for his Bampton Lectures of 1851 on the communion of saints. In these he had given great offence by his advocacy of Zwingli's sacramental theology as that best adapted to the modern age, by his description of prayers for the dead as the relic of a hopeless paganism carried over into Christianity, and by his refusal to give the name of Catholic to any who held a rigorist interpretation of *extra ecclesiam nulla salus*. The Tractarians had little liking for Wilson's comprehensive view of the church.

The Church to which we have the happiness to belong, allows us to acknowledge the ambiguity ... of the word Church and of the word Salvation. It neither obliges its members to restrain the application of the word Church to a partial material succession, nor to define it by imaginary, invisible properties nor to believe the absolute perdition of those who are not 'saved' in a technical and theological sense. She is not thus engaged in making proselytes of fear; is not driven and goaded to it, as though she were compelled to pull all out of the fire, who do not as yet embrace her forms.[2]

To those already alarmed by such ideas *Essays and Reviews* was a betrayal of the Christian faith which had to be combated. Moreover, 1861 had also seen the appearance of another substantial work casting doubt on the doctrine of eternal punishment, the *Commentary on Romans* by Bishop Colenso of Natal.

Colenso, like Wilson, had already stated his position on the question. In his *Village Sermons* (1853), which were dedicated to F. D. Maurice, he had first put forward the view, which he developed at greater length in his commentary, that the universalist passages in Paul's epistles, and the belief of a large part of the Church that there

---

[1] *Essays and Reviews*, 1860[2], pp. 205–6.
[2] H. B. Wilson, *The Communion of Saints*, 1851, pp. 16–17; 245–6.

was some kind of remedial process after death, amounted to a refutation of the popular doctrine of eternal punishment and fitted better with the infinite gradations of good and evil found amongst men, and the 'law of progress', than theories suggesting absolute division, either morally or temporally. Colenso's missionary experience undoubtedly lay behind his doctrine. In 1855 he had asked how a Christian could 'comfortably eat butter with his bread, ride in a carriage, wear a fine nap upon his coat, or enjoy one of the commonest blessings of daily life' if he believed heathen souls to be perishing in their millions.[3] In his commentary he went as far as to state that the doctrine of eternal punishment was a positive hindrance, rather than a spur, to missionary endeavour. To teach 'the state of everlasting torment after death, of all impenitent sinners and unbelievers, including the whole of the heathen world', as many missionaries taught, was, Colenso wrote, to make incredible 'the cardinal doctrines of the Gospel, the Fatherly relation to us of the Faithful Creator', and it was not surprising that so many missionaries, preaching a hell-fire gospel, found little response amongst their hearers.[4] The victory of Christ, Colenso maintained, was not a victory won by the banishment of sinners, but by the extirpation of sin.[5] In Colenso's case the publication of his commentary on the Pentateuch soon diverted attention from his views on eternal punishment, but the defenders of orthodoxy noted that, as with the essayists, denial of the veracity of Scripture and doubt concerning eternal punishment appeared to be linked.

In June 1862, in the Court of Arches, Dr. Lushington delivered his judgment in the case brought against Wilson. Lushington, though personally unhappy about his decision, believed that he was compelled by the words of the Athanasian Creed, 'and they that have done good shall go into life everlasting; and they that have done evil into everlasting fire', to condemn Wilson. Wilson's opinion could not be reconciled with their plain, literal, and grammatical sense, and a sentence of a year's suspension from his living was passed on him.

[3] J. W. Colenso, *Ten Weeks in Natal*, 1855, pp. 252–3.

[4] J. W. Colenso, *Commentary on Romans*, 1861, p. 218.

[5] Liddon thought that Colenso's theology would 'empty his own labours as a missionary to the heathen of their meaning and value—if, indeed, it does not represent them as mischievous'. (J. O. Johnston, *Life of Liddon*, 1904, p. 64). The Wesleyan *London Review* stated that the heathen were damned for their immorality, not for the fact of their being heathen, and asked whether, if Tennyson, Byron, Maurice, and Colenso were right, 'the consummation of all our labours' was a possibility of one day 'sitting down with "Lucifer" in the Kingdom of God?' (xviii, 1862, 39n, 41).

He was found guilty of maintaining that men's condition in the
future state was determined by their moral conduct exclusive of the
religious belief they professed, and of denying that God judged men
'after this life and at the end of the existing order of things on this
Earth', awarding to those whom he approved 'everlasting life or
eternal happiness', and to those whom he condemned 'everlasting
death or eternal misery'. Wilson appealed to the judicial committee
of the Privy Council in June 1862, but it was not until February
1864 that Lord Chancellor Westbury delivered his celebrated
judgment, allowing Wilson's appeal, and declaring that:

> We are not at liberty to express any opinion upon the mysterious question
> of final punishment, further than to say that we do not find in the
> Formularies ... any such distinct declaration of our Church upon the
> subject as to require us to condemn as penal the expression of hope by a
> clergyman, that even the ultimate pardon of the wicked, who are con-
> demned in the day of judgment may be consistent with the will of Almighty
> God.[6]

The three years spent in legal wrangles delayed the orthodox
explosion of wrath against the essayists. As early as 1861, however,
Keble had suggested to Liddon that replies ought to be considered
on two fronts, one in the style of the *Provincial Letters* of Pascal and
the other in the form of a remonstrance showing the divergence
between the teaching of Christ and the views of the essayists.[7] Pusey,
who had been well satisfied with Lushington's judgment, had
gloomy forebodings about the result of Wilson's appeal to the
judicial committee. He foresaw a danger in the judicial committee
issuing an explanation of what was meant by eternal punishment,
regardless of whether or not Wilson was acquitted. He wrote to
Bishop Hamilton of Salisbury:

> A sentence which should declare that 'eternal punishment' only meant
> 'very long', in fact a sort of Purgatory, or that the Athanasian Creed was
> not a matter of faith would be most fatal. For if the word 'eternal' were
> taken out of its known historical meaning in the Church, then so may the
> word be used of God the Son with Arius, or 'grace' might be said to mean

---

[6] *Fendall* v. *Wilson* in Brodrick and Fremantle, *Ecclesiastical cases relating to doctrine
and discipline*, 1865, pp. 289, 247–90. Robert Jenkins, a friend of Lushington's told
Dean Farrar that Lushington was 'grieved that he was compelled by the words of the
Athanasian Creed to condemn Mr. Wilson' (Farrar MSS. 8/34. 9 Oct. 1888).

[7] Liddon's Diary, 27 Mar. 1861.

God's favour and assistance by man's natural endowments, as the Pelagians taught. There would in this case be an end of all teachings.[8]

And not only would theological language be rendered meaningless, hell would cease to be a valid moral sanction. 'I am sure nothing will keep men from the present pleasures of sin, but the love of God or the fear of Hell: and that the fear of Hell drives people back to God, to seek . . . Him, and in seeking Him to love Him first because He delivered them from Hell, then for His own sake.'[9]

Although the 1864 judgment did not contain any explanation of what was meant by eternal punishment, it caused grave concern to both High Churchmen and Evangelicals. A furious correspondence began amongst the leading Tractarians to consider what action should be taken. Pusey wrote to Hamilton hoping that convocation would declare that eternal punishment was the doctrine of the Church of England, for 'its denial would open a floodgate of immorality'; he lamented that the *Guardian*, which had failed to condemn the judgment, had long been drifting away from Church principles; and he suggested to Keble that the Church Union might well take eternal punishment as one of its annual subjects for discussion.[10] Pusey found the hazard men's souls were exposed to by the judgment almost too horrible to contemplate:

People risk too much now. They would risk everything, if they did not dread an eternity of suffering. A mere Purgatory for the bad would not move them. That title 'Purgatory' I see takes with people; for it sets it before their eyes. They are familiar with the idea of Purgatory as a passing punishment, and it sets before them what these people bring hell down to.[11]

God, Pusey said, when he revealed hell knew his creatures better than the Privy Council judges. He hoped that the *Litany of our Lord's Warnings*, which Keble had composed, would not only bring solemn thoughts into people's minds but would also show the evidence for eternal punishment. Keble published the Litany in 1864. Its suffrages prayed that men might be delivered from both the pains of hell and from specious interpretations of Scripture.

[8] Pusey MSS., Pusey to W. K. Hamilton, 22 June 1861/2?.
[9] Tait MSS. 80/109, Pusey to Tait, 25 June 1863.
[10] Pusey MSS., Pusey to W. K. Hamilton, 9 Feb. 1864; Pusey to John Keble, 10–12 Feb. 1864. (Cf. Liddon: *Life of Pusey*, iv, 48, 50.)
[11] Pusey MSS., Pusey to John Keble, 14 Feb. 1864.

Jesu, from Whose lips full of grace, came thrice the terrible mention of 'the whole body cast into hell' . . . *Have mercy upon us.*

Jesus, Who didst mention not only the worm and the fire, but *their* worm and *their* fire—what *each one* suffers—as undying. *Have mercy upon us.*

From wresting Thy Holy Scripture; from mistrusting Thy Holy Church; from bigotry and indifference; from partiality and prejudice; from respect of persons; from making God's Word of none effect by man's tradition: *Good Lord deliver us.*

That it may please Thee to convert and pardon all who disbelieve Thy threatenings of eternal woe, and consciously or unconsciously cause any to disregard them. *We beseech Thee to hear us Good Lord.*[12]

The Litany appealed to the authority of Scripture, which had been the subject of the other prosecution which had arisen out of *Essays and Reviews*, and it is not surprising that the Oxford declaration against the essayists linked a confession of faith in the inspiration of Scripture with eternal punishment. It was signed by 11,000 clergy, both Tractarian and Evangelical, and affirmed that the Church of England believed and taught, 'in the words of our Blessed Lord, that the "punishment" of the "cursed" equally with the "life" of the "righteous" is "everlasting"'.[13] H. B. Wilson condemned the declaration as 'a presumptuous and unwarrantable interference', but both archbishops showed themselves sympathetic to its tone. Longley of Canterbury insisted that no wedge should be driven between the word 'eternal' applied to the future life of the righteous and applied to the future punishment of the wicked, but judiciously considered that Wilson's obscurity of expression had prevented him from actually denying eternal punishment.[14] Archbishop Thomson of York set his face firmly against any qualitative use of the word 'eternal'. 'Everlasting', he wrote, 'must mean lasting for ever, never coming to an end', and he gave a solemn warning that tampering with this meaning, disturbed men's faith in the plain declarations of the Bible.[15]

Others took a different view. F. D. Maurice, whilst ready enough

[12] *Record*, 19 Feb. 1864; J. Keble, *A Litany of our Lord's Warnings*, 1864, pp. 15, 19, 21; Pusey MSS., Pusey to John Keble, 19 Feb. 1864.

[13] 1864 Declaration. Among the signatories is to be found F. N. Oxenham, who, by the time of Dean Farrar's *Eternal Hope*, had become an opponent of Pusey and an advocate of universalism.

[14] C. T. Longley, *Pastoral Letter*, 1864, pp. 11–13; *Daily News*, 7 Apr. 1865.

[15] W. Thomson, *Pastoral Letter*, 1864, p. 18.

to agree with the signatories of the declaration that the punishment of the wicked and the life of the righteous were both 'eternal', refused to be party to any action which would narrow the interpretation of the Anglican formularies, and suspected that the declaration had hidden implications. It could be read, he suggested, as meaning that 'eternal life is not the life of the eternal God, that eternal punishment is not the punishment of losing that life, that righteousness is not to prevail over evil' and that 'God's purpose is to keep man for ever and ever in evil'. He found such an interpretation abhorrent. If that was what Pusey and the other signatories meant, their God was not his. Whatever Maurice's views, Pusey was quite clear that the signatories of the declaration and Wilson and his supporters believed in different gods. 'God, whom we adore in His awful and inscrutable justice and holiness, these writers affirm to be cruel. The God whom they acknowledge we believe to be the creature of their own minds, not the God who has revealed Himself to men.' The Oxford declaration was the least that could be done by those who 'feared lest people should be encouraged to disbelieve the Bible and Hell and that they were in risk of losing their faith and their souls'.[16] Gladstone was more optimistic. 'It may be,' he wrote, 'that this rude shock to the mere Scripturism which has too much prevailed is intended to be the instrument of restoring a greater harmony of belief, and of the agencies for maintaining belief.'[17]

The *Essays and Reviews* judgment, after the theological polemics had died away, was seen to have lead neither to a gross increase in immorality, nor to a wholesale abandonment of the doctrine of eternal punishment. In his 1866 charge to the clergy of London Tait had to condemn a clergyman who had told his congregation that 'at every ticking of the clock in every four-and-twenty hours God sends a heathen soul straight to never-ending misery'.[18] Such methods Tait thought inappropriate as a means of encouraging missionary zeal, and his sensitivity on the point indicates something of the caution which the *Essays and Reviews* judgment had brought about in the discussion of eternal punishment. When the issue was debated again in the seventies, not only was the argument conducted against a background of a more decided agnosticism, the general tone

[16] Liddon, *Life of Pusey*, iv, 57, 60, 62.
[17] D. C. Lathbury, *Correspondence on Church and Religion of W. E. Gladstone*, ii, 1910, p. 82 (8 Feb. 1864).
[18] A. C. Tait, *Charge to London clergy*, 1866, p. 39.

of the debate was much calmer. A growing appreciation of the achievements of biblical criticism did much to weaken the simple appeal to the authority of texts, which had been so frequently employed by the defenders of eternal punishment. The part played by the damnatory clauses of the Athanasian Creed in the *Essays and Reviews* controversy undoubtedly contributed to the wrangles over the use of the creed in worship, which produced many tedious arguments but no definite decision.

Several points emerge from the opposition to Wilson's views on eternal punishment. First there is a clear connection between belief in an infallible Bible and belief in hell. Those who attack hell are in fact saying that the Bible is untrue, and that outweighs any arguments about the morality of eternal punishment as far as the majority of its defenders are concerned, and for them it was no accident that the second legal action deriving from *Essays and Reviews* should have been concerned with the inspiration and authority of Scripture. Secondly there was a genuine fear of theological language being rendered meaningless, and in particular of the way being laid open to Arianism. This was not only the result of the ambivalence introduced into the meaning of the word 'eternal', but was also connected with the debasement of Christ which, it was thought, the denial of hell entailed, for, in the minds of many, there was an inverse correlation between the intensity of the pains of hell and the status of the Saviour. They could find support for this view by pointing to the low Christology of the Unitarians and other sectarian universalists. The moral-sanctions argument still weighed heavily, as Pusey's correspondence makes plain, and it was used, not only to promote moral behaviour but also to encourage religious belief. Finally, in the background of the whole controversy, lay the issue of authority in the Church. The belief that this was being undermined by both liberalizing theologians and the decisions of the courts undoubtedly rallied a certain amount of support for those opposed to the 1864 judgment from those who might otherwise have been prepared to concede something to the essayists. But what is notable in all this is how little part the central issues of eschatology played in the whole debate.

T. R. BIRKS AND THE EVANGELICAL ALLIANCE

The controversy over *Essays and Reviews* made the inspiration and authority of the Bible and the doctrine of eternal punishment matters of public debate to a much greater extent than had previously been the case. After it those who wished to maintain belief in a traditional hell had to make some attempt to do justice to the protests of those to whom such an idea was abhorrent, though all too frequently this amounted to little more than a refusal to go beyond the actual words of Scripture in asserting the doctrine. Occasionally, however, more constructive attempts were made.

One such was Thomas Rawson Birks's *Victory of Divine Goodness*, which appeared in 1867. Birks was the son-in-law of Edward Bickersteth, one of the founders of the Evangelical Alliance, and was himself secretary of it. Having been rector of Kelshall in Hertfordshire, he had been appointed to Simeon's old parish, Holy Trinity, Cambridge, and he later succeeded F. D. Maurice in the chair of Moral Philosophy in the university.[19] Although he could not be described as an outstanding scholar, he was definitely to be ranked amongst the leaders of Evangelicalism, and the young Gerard Manley Hopkins could describe him in 1864 as 'almost the only learned Evangelical going'.[20] Birks described his theology as a moderate Calvinism, though there would seem to have been some justice in Candlish's suggestion that he was an Arminian despite Birks's repudiation of the idea. Birks, nevertheless, told Candlish:

I have never become an Arminian for a moment, or ceased to be, like most of the Evangelical clergy, moderately Calvinistic, or, to speak more correctly, temperately Augustinian, in my views on theology. I accept the doctrine of the catechism with equal heartiness in its second and third clauses, that 'God the Son hath redeemed all mankind', and that God the Holy Ghost 'sanctifieth all the elect people of God'.[21]

The Victory of Divine Goodness, which was the major statement of his position, was preceded by two other works, *Difficulties of Belief in connexion with the Creation and the Fall* (1855) and *The Ways of God* (1863), in which there are some indications of the development of his eschatology.[22]

---

[19] Some considered his appointment retrograde. Cf. 'T. R. Birks' in *DNB*.

[20] C. C. Abbott (ed.), *Further Letters of Gerard Manley Hopkins*, 1956, p. 18 (6 June 1864).

[21] T. R. Birks, *The Atonement and the Judgment: a reply to Dr. Candlish's inaugural lecture, with a brief statement of facts in connexion with the Evangelical Alliance*, 1876, p. 11.

[22] In *The Ways of God* Birks denied that the Fall of Adam was a physical necessity imposed on all men. It was rather a precedent which was invariably followed, the personal and deliberate choice of evil by all who reached the years of discretion.

For Birks the problem of eternal punishment was the old problem of the relation between God's justice and mercy. To assert that God is both perfect justice and mercy was, Birks maintained, only to point a contrast not to state an absolute contradiction, and he believed those who equated eternal punishment with 'the infliction of pure, perfect, merciless misery' to be guilty of turning this contrast into just such a contradiction.[23] He held that much contemporary theology distorted the perspective of biblical eschatology. Death had usurped the place of resurrection, and ideas of immortality had obscured the second coming and general resurrection. It was, therefore, necessary to recover the biblical perspective and to set eternal punishment once again within the context of the 'historical plan of redemption', centring on the 'death and resurrection of Christ . . ., his future return and the resurrection of his people'.[24] He consequently attempted to draw into the debate about eternal punishment the neglected 'cosmic dimension' of eschatology, and stressed that salvation was not only to be spoken of in individual terms but also corporately. 'Every created being,' he wrote, 'has a personal and individual, but also a relative and federal character.'[25] Biblical references to eternal judgment and the resulting blessing and punishment were indeed to be interpreted with reference to the individual, for Birks believed that a personal misery suffered by lost souls in hell was quite clearly taught in Scripture, but, having said this Birks went on to ask what was the purpose of God's judgment. To say that its purpose was such individual misery would mean that its purpose was 'to stereotype and eternize active rebellion against God'. Its purpose was rather, as Scripture also taught, to abolish such rebellion.[26] For one like Birks who believed in a universal atonement only three positions were possible regarding lost souls: that God ceased to love those whom he once loved; that the power of sin in the lost was so great that it was capable of defeating the love of God; or that the punishment was of such a nature that it did not exclude the lost from some passive, but real, contemplation of the divine goodness.[27] Birks adopted the third of these options, and argued

[23] *The Atonement and the Judgment*, pp. 27, 40.

[24] *The Victory of Divine Goodness*, 1867, pp. 11, 53, Calvin connected the bliss of heaven with death rather than with the Last Judgment. (Cf. J. P. Martin: *The Last Judgment in Protestant theology from Orthodoxy to Ritschl*, 1963, p. 16.)

[25] *Victory*, p. 42.

[26] p. 179.

[27] *The Atonement and the Judgment*, p. 15.

that 'the future condition of the lost' would 'combine, with the utmost personal shame and humiliation and anguish the passive contemplation of a ransomed universe and of all the innumerable varieties of blessedness enjoyed by unfallen spirits and the ransomed people of God'.[28] To maintain such a position was, he suggested, no more difficult than to believe in the co-existence of perfect mercy and perfect justice in God.[29] He supported his theory with an idiosyncratic exegesis of the text 'Good were it for that man if he had never been born' (Mk. 14:21):

The word is καλόν and not ἀγαθόν . . . In respect of honour it were far better for them not to have been born . . . May we not rather believe that their condition will be a mysterious paradox, an eternal contrast where the καλόν has been reversed into utter shame thro' the perverseness of evil; but the ἀγαθόν remains because of the love of the Creator and the grace of the Redeemer?[30]

Because of this co-existence of righteous punishment and the enjoyment of the passive contemplation of the goodness of God, any idea of lost souls perpetually tormenting each other, or being given into the power of Satan to be tormented, was abhorrent. Such a theory assumed 'the perpetual continuance of active malice' and ascribed to God 'a dominion shared for ever with the powers of evil'.[31]

As Birks's theology is in many points sharply opposed to that of Aquinas it is somewhat surprising to find that he adopts similar arguments to Aquinas in repudiating annihilationism.[32] Aquinas argued against annihilationism because he believed the glory of the blessed to be enhanced by their knowledge of the torments of the damned; Birks suggests that the continuing knowledge of the lost by the blessed makes redemption a perpetually revealed, present reality, whereas, if the wicked were annihilated, redemption would only be the recollection of an ever-fading past as far as the blessed were concerned.

In keeping with his belief in a universal atonement Birks did not limit the saved to the ranks of the Church. The Church was the 'first-fruits', and its glory was the manifestation of the electing grace of God, but 'a wider truth of redeeming love', Birks wrote, 'would be seen in successive and unlimited generations of holy men, the subjects of Christ's kingdom, over whom He will reign with His

[28] *Victory*, p. 45.   [29] p. 187.   [30] pp. 194–5.   [31] p. 47.
[32] Cf. *Summa Theologica*, III, Supp. Q.98, Art. 5, 8, 9, on the attitude of the lost to God and to the blessed; *Victory*, 1870², p. 205.

Church in that new earth, where righteousness shall dwell for ever'.[33]
In both *The Victory of Divine Goodness*, and in the second edition of
Difficulties of Belief the increasing interest of English theology in the
perspective of creation and incarnation can be seen:

> The contrast between the obedient and the disobedient, the faithful and
> the unbelieving, in their relation to God as the righteous Judge, cannot set
> aside their common relation to Him as the bountiful Creator of all men,
> and the God of grace towards all who are sunk in guilt or misery.[34]

There is a strong echo here of Maurice's concept of the Kingdom of
Christ, and, as E. H. Plumptre recognized, there are many affinities
between the theology of Maurice and Birks. Plumptre went so far as
to comment that *The Victory of Divine Goodness* 'in not a few passages
. . . presents so close a verbal identity with the language of Mr.
Maurice's *Theological Essays*, that in a writer of inferior calibre it
would suggest the thought of a literary plagiarism'.[35] He also pointed
out the resemblance of Birks's teaching to that of some parts of
E. H. Bickersteth's poem, *Yesterday, Today and for Ever*, published
the year before *The Victory of Divine Goodness*.[36] That convinced
Evangelicals like Birks and Bickersteth should have come so close to
views akin to those of Maurice is a clear indication of the extent of
the reaction against the harsh eschatology of popular Protestantism.

Nevertheless many Evangelicals remained firmly convinced that a
doctrine of eternal punishment free from any reinterpretation was a
corner-stone of the Christian faith. When, in 1846, the confession of
faith of the Evangelical Alliance had been expanded, a clause
affirming eternal punishment had been added, chiefly at the request
of American delegates, alarmed by the spread of universalist and
annihilationist ideas. Since Birks occupied the position of secretary
of the Alliance for nineteen years, it was not surprising that some
would consider that his publication of *The Victory of Divine Goodness*
to be incompatible with his subscription to the Alliance's basis of
faith, and so it proved. The attack was led by a solicitor, R. Baxter,
who, whilst admitting Birks's claim to teach eternal punishment,
questioned his interpretation of it, and demanded the use of the

---

[33] *Victory*, 1870², p. 208; cf. Birks: *The Four Prophetic Empires*, 1844, and *Outlines of Unfulfilled Prophecy*, 1854.

[34] *Difficulties*, 1876, p. 240.

[35] E. H. Plumptre, *The Spirits in Prison*, 1884, p. 229.

[36] e.g. p. 232, the acknowledgement by Satan and the lost souls of the righteousness of their punishment.

plain words of Scripture alone to put an end to all speculation. In the face of this challenge Birks resigned his office, but announced his intention of remaining a member of the Alliance without retracting his opinions. He confessed to being somewhat surprised by the controversy in the Alliance, which he had expected to encounter not there but in the Church. In December 1868, the treasurer of the Alliance, R. C. L. Bevan, asked Birks to make 'an unqualified contradiction' of the charge that he held 'modified views' on eternal punishment. Birks replied by sending Bevan a private statement of his position, but shortly afterwards discovered that Bevan intended to use this reply publicly in an attempt to expel him from the Alliance, and that James Grant, the powerful Evangelical editor of the *Morning Advertiser* had received an account from Bevan of Birks's teaching. Grant denounced Birks and published a rambling attack on him under the title of *The Religious Tendencies of our Time*, which tediously re-asserted the necessity of belief in hell. Such belief was, Grant believed, 'a preliminary step to saving faith in Christ', and claimed that 'there was not a single case of conversion recorded in the New Testament, in which there was not the previous consciousness of deserving hell, and the consequent dread of being doomed to endure the Divine displeasure in a future state.'[37]

Baxter's move to have Birks expelled failed as a result of the unwillingness of the majority of the Alliance council to set themselves up as a theological tribunal, and they agreed to accept a statement from Birks that those who died in their sins would be punished by God as a sufficient statement of his Evangelical faith. It is an indication of the changed climate that only sixteen members of the Alliance felt so strongly about the dispute that they resigned.[38]

Birks's success in remaining a member of the Evangelical Alliance, and his subsequent promotion to a Cambridge professorship, shows how, by the late 1860s, it was becoming possible for Evangelicals cautiously to reinterpret the doctrine of eternal punishment. It also points to a growing sensitivity to the harshness of the

[37] J. Grant, *The Religious Tendencies of our Times*, 1869, p. 98.

[38] For the history of Birks's conflict with the Alliance, cf. *Evangelical Christendom*, xxiv (N. S. II), 1870, 33–7, 66, 104–5, 198. The sixteen who resigned were: R. C. L. Bevan; A. Kinnaird; R. Baxter; H. M. Matheson; C. Skrine; R. Alexander; M. Rainford; F. A. Bevan; C. J. Glynn; G. Curme; D. T. K. Drummond; J. H. Balfour; R. S. Candlish; A. Thompson; J. Jordan, and H. Bewly. An account of the doctrinal basis of the alliance can be found in D. King, *Historical Sketch of the Evangelical Alliance*, Glasgow, 1851.

Calvinist assertion that Christ died for the elect alone. Birks saw more
clearly than most that the conflict between universalism and a rigor-
ous understanding of eternal punishment was paralleled by the
problem of the relation of God's justice and mercy. His attempted
solution may have been paradoxical, but he did at least recognize that
the problem existed, and at the same time pointed the way to an
emphasis on a corporate as well as an individual salvation.

TWO UNIVERSALISTS: ANDREW JUKES AND SAMUEL COX

In the same year as Birks published *The Victory of Divine Goodness*
Andrew Jukes brought out *The Second Death and the Restitution of
all things*, a book which marked him as one of the leading universalists of the 1870s. Jukes had been a contemporary of F. W. Faber at
Harrow and had then gone up to Cambridge where he won the
Hulsean Prize for an essay on the principles of prophetic interpretation. He records that he had felt a desire to live for God quite early
in life, but had only been converted through reading the works of
the great Evangelical, Thomas Scott. In 1842 he was ordained deacon
to the parish of St. John's, Hull, but almost immediately began to be
doubtful about baptismal regeneration, left the Church, and was re-
baptized by a Baptist minister. He succeeded in gathering his own
congregation in Hull, to which he ministered for the next twenty-five
years, during which he devoted himself to a study of the Bible, the
Fathers, and the works of Boehme and William Law. He also corresponded with F. D. Maurice. The publication of *The Restitution of
all things*, however, led to a controversy with his congregation, and
in 1868 Jukes left Hull and came to live in Highgate. He returned to
the Church of England, and was increasingly drawn into the orbit of
Anglo-Catholicism, though he never took the step of taking priest's
orders.[39] In 1870 a meeting with the Pearsall Smiths led to an
introduction to Lord and Lady Mount Temple and an invitation to
the Broadlands conferences, which they organized. At these religiously eclectic gatherings he soon became a well-known figure.
H. B. Macartney, who attended the 1878 conference, met Jukes and
was much impressed by him:

[Mr. Jukes] has so much light and so much love and yet has done so much
harm! He was very kind to me. He is as simple as a little child, sorrows
over his position, in, or rather outside, the Church, has published his book

[39] His son, however, was ordained and became curate to T. T. Carter at Clewer.

on Restitution, much against his will, at the urgent insistence of friends, and believes that he is generally misunderstood . . . I never met anyone more humble or less dogmatic.[40]

Jukes's doctrines were in many respects idiosyncratic. He was interested in numerological and typological interpretations of Scripture, regarded Spiritualism as a sign of the last times, and believed Boehme superior to Swedenborg because he maintained the final unity of male and female angels.[41] For all this his works aroused serious interest.

Jukes had been brought up to believe the traditional doctrine of eternal punishment, but, whilst at Cambridge, had become doubtful on the matter, through discovering that the Bible described the Aaronic priesthood, which was certainly not eternal, as lasting 'for ever'.[42] He came to believe that the traditional doctrine was at variance with the teaching of Scripture, and devoted himself to a search for ways of reconciling them. By the time he published *The Restitution of all things* he had been led to three main conclusions. First he put forward the idea of the 'first-born', those whose office and duty it was to intercede for others. Christ, he believed, entered on his priestly work of intercession only after passing through death and judgment, and he was the pattern for the ministry of the redeemed after their death. They would be set as priests and kings over the lost 'until all things are restored and reconciled unto God'.[43] His second principle was that God's activity was always an activity by degrees, and he saw in the days of creation, and the various periods of ritual purification prescribed by the Mosaic Law, types of the ages initiated by the coming of Christ. Ζωὴ αἰώνιος was quite rightly translated in this context as 'life "for the age" or "for the ages of ages"'.[44] Finally, it was at the end of these ages that the redeemed would be made 'partakers of the divine nature'.[45] This ultimate goal was only to be reached through death. All were subject, like Christ, 'to the same great law of progress through death', which was another baptism enabling man to enter heaven, and a deliverance

---

[40] H. B. Macartney, *England, Home and Beauty; sketches of Christian Life and work in England in 1878*, n.d. pp. 88–9.

[41] Broadlands Archives, Winchester. Mount Temple MSS., Andrew Jukes to Lord Mount Temple, 9 Oct. 1875.

[42] *Literary Churchman*, xxxiv, 1891, pp. 103–6.

[43] *Restitution of all Things*, 1867, p. 38.

[44] pp. 53–54.   [45] II Pet. 1:4.

from man's earthly nature and so a deliverance from sin.[46] Jukes's doctrine has a somewhat Gnostic flavour, but it enables him to argue that as death is the deliverance from sin for the godly, the second death is a similar deliverance for the ungodly, who have not died to sin, and therefore have not really passed out of this world.[47]

In Jukes's theology death is given an almost boundless moral significance, and, although he is careful to point out that death is by no means devoid of suffering, it is for him an almost entirely positive event. His conception of the role of believers after death as channels through which unbelievers are brought to the possession of the divine life is akin to the appreciation of the communion of saints in Tractarian theology, and it is perhaps hardly surprising that it was this theory which was most fiercely attacked by J. N. Darby, the founder of the Plymouth Brethren, with whom Jukes had for a time been associated. Darby charged Jukes with ignoring the atonement, guilt, and judgment, and reducing salvation to a change of nature produced by dying. 'Is Christ no more than a channel, or do we bless as Redeemers?' Darby asked.[48]

Jukes was idiosyncratic in his theology; this was not the case with Samuel Cox. Cox was born in 1826, one of a large group of brothers. At fourteen he began work in the London docks, but, feeling drawn to the ministry, entered Stepney College as a student, and in 1852 became pastor of a Baptist church in Southsea. Four years later he accepted a charge at Ryde in the Isle of Wight, and it was whilst he was there that he adopted the universalist views for which he became known. Although his change of opinion occasioned some distrust, it was not sufficient to prevent him from being appointed in 1861 as secretary to the committee responsible for the commemoration of the Great Ejectment, nor from becoming minister of the Mansfield Road Baptist Church in Nottingham two years later.[49] It was at Nottingham that Cox gave the series of lectures which was published under the title of *Salvator Mundi*.

Judging by what Cox says in *Salvator Mundi* it would appear that the problem which led him to reconsider popular eschatology was the disparity of opportunity afforded to men to achieve that state of grace which was held to be requisite for salvation. Christ's words

[46] *Restitution*, p. 65; A. Jukes, *The New Man and the Eternal Life*, 1884³, pp. 53-4.
[47] *Restitution*, p. 87.
[48] J. N. Darby, *Works: Doctrinal*, ix, 130ff., 166-7.
[49] Prefatory memoir by Mrs. Cox attached to S. Cox, *The Hebrew Twins*, 1894.

about the refusal of Bethsaida and Chorazin to repent, when Tyre
and Sidon would have done so on the same evidence, seemed at
face value 'to charge Divine Providence with a double blunder'.
'What would have sufficed to save one set of men was withheld from
them; it was granted to another set of men, whom it did not suffice to
save.'[50] Rejecting the argument that God did in fact give Tyre and
Sidon every opportunity to live virtuously, Cox suggested that the
possibility of their repentance in other circumstances clearly pointed
to a state of probation after death. The wrath of God, which the lost
were supposed to suffer, had, Cox believed, only a reformatory
purpose. It was to convict men of sin and lead to their abandoning
of it. Like Jukes, to whom he acknowledged a debt, he believed that
salvation was always for a purpose, and was never selfish, and that
all punishment mentioned in Scripture was redemptive and creative,
apportioned in just degrees to the state of the offender.[51] As the
reward of the righteous could be regarded as their just retribution
which also perfects them, so the punishment of the wicked could be
seen as being similarly retributive and, at the same time, remedial.
But Cox went beyond these somewhat specious arguments and
maintained that there would be a new and fuller revelation of the
grace of God, which would have a converting and saving efficacy.

As with many universalists Cox did not regard death as a sudden
break in man's history, with man's future indeterminate on one side
of it and irrevocably fixed on the other. To suppose that death had
such an effect was, he argued, to say that it had the power of effecting
an unaccountable change in a man's character, which, curiously
enough, was one of the main charges Darby brought against Jukes.
Cox believed that theologies which made death a sharp dividing line
had been too much influenced by questions concerning the ontological, rather than the moral, aspects of the future life.[52] In thus
playing down death as a shattering event, Cox is typical of many
nineteenth-century divines who were influenced by ideas of gradual,
evolutionary progress.

When *Salvator Mundi* was published in 1877 Cox's theology does
not seem to have occasioned much controversy, but in 1884 the
publishers of the *Expositor*, which Cox edited, demanded that he
gave an undertaking to exclude from the journal in future 'all

---

[50] S. Cox, *Salvator Mundi*, 1877, p. 20.
[51] p. 161.
[52] S. Cox, *Expository essays and discourses*, 1877, p. 96.

allusions to "the larger hope" and even to the general tone of thought, which it carried with it'.[53] Rather than do this Cox resigned. His own congregation, however, remained unperturbed, and when a presentation was made to him in that same year, the address referred specifically to his 'vindication of the infinite love of God and of its final triumph over all men through Jesus Christ'. It went on to claim that 'since the publication of *Salvator Mundi* there has been a marked change of religious thought' concerning eternal punishment. In his reply to this address Cox stressed that he wished to make it clear to the younger members of his congregation that, in adopting a universalist theology, 'we have not loosened our hold on any of the truths to which our fathers held and by their faith in which they were saved, but have simply learned to hold them in a broader and more reasonable form, and, as we trust, in a more catholic spirit'.

We still believe in the sinfulness of man, especially our own sinfulness, but we believe that evil will finally be overcome by good. We still believe in the Atonement, that the forgiving and redeeming love of God is revealed in the life, death and passion of our Lord Jesus Christ, but we also believe in an Atonement of wider scope, that Christ will see of the travail of his soul and be satisfied in a larger and diviner way than some of our theologians have supposed.[54]

IMMORTALITY UNDER DEBATE

In 1877, the year of the publication of *Salvator Mundi*, a series of articles devoted to the discussion of 'the soul and the future life' appeared in Sir James Knowles's newly established review, the *Nineteenth Century*, under the title of 'A Modern "Symposium"'. It consisted of nine articles written as a reply to an earlier article by the Positivist, Frederick Harrison, who himself added a reply to his critics at the end of the series. The articles are of some importance in the history of nineteenth-century religious thought as they appeared at a time when eschatology was again under debate and they were all written by men of distinction: R. H. Hutton; T. H. Huxley; Newman's old friend, Frederick Rogers, Lord Blachford; the poet,

[53] A. Peel, *Letters to a Victorian Editor*, 1929, p. 292. S. Cox to Henry Allon, 30 Aug. 1884. Cox's universalist preaching had earlier disturbed R. W. Sibthorp, who had drawn the attention of Bishop Wordsworth of Lincoln to it. Wordsworth had then preached two sermons in Nottingham to combat it. (J. Fowler, *R. W. Sibthorp*, 1880, p. 340.)
[54] Cox MSS. (Mansfield Road Baptist Church records, Nottingham University Library.) I am indebted to Mr. F. M. W. Harrison for these quotations.

Roden Noel; Lord Selborne; Canon Barry; W. R. Greg; James Baldwin Brown; and W. G. Ward.

Frederick Harrison had defended the Positivist position that the only sense in which it was meaningful to talk of a man's future life was in the sense of a man's posthumous influence on other men, and he had charged orthodox Christianity with teaching a selfish immortality, and the 'eternity of the tabor, . . . an inane and unworthy crown of a human life'.[55] In his reply, R. H. Hutton charged Harrison with inconsistency. The Christian hope, he argued, was centred on an adoring relationship with God, and that could not easily be described as selfish. Moreover Christianity recognized the existence of moral distinctions in a future life as important in a way that Harrison's view of an immortality of 'posthumous energy' failed to do. He was, however, sufficiently sympathetic to some of Harrison's ideals to emphasize that, in his opinion, for a man to believe in a future life was to believe in his becoming 'an altogether better member of a better society'.[56]

T. H. Huxley defended a thorough-going materialism, and found Harrison's acceptance of a 'distinct correspondence between every process of thought or of feeling and some corporeal phenomenon' strangely at variance with his condemnation of the 'irrational and debasing physicism' of materialists.[57] For Huxley, Harrison's admission of the influence of physical factors on mental states and moral decision immediately brought moral and religious concepts fully within the purlieus of physiology.

If impaired secretions deprave the moral sense, it becomes an interesting and important problem to ascertain what diseased viscus may have been responsible for *The Priest in Absolution*, and what condition of the grey pulp may have conferred on it such a pathological steadiness of faith as to create the hope of personal immortality, which Mr. Harrison stigmatizes as selfishly immoral.[58]

[55] *Nineteenth Century*, i, 841; ii, 536.

[56] ii, 330, 332. R. H. Hutton (1826–97), theologian, journalist, and man of letters, was editor of the *Spectator* from 1861. Theologically he began as a disciple of Martineau, then became an Anglican under the influence of F. D. Maurice and F. W. Robertson, and towards the end of his life became increasingly sympathetic to the teaching of Newman, though he never joined the Roman Church.

[57] I, p. 627.

[58] II, p. 337. *The Priest in Absolution* was a manual for confessors, circulated amongst members of the Anglo-Catholic Society of the Holy Cross. It became a centre of controversy, because of its advocacy of confession and the personal nature of the questions the confessor was encouraged to ask, and was fiercely attacked in the House of Lords by Lord Redesdale in June, 1877.

Harrison's Positivism, in Huxley's opinion, halted between two opinions, and could only be regarded as 'a half-breed between science and theology' that used too much metaphysical jargon to be acceptable. Whilst he understood the word 'soul', when it was used by pagan or Christian writers, without being able to believe in it, Harrison's use of the term could only be described as nonsense.

In the interests of scientific clearness, I object to say that I have a soul, when I mean, all the while, that my organism has certain mental functions which, like the rest, are dependent upon its molecular composition, and come to an end when I die; and I object still more to affirm that I look to a future life, when all that I mean is, that the influence of my sayings and doings will be more or less felt by a number of people after the physical components of that organism are scattered to the four winds.[59]

But the very dependence of the body on the mind, which Huxley had proclaimed as the creed of a triumphant materialism, was a source of deep anxiety to Roden Noel. 'The discovery', he wrote, 'has no doubt gone far to shake the faith of many in human immortality . . . It has been so with myself', and, to salvage something of his former faith, he clung to a belief in the vitalistic universe, which James Hinton had depicted in *Life in Nature* in 1862, in which the interdependence of body and mind was of such a kind that eternal consciousness formed the basis of the physical, the composite and the temporal.[60] This idealist pantheism seemed to offer Noel more than the cold and unsatisfactory promises of Positivism, a need which he felt acutely because of the death of his small son, which weighed heavily upon him.[61]

What of those we have lost, who were dearer to us than our own selves, full of fairest hope and promise, unaware annihilated in earliest dawn, whose dewy bud yet slept unfolded? If they were *things*, doubtless we might count them as so much manure, in which to grow those still more beautiful, though still brief-flowering human aloes, which Positivism . . . is able confidently to promise us in some remote future. But alas! they *seemed* living spirits, able to hope for infinite love, progressive virtue, the beatific vision of God Himself! And they really *were*—so much manure! . . . I could believe in the pessimism of Schopenhauer, not in this jaunty optimism of Comte.[62]

[59] p. 340.
[60] pp. 351, 353. Roden Noel (1834–94), a poet and 'an almost pure romantic who, except in occasional moments of despairing scepticism, was able to regard himself as a Christian by identifying Christianity with the romantic faith'. (H. N. Fairchild, *Religious Trends in English Poetry*, iv, 217.)
[61] Cf. H. N. Fairchild, ibid. p. 222.   [62] *Nineteenth Century*, ii, 353–4.

W. R. Greg, of whom Morley said that it was impossible to decide whether he were a Theist or an agnostic,[63] admitted the power of immortality, not only as a consoling belief, but as an ennobling conception with a beneficient, practical influence. It was, he suggested, the one religious doctrine possessed of an overriding demand to be believed, not for its truth, but for its comfort or consequences.[64] For Greg himself, however, the future life remained an insoluble enigma, for where there was a clear, dogmatic belief in a future life, it seemed to coincide with a heaven made up of 'mundane and material elements', in which it had become impossible for any intelligent man to believe. On the other hand, any attempt to frame a theology of the future life without recourse to such 'physical' imagery seemed doomed to failure. Those who had attempted it, had only discovered that 'in renouncing the "physical" and inadmissible they have been forced to renounce the "conceivable" as well'.

A dimness and fluctuating uncertainty gathers round a scene, from which all that is concrete and definable, and would therefore be incongruous, has been shut out. The next world cannot, it is felt, be a material one; and a truly 'spiritual' one even the saints cannot conceive so as to bring it home to nature still shrouded in the garments of the flesh.[65]

Greg thus treats imagery with a typical Victorian literalism, combined with an idealist yearning for a 'spiritual' realm freed from the ambiguities of such imagery, a position which is not surprising when one remembers the crudity with which eschatological imagery was used by many contemporary divines.[66] He also refused to accept the popular argument that the universality of belief in immortality was an important witness to its truth, for he very much doubted whether the universality claimed had ever existed. In pagan nations it had often been vague, amongst the Chinese it was scarcely recognizable, Nirvana was 'more a sort of conscious non-existence than a future life', and even amongst the Jews it had developed relatively late.[67] His argument is an indication of how the new awareness of other cultures, brought about by the development of anthropology and the study of other religions, was beginning to have an effect on the beliefs of educated men. Greg linked this argument with another, a curious reversal of the common belief that men were more occupied

[63] J. Morley, *Critical Miscellanies*, 1901 ed., pp. 252–3.
[64] *Nineteenth Century*, ii, 507.   [65] p. 509.
[66] Greg cites an extract from Chalmers's sermons as an example of this crudity.
[67] ii, 509–10.

with the future life in old age than in youth. 'For the old,' he wrote, 'today, which may be our last engrosses us far more than tomorrow, which may be our FOREVER' and it was the young who held most firmly to a belief in the future life.[68] It was curious argument, for which there would seem to have been little evidence, and it was not repeated.

James Baldwin Brown put forward a basically Mauricean viewpoint. He castigated much Evangelical language as self-indulgent, with its picture of 'souls mooning on the mount', and wished that such Christians would be given 'a vigorous shake . . . to set them with some stinging words about some good work for God and for their world'. He entirely agreed with Harrison's protest against 'the vague, bloodless, bodiless notion of the life of the future, which has more affinity with Hades than with Heaven'.[69] Taking the Resurrection of Christ as his basis, Brown declared that the life of the future was of the same character as that of the present, the life of an embodied spirit, and that it was because Christianity was concerned with the totality of man that it was so powerful. The 'new life', which was revealed by the Resurrection, he wrote, 'has been near the heart of all the great movements of human society from that day until now. I do not even exclude "the Revolution"'.[70] He saw in the growth and development of a Christian society a far stronger argument for the truth of immortality than pale survivals of personal ghosts. Yet Brown did not defend an unthinking optimism. He protested against Harrison's assumption of the continual progress of humanity, which would provide the individual with his posthumous immortality, and stressed that the world itself was a disordered world, which perpetually frustrated the coming into being of any perfection, social or individual. Immortality was, therefore, to be seen as the complement to both the 'unshaped and unperfect' life of the individual, and to the world which frustrated his development. 'The sad strain and anguish of our life, social, intellectual, and spiritual,' was 'but the pain by which great stages of growth accomplish themselves.'[71] It was a social and evolutionary picture, which Brown presented, which attempted to do justice to the material order, and to man as belonging to that order. But, for all his recognition of man's embodied nature, he still referred to the material world as 'Bare, heartless' and 'hopeless', and described life in it as a 'ghastly drearihood', and he made little attempt in his article to show exactly how the Resurrection supported his thesis.

[68] pp. 510–11.   [69] p. 513.   [70] p. 515.   [71] p. 517.

Frederick Harrison, in his reply to the symposiasts, strongly emphasized man's social nature. Possibly because he considered the linking of social and evolutionary views with Christian eschatology as the greatest threat to his own theories of posthumous futurity, he strongly denied that the Bible supplied any grounds for believing that 'grander activity' was the main characteristic of the future life, and he quoted with relish a Scottish preacher, whom he had once heard exclaim, 'O dear brethren, who would care to be *saved in a crowd?*'.[72] For him, the traditional understanding of the future life was a live option only for those who denied all physical grounding for mental and moral activity, and if this were not admitted, it was useless to talk of moral perfection, or boundless good works for the saved to perform on behalf of the lost. 'Moral development,' he wrote, 'does not grow like a fungus; it is continual struggle in surrounding conditions of a specific kind, and an active putting forth of a variety of practical faculties in the midst of real obstacles.' Like Francis Newman he believed that pain and suffering were necessary for moral growth, and therefore a heaven of moral growth which excluded them was impossible.[73]

The 'Modern "Symposium"' clearly illustrates both the growing doubts about a future life and the need felt, by those who were no longer able to accept the traditional doctrine, to find some kind of adequate substitute for it. It is perhaps a commentary, both on the way in which hell was used primarily as a moral sanction, and on the extent to which belief in eternal punishment had diminished, that arguments about hell do not appear in the articles, not even in those of the High Anglican, Lord Selborne, or the Roman Catholic, Ward. Those who still wished to argue for a future life made little reference to it, and their doctrine was usually both evolutionary and activist in its emphasis. Improving activity rather than passive contemplation was the keynote, combined with an awareness of the challenges posed to the concept of the soul by scientific theories concerning the relation of mind and matter.

[72] p. 524.
[73] p. 525. Cf. F. W. Newman, *Life after death? Palinodia*, 1886, p. 34. It was thought at one time that Robert Browning, in his poem *La Saisiaz*, had intended to make an unofficial contribution to the symposium. H. N. Fairchild has shown that this speculation is unfounded, but the poem remains an interesting contemporary expression of belief in a future life. Cf. H. N. Fairchild, '*La Saisiaz* and the *Nineteenth Century*', *Modern Philology*, 48, 1950, 104–11.

VII

Eternal Hope

At the end of 1877 F. W. Farrar, then archdeacon of Westminster, preached a series of sermons on eternal punishment, which initiated another debate on the subject. It was not, in intellectual terms, as significant as the 'Modern "Symposium"', but the large amount of background correspondence which has survived gives it an importance beyond the arguments actually employed. It is perhaps only in this controversy, of all the many in the nineteenth century, that it is possible to see clearly the whole spectrum of reactions to the debate about hell.

Reginald Farrar believed that his father was led to preach on the subject as a direct result of the 'Modern "Symposium"' and the articles by W. H. Mallock on the theme 'Is Life worth Living?'.[1] The sermons were delivered in November and December 1877, the most controversial, 'Hell, what it is not', being preached on 11 November. Farrar later recalled how he had walked over to Westminster Abbey to preach it on a 'dim, drizzling afternoon', and how afterwards Dean Stanley had thanked him 'with unusual energy of emotion and approval'.[2] The series excited considerable interest, and much of what Farrar said was reported in garbled form before the official version appeared the following year under the title *Eternal Hope*. Despite the fact that it was both prolix and moralizing, and was marked all too clearly by Farrar's characteristic 'thinking in quotations' and florid, oratorical style, the book had a considerable impact. Farrar's standing as a revered headmaster and the author of the popular *Life of Christ* and *Eric, or little by little* ensured that he got a ready hearing, particularly on a subject which had long troubled many minds.[3]

Farrar argued for a heaven that was 'a temper rather than a habitation,' and he protested against pictures of hell, confidently put forward by both popular preachers and eminent theologians, which

[1] R. Farrar, *The Life of F. W. Farrar*, 1904, pp. 266–7.
[2] F. W. Farrar in *That Unknown Country*, (Anon.), 1888, p. 271.
[3] Cf. H. Gresford Jones: 'Universalism and Morals', *Scottish Journal of Theology*, iii, 1950, 28; R. Farrar, *Life of Farrar*, p. 261.

were little more than 'acrid fumes from the poisoned crucible of mean and loveless conceptions'.[4] To preach in such a way was in his opinion to make a mockery of any claim that God was just and loving. He cautioned his hearers against easy appeals to Scripture, reminding them, as became a strong advocate of Temperance, that gin-drinking had been defended out of the epistles to Timothy and slavery out of Philemon.[5] He believed the doctrine of an endless hell depended on a misinterpretation of αἰώνιος.[6] But, having repudiated it, Farrar was reluctant to declare his belief in any of the common alternatives, seeing no proof for purgatory, being unable to accept conditionalism, and lacking the certainty to preach universalism.[7] He preferred to maintain a reverent agnosticism, though he was prepared to affirm that the fate of man was not 'finally and irrevocably sealed at death'.[8]

The comments on *Eternal Hope* show, that, however much he had denied preaching universalism, he was widely believed to have done so. The *Contemporary Review*, perhaps attempting to emulate the success of the *Nineteenth Century*'s 'Modern "Symposium"', began a series of articles in reply to Farrar's book. John Tulloch, the liberal Scottish theologian, who was Principal of St. Andrews, and J. H. Jellett, the professor of natural philosophy at Trinity College, Dublin, were largely appreciative. Baldwin Brown, a Congregationalist, who was a disciple of Maurice, contributed a mild essay largely concerned with condemning Calvinism, whilst John Hunt, a Broad Church divine, pleaded that Farrar had perhaps been too ready to describe the preaching of revivalists as 'hell-fire'. Edward White, as an upholder of conditional immortality, sharply criticized Farrar, whose doctrine, he declared, differed '*toto caelo* and *toto inferno* from the fearful doctrine of Christ and His Apostles'. The Anglo-Catholic Beresford Hope castigated the sermons as 'an incomplete and emotional exposition of an arbitrarily chosen fragment of a complex mystery',[9] but surprisingly, Samuel Cox, who as a universalist might have been expected to show some sympathy for Farrar's position, was alarmed by Farrar's use of Scripture, which, he declared, would end by making it necessary to believe in transubstantiation![10] But the most significant contribution to the series was E. H. Plumptre's publication of his earlier correspondence with Newman on eternal

---

[4] F. W. Farrar, *Eternal Hope*, 1878, pp. 19, 64.   [5] p. 75.   [6] pp. 78–9.
[7] p. 84.   [8] p. 86.   [9] *Contemporary Review*, 32, 1878, 181, 549.
[10] p. 310.

punishment, though the letters were merely stated as being from a Roman Catholic priest. It was left to H. N. Oxenham to reveal Newman's identity in the second edition of his *Catholic Eschatology* (1878).

Dr. Pusey was much disturbed by Farrar's sermons and the publicity which they had attracted. He welcomed H. N. Oxenham's work as a valuable statement of the traditional understanding, and wrote to him lamenting that St. Catherine of Genoa's doctrine of a future happiness co-existing with an intense suffering had not prevailed.[11] He thought some reply needed to be made to Farrar, and at first, in view of his age, was prepared to leave this to others, but when none was forthcoming decided at the end of 1878 to undertake it himself. Liddon rejoiced at the decision, for in many whom he had met *Eternal Hope* seemed to have caused great unsettlement of faith, even though, to his mind, the book was full of contradictions, such as Farrar's contention that eternal punishment was inconsistent with the character of God whilst at the same time conceding that a few souls might be lost.[12]

Farrar had quoted in support of his position some French Catholic writers, and Pusey, more than a little puzzled by some of their reported teaching, wrote to Newman for advice on the subject. Farrar, he claimed, had suggested that certain important points were, according to these writers, not *de fide* for Catholics.

1. That the fire is other than a metaphor of extreme suffering;
2. that the *poena sensus* is not gradually mitigated in degree;
3. that the lost (as I understand them) are in actual rebellion against God;
4. that neither Holy Scripture or the Church lay down an absolute eternity of punishment, but only 'aeonian', it being supposed that 'aeonian punishment' should be boundlessly long compared with the relatively short period of purgatory.[13]

Pusey, believing that these ideas were contrary to punishment that was stated to be 'to the ages of ages', asked Newman to comment on the point, and on the opinion of the eighteenth-century Bishop of Boulogne, de Partz de Pressy, that 'the lost do not desire death, do not hate God, do not curse Him', and that of the abbé le Noir, that

[11] Pusey MSS., Pusey to H. N. Oxenham, ?1878. [Chest B. Drawer 4.]
[12] Pusey MSS., H. P. Liddon to Pusey, 22 Nov. [1878.] Liddon–Pusey, ii, f. 53.
[13] Newman MSS., Birmingham Oratory, Pusey to Newman, ? December, 1878. Pusey–Newman clxix., f. 199.

the church had never condemned simple universalism. He quoted with alarm the remark of a poor woman, 'they say now, there is no hell, it is only being miserable ourselves'.[14]

Newman replied to Pusey at the beginning of 1879. He discounted le Noir and de Pressy as being of minimal authority for Catholics, and devoted most of the letter to a discussion of the 'non-materiality' of hell-fire, a theory which had been suggested by two Catholic theologians in Germany, Hettinger and Kiel.[15] Newman had little sympathy with their ideas as he had developed an idiosyncratic doctrine of his own which used the idea of the material fire of hell inducing a numbness in those who suffered it as a way of mitigating eternal torment.

I cannot conceive what is gained by liberty to consider the fire non-material. At least it is called in Scripture *fire*. If in its properties and its effect it is fire, what is the good of quarrelling about its name? Nay, if you lay a stress upon its non-materiality, as so much gained in the mitigation of suffering, be quite sure, before you proceed, that you do not make the suffering greater not less. We know that material pain cannot continue intense—the martyrs at Lyons did not feel the red-hot chair a second time —men do not fear the rack after several applications of it—a spiritual pain may be living and enduring. An eternity of physical fire would perhaps be no eternity of physical suffering—it might so shatter the material constitution of our nature, as to make us incapable of suffering. Certainly, judging by such experience as I have had, I should say that intense pain destroys the recognition of time, or a succession of minutes and hours.[16]

Pusey was disappointed by Newman's reply, and told Liddon that he thought it unsatisfactory, though he was glad to know that the writers Farrar had cited could safely be ignored as being of little consequence.[17] Liddon told him that Dean Church had suspected that Newman would not let himself be drawn on the subject.[18] He himself saw Farrar as 'a symptom rather than a cause', the representa-

---

[14] Cf. J. J. de Partz de Pressy, *Oeuvres très-complètes*, I, Paris, 1842, cols. 643, 650–1; For le Noir cf. J. P. Migne, *Encyclopédie théologique troisième et dernière*, XIX (*Dictionnaire des harmonies de la raison et de la foi*), Paris, 1856, article: 'Vie éternelle', cols. 1688–94. Newman MSS., Pusey to Newman, Pusey–Newman, clxix, f. 199.

[15] Cf. F. Hettinger, *Apologie des Christentums*, II, Freiburg-im-Breisgau, 1867, p. 312. 'Wie sind jene Strafen zu denken? Ist es ein wirkliches (wennglich kein materielles) oder nur im metaphorischen Sinne ein Feuer, von dem der Herr rekt? Die Kirche hat hierüber keine Entschiedung.'

[16] Newman MSS., Newman to Pusey, 4 Jan. 1879, Pusey–Newman, clxix, f. 201.

[17] Pusey MSS., Pusey to H. P. Liddon, 6 Jan. 1879. Pusey–Liddon, ii, f. 218.

[18] Pusey MSS., Liddon to Pusey, 9 Jan. 1879, Liddon–Pusey, ii, f. 58.

tive of 'the passion rather than the logic of the attack on the old doctrine', and thought that the true answer to Farrar was 'a very full statement of the doctrine of the Intermediate State with its practical corollary of prayers for the Faithful Departed'. He accurately pointed out that:

The mass of people do not think about the texts of Scripture . . . they ask what has become of A. B. and C., whom they have known in this life and who have died and who cannot be thought of as at once either in heaven or in hell without moral violence. The popular Protestant doctrine, with its two categories of the dead gets into endless difficulties when applied to the facts of life: and Farrar is on strong ground when he urges this. But unless the graduated relief afforded by the belief in a state of suspense and training for heaven be granted, the majority of modern men *will* resolve hell into a purgatory—probably into a very brief and endurable purgatory— and will persuade themselves that Scripture allows them to do this, or that it must be done whether Scripture allows it or not.[19]

Others, like the fiery High Churchman Archdeacon Denison, refused to admit the right of anyone to question the justice of eternal punishment.

I cannot tell you how my nature revolts against these searchings into the mysteries of God, you believe that His Love, Justice and Mercy are all of them perfect, also His Wisdom. You know that it is not given to you or to any human being to comprehend His Mysteries. You know that those who come to the Beatific Vision will comprehend them in their new nature. To what good purpose to make argument about that you cannot comprehend?

. . . I have dipped into the book in some places. It seems all of it to me to be founded in a misconception of what Faith is.[20]

Pusey's reply to Farrar appeared in 1880 under the title *What is of Faith as to Everlasting Punishment?* Pusey himself was full of misgivings about it. He described it as a dry work, answering Farrar 'sentence by sentence and hint by hint', 'an odd mish-mash'.[21] Newman wrote, however, to say that he found Pusey's argument 'very forcible', and the admiring Liddon considered that Pusey had

[19] J. C. Johnston: *Life of Liddon*, 1904, pp. 286–7. Liddon to R. W. Church, 28 Oct. 1879.
[20] G. A. Denison, *Fifty Years at East Brent*, 1902, p. 203. Denison to Miss Phillimore, 13 Mar. 1878.
[21] Liddon, *Life of Pusey*, iv, 349, 352.

succeeded in making an impression on Farrar.[22] Nevertheless, in terms of popular appeal, a catena of Rabbinic quotations was not altogether the best reply to *Eternal Hope*, and Pusey's book was a dry and scholarly tome, not likely to have the same popular appeal as Farrar's emotional rhetoric. Surprisingly, on some points Farrar and Pusey were shown to be in agreement. There was, Pusey declared, no ground for believing that the majority of mankind were lost, nor could it be known who had died out of grace.[23] But Pusey gave a greater significance to the moment of death than Farrar did, and described it as an 'almost sacrament', a time when God's mercy and grace was particularly shown, and one might believe, for instance, 'that Absalom, parricide as he was in intention, repented, when hanging between heaven and earth by the hair which had been his pride'.[24] He conceded, moreover, that Farrar's arguments could lead to a recognition of the value of a belief in the intermediate state, and he emphasized how closely this belief was linked with much Patristic thought. He even, following the teaching of St. Catherine of Genoa, criticized Farrar for depicting the souls in the intermediate state as suffering the willing agony of God's remedial fire, a hell which was not eternal. Such a concept, he thought, resembled some of the cruder Roman formulations of purgatory.[25]

Although Farrar and Pusey differed on the state of Jewish opinion concerning Gehenna at the time of Christ, Farrar viewed Pusey's work as in many ways a vindication. In a new preface to *Eternal Hope* he pointed out that in correspondence with him Pusey had admitted that belief in the *poena sensus* was not a vital part of belief in hell, though he himself accepted it; that he had confessed to a hope that the greater part of mankind would be saved; and that he had accepted with gratitude Farrar's willingness to substitute 'future purification for those who have not utterly extinguished the grace of God in their hearts' for some of the expressions in *Eternal Hope*.[26] Pusey, for his part, did not consider that they had been so easily reconciled, and wrote to Liddon: 'Poor Farrar, he thinks that he has made up matters by professing agreement with me up to a certain point, while in his book he propagates universalism as passionately

[22] Newman MSS., Newman to Pusey, 20 June 1880, Pusey–Newman, clxix, f. 203; Pusey MSS., Liddon to Pusey, 21 July 1880, Liddon–Pusey, ii, f. 122.

[23] E. B. Pusey, *What is of Faith as to Everlasting Punishment?* 1880, pp. 7, 12.

[24] pp. 113, 13.

[25] p. 120.

[26] *Eternal Hope*, 1898 ed., pp. viii–ix.

as he can . . .'[27] He was nervous lest Farrar's apparent willingness to endorse his position should give encouragement to those who wished to justify moral indifference by banishing the fear of hell. Why, he lamented, had he not asked more clearly what to him was the basic question, 'What do those who disbelieve Eternal Punishment think that God became Man for?'.[28]

The difference between the two men is clearly shown by their different attitudes to the Revised Version of the New Testament, when it appeared in 1881. Pusey wrote sorrowfully to Dean Lake about the new translations of κρίσις, γέεννα, and αἰώνιος:

Alas for England! Everything seems let loose against the faith now . . . 'Doctrine' and 'heresy' are to lose their meaning which they have had since the Apostles' times and to become mere 'teaching' and 'party spirit'. All the modern fancies which have congregated round the words 'hell', 'everlasting' and 'damnation' have, from different causes, been exploded in the version.[29]

Farrar, on the other hand, wrote in a very different vein to one of the members of the Revision Committee. He called the committee's attention to the 'immense and dangerous responsibility' they incurred by treating the word 'Gehenna' on different principles to those on which it was treated by Christ and His Apostles.

By retaining the word 'Hell' they will inevitably stereotype in the minds of the ignorant, many conceptions which probably every one of them would reject as false; if they use the word 'Gehenna' *they use the word which our Lord Himself taught them to use*, and follow the example of the Evangelists. Dare they do otherwise? More perhaps than any of us can at present decide may hang on the issue of their decision.[30]

Pusey's scholarly reply forced Farrar into a fuller defence of his position, which was published as *Mercy and Judgment*, and dedicated to Tennyson, the poet of 'the larger hope', as *Eternal Hope* had been dedicated to E. H. Plumptre. It was little more than an extensive reworking of the material which Pusey had collected in his book, but Farrar devoted some attention to death-bed repentance, from which

[27] Pusey MSS., Pusey to Liddon, 23 Aug. 1880, Pusey–Liddon, iii, f. 106.
[28] Liddon, *Life of Pusey*, iv, 357.
[29] Katherine Lake (ed.): *Memorials of Dean Lake*, 1901, p. 251. Pusey to Lake, 1 Oct. 1881.
[30] Farrar to Troutbeck, 20 Dec. 1881 ?. Cambridge University Library, Add. MSS., 6947, f. 123.

Pusey had argued that it was not necessarily true that a large number of men were destined to damnation. Farrar claimed to have met with very few such cases in his own experience, and considered it a weak argument, and if all that could be said of the large number of people remarkable neither for their virtue nor their vice was that they were left to God's 'uncovenanted mercies' further explanation of that phrase was called for. His own belief was that the intermediate state allowed all 'except the absolutely reprobate' to progress and improve.[31]

Whilst Pusey was willing to accept Farrar's assurances that he was not a universalist, he continued to believe that his arguments were, and 'were used as an encouragement in sinful living', but at eighty-one he was too old to engage in further controversy. Liddon echoed Pusey's feelings, and believed Farrar had been led by a desire for popularity to attempt to curry favour with 'his Latitudinarian friends,' whilst refusing to break with more conservative churchmen.[32]

In many respects, as was perhaps to be expected, the debate between Farrar and Pusey only echoed the established arguments of earlier controversies: the appeal to a fixed, revealed doctrine on the one hand, and the protest against its morally intolerable nature on the other; a fear of giving a licence to sin on the one hand, and a fear of making it impossible for men to believe in a good God on the other; the pitting of text against text, and authority against authority. But there are also some changed emphases. Pusey and Liddon, as defenders of the traditional hell placed far more weight on the damage caused by an inadequate doctrine of the intermediate state, and on the possibility of death-bed repentance than earlier protagonists had done. They were prepared to allow that much of the traditional picture of hell was unwarrantable imagery, and concentrated on its essence as separation from God. They were willing to allow that there was some validity in the moral protest against the doctrine,

[31] F. W. Farrar, *Mercy and Judgment*, 1894 ed., pp. 166, 174. F. N. Oxenham, the cousin of the author of Catholic eschatology, also replied to Pusey in the form of an expanded version of his pamphlet, *What is the truth as to everlasting punishment?* This had first appeared in 1875, when Oxenham had considered that hell was 'driving back thoughtful and honest men from the acceptance of Christianity'. (Oxenham to Gladstone, British Museum, Add. MSS., 44,447, f. 337.) Like *Mercy and Judgment* it largely consisted of a detailed examination of Patristic teaching, particularly the condemnation of Origenism in 541.

[32] *Life of Pusey*, iv, 358; Pusey MSS., Liddon to Pusey, 16 Aug. 1881, Liddon–Pusey, ii, f. 163.

providing that it was the doctrine of the Calvinist decrees and not of the Fathers. In short, although the presuppositions of the defenders of both positions remained much the same as in the earlier debates, the presentation of the traditional case had, by the late 1870s, been brought closer to that of the liberalizers than ever before.

WIDER REACTIONS

The unsettlement of Christian faith in nineteenth-century England has frequently been considered from the viewpoint of an important, but small, intelligentsia. This is not surprising, both because this group was remarkably articulate about its loss of faith, and because of the difficulty of obtaining similar information about the opinions of those outside it. Where such information exists, however, as in the obituaries of the adherents of the Secular Movement, doubts about hell and a repudiation of popular ideas about death-bed repentance have been shown to have played an important part in the rejection of Christian belief.[33] More can be learnt of these doubts about hell amongst a wider public from the correspondence which Farrar received after the publication of his two books and of which a considerable amount has survived, though there is no means of telling how representative this sample is.

The most important letter amongst the few from professional theologians is one from Westcott, sympathizing with Farrar's endeavours to reinterpret traditional eschatology. 'You cannot have the subject more at heart than I have,' Westcott wrote, 'but you can bring it home to men and that is a great privilege. I rejoice to hear of the sermons and of their effect.'[34] Support also came from A. R. Symonds and Angus Mackay, both of whom had adopted more definitely universalist positions than Farrar, Mackay under the influence of Baldwin Brown.[35]

Many correspondents underline the extent to which hell was a cause of unbelief, especially amongst working men. A London correspondent wrote:

The necessity of this is really urgent ... there is no one thing which oppresses the minds of thoughtful men at the present day more than the

[33] Cf. Susan Budd: 'The Loss of Faith, Reasons for Unbelief among members of the Secular Movement in England, 1850–1950', *Past and Present*, 36, April 1967, pp. 106–25.
[34] *Life of Farrar*, pp. 277–8.
[35] Farrar MSS., Bundle 8, f. 3; 8, f. 7. A. R. Symonds, a former missionary in India, was vicar of Walmer and author of *The Ultimate Reconciliation and Subjection of all souls to God* (1873).

popular idea that Christianity is committed to the affirmation of the everlasting damnation of the overwhelming majority of mankind. Among the
lower class of unbelievers (I allude to such as frequent Bradlaugh's hall)
there is no greater stumbling block in the way of their acceptance of
Christianity; and I know of no thoughtful man on whose mind the idea is
not acting with [great?] might. It is one of the most fruitful sources of
modern unbelief.[36]

A Cambridge graduate, who had been working for six years amongst
the London poor, supported this view, adding that the popular
doctrine of hell excited the scorn of working men and quite failed to
deter them from sin.[37] A Manchester curate wrote that many working men would become atheists, if Spurgeon's Hall, renowned for
the hell-fire preaching of its founder C. J. Spurgeon, were to continue much longer, and the secretary of the Bethnal Green Working
Men's Club expressed much the same opinion.[38] The vicar of
Aylesford in Kent told Farrar that he longed for *Eternal Hope* to be
'in the hands of every man in England and especially every working
man'. Hell, he said, was a 'cruel misrepresentation of God's love
towards mankind', and was responsible 'for much of the infidelity of
so-called Christian England'.[39] Only two letters, however, claim that
Eternal Hope had in fact prevented working men from becoming
atheists. One was from a lady in Cornwall, who wrote to Farrar to
tell him that his book had been:

... the means of saving from Atheism a young and thoughtful man—a
carpenter in our village. Brought up strictly in the narrow views of the
United Free Methodists his danger was, from feeling the terrible inconsistency of the hell preached by them with the doctrine that God *is*
love. I lent him *Eternal Hope*, which he has since told me saved him when
on the verge of Atheism.[40]

The other letter was from a working man of Stafford, Walter
Saunders, who thanked Farrar for his book, which he had read at a
time when he had been 'almost demented with the thought of eternal
punishment'.[41]

There are a number of letters expressing horror at the doctrine of

[36] 8, f. 21. Letter of 4 Feb. 1878 (signature illegible).
[37] A. H. Coles to F. W. Farrar, 27 Nov. 1886; 8, f. 80.
[38] 8, f. 92. Letter of 4 Jan. 1878; W. A. Buck to F. W. Farrar, n.d. 8, f. 6.
[39] 8, f. 66. Letter of 20 Apr. 1892.
[40] Mrs. L. M. Treffry to F. W. Farrar, n.d. 8, f. 30.
[41] 8, f. 84.

eternal punishment and its apparently arbitrary character. A. J. Duffield saw in it 'the same spirit that says in the politics of our day that the foundation of the English throne is the English workhouse', and Robert Jenkins, a friend of Dr. Lushington, vehemently condemned the 'unmerciful divines', who delimited God's mercy 'as our Indian commissions would a disputed Afghan frontier'.[42] A more reasoned protest came from W. W. La Barte, a clergyman living near Walsall, who criticized the traditional doctrine for making no apparent allowances for the influence of heredity and environment.

Could we trace the history of many of those whom you class amongst the 'reprobate' ... how many should we find ... 'Base-natured beings' ancestrally organised to evil? Of course all who have not sufficient daring to call these so many 'logs' already prepared for 'Hell-fire' will say, that their guilt will be proportioned to their opportunities, (tho' I am contending that they have had *no* opportunities at all, none at least, which, compared with those of other men, are worthy of being called opportunities) ... How are these Ethiopians to change their skin? How are these leopards to change their spots? In *this* world? Believe it who can. This world seems to have no appliances for such cases ... To them the life beyond the grave seems to be not only the *first* opportunity they *can* have but it also seems, from its very conditions, to be *the* opportunity—the instrumentality needed.[43]

Another correspondent claimed that many Evangelicals, who had preached eternal punishment for most of their lives, gravitated towards Universalism as they approached death, and he wondered whether this was to be ascribed to 'failing judgments or dawning illumination!'.[44] Farrar was also told of some clergy who themselves disbelieved in eternal punishment but thought that it was inexpedient to admit to this publicly. Lonsdale, the Bishop of Lichfield, was stated to be amongst this group, a Derbyshire lady reporting that she had once asked him about the harshness of the gospels, and he had told her, 'I have a hope for men beyond this life, but I am afraid it would not do to preach it, people are careless enough'.[45]

---

[42] 8, f. 91. Letter of 9 Jan. 1879; 8, f. 34. Letter of 9 Oct. 1888.
[43] 8, f. 3. Letter of 17 June 1878.
[44] C. J. Young to F. W. Farrar, 27 Sept. 1880. 8, f. 58.
[45] Helen Currey to F. W. Farrar, 17 Apr. 1882. 8, f. 15. Lonsdale shared the opinion of Archbishop Tillotson in wishing to dispose of the damnatory clauses of the Athanasian Creed, and may well have followed him in attitude to hell also. (Cf. D. P. Walker, *The Decline of Hell*, p. 6; E. B. Denison: *Life of Lonsdale*, 1868, p. 111).

Only a very few of the letters which Farrar received were opposed to his liberal views. One described his book as a 'soul-destroying error' and prayed that Farrar's eyes might be opened before it was too late and he found himself 'in the lake of unquenchable fire'.[46] Others accused him of ignoring the 'horrible law' of the formation of character and the closing of the book of life, and that the essence of eternity was 'unchangeableness and immortality': 'the sinner dying a sinner unpardoned and unpurified, remains a sinner and *must* remain such for ever'.[47]

There were some letters from overseas. An army chaplain in Barbados reported that *Eternal Hope* had aroused some interest amongst privates and officers, even though most of the soldiers treated hell as a joke, and from America it was stated that the book was being widely discussed in the Press.[48] Julia Margaret Cameron, the photographer friend of Tennyson and Jowett, wrote from Ceylon of her difficulties with a bishop who believed Maurice to have done great harm to the church.

He will not believe that, as our Alfred Tennyson has so often said in my presence—the words *everlasting* punishment the clergy utter so glibly are beyond comprehension; that no Theodore of Abyssinia . . . was half as dreadful in his vengeance as the God they preach, who for the sins of time condemns the sinner to the torments of eternity, heating the furnace with yet more fuel . . . to keep the flames at white heat through all the ages.[49]

The pamphlet literature occasioned by *Eternal Hope* was more hostile to Farrar than the correspondence, though support came from A. Goodfellow, who pleaded for an 'Aeonian God' associated with the 'principles of progression, justice and love'.[50] Goodfellow wrote in opposition to Dr. Alexander Thomson, minister of Busholme Chapel, Manchester, who had produced a particularly vehement attack on Farrar. Although Thomson conceded that the imagery of hell was only imagery, he insisted that hell was a necessary consequence of the Divine law, and explicitly connected the development of liberal theology with social changes. Such changes, he wrote, were to be seen:

[46] *Life of Farrar*, p. 281.
[47] 8, f. 85. Letter of 12 Nov. 1877; J. H. Stephenson to Farrar, n.d., 2, f. 21.
[48] 23, f. 33. Letter of 28 Feb. 1879; 39, f. 21. P. H. Hayne to Farrar, 19 Jan. 1878.
[49] 8, f. 89. Letter of 18 Dec. 1877.
[50] A. Goodfellow: *Farrar and Cox versus Dr. Thomson*, 1878, p. 16. Goodfellow's 'Aeonian God' was distinguished from the God of the orthodox who inflicted eternal punishment.

. . . in the large philanthropic movements of the time; in the soften-
ing of our manners and the prevailing kindliness of sentiment; in the deep
sympathy aroused by the reports of cruelties and outrages perpetrated on
those with whom we have no direct connection; in the greater humanity of
our laws; in the improved temper and spirit of our social arrangements and
proceedings. The brotherhood of man is generally acknowledged: it is
even exalted by infidel teachers into a religion. The stern dictates of the
Christian conscience are more and more mitigated by the tender feelings
of the heart. Compassion for misery—especially when that misery looms
in the future, vast, boundless, unrelieved by hope—is very apt to supersede
and absorb the condemnation of sin. We fail to realise the intense hateful-
ness of sin in God's sight; we forget its deadly, destructive effect on the
soul . . . a specious error spreads, clothing itself in the garb of sanctity and
gentleness.[51]

The time, wrote Thomson, was one of 'Broad Churchism, a pre-
tentious, conceited, hollow posture, which decks itself out in the
parti-coloured garb of a semi-philosophic Christianity, while it
empties the Gospel of all definite doctrine and life-giving power'.[52]
He regarded it as a product of sentimentalism. H. R. Bramley, a
High Church divine of Magdalen College, Oxford, published a more
reasoned criticism. Farrar, he thought neglected the voluntary
character of sin, talking too much of the evil of sin itself and not
enough of the evil character of the sinner, and he looked with grave
suspicion on a view of evil which saw it primarily as the deprivation
of good.

It must be remembered that wickedness is not the mere absence of goodness. An inveterate preference for evil is engendered by continual ill-doing;
the will is warped, the motives of choice corrupted. The confirmed sinner
is not indifferent to God: he hates Him; he hates His character: he hates
obedience; he hates the principles on which God rules, and to which He
requires adhesion. This is the result of a life of sin. Evil is chosen first for
its accompaniments, and afterwards in itself.[53]

These opposing viewpoints show clearly the presuppositions of
both sides in these debates. Personal choice is stressed on the one
hand, the effects of heredity and environment on the other. The
defenders of the traditional hell emphasize the cumulative effect of
numerous individual decisions on the formation of character, whereas
the advocates of a more liberal theology regard God's loving purposes

[51] A. Thomson: *The Scripture Doctrine of Future Punishment*, 1878, pp. 42–4.
[52] p. 58.
[53] H. R. Bramley: *Eternal Punishment*, 1878, pp. 6, 15.

for the whole universe as having a greater ultimate significance than the particular choices of individuals. There is a certain amount of evidence that the defenders of hell were more likely to be politically conservative, although few go so far as to maintain that the fear of eternal punishment was the chief bulwark against revolution. Men like Thomson connected Farrar's theology with changed social attitudes, just as the conditionalist, Edward White, searching for a credible doctrine of future punishment, believed Benthamite influence to be responsible for much of the questioning of eternal punishment.[54] Conversely, those arguing for some mitigation of the popular doctrine, are prepared to cite the increasing humanitarian-ism of social policy in their support, as well as extending the idea of progress into the realm of the future life. By 1880 the debate had quite clearly moved from whether eternal punishment was, or was not, the teaching of Scripture, to whether it could be shown to be morally defensible and consistent with contemporary ideas of progress and humanitarianism.

[54] Cf. an anonymous pamphlet, *Eternal Punishment: a critique of Canon Farrar's 'Eternal Hope'*, 1878, pp. 30–1, for the linking of the denial of hell and the threat of revolution; E. White, *Life in Christ*, pp. 502–3.

VIII

The Bounds of Purgatory

THE nineteenth century was a time of unprecedented revival and change for Roman Catholicism in England. Already, at the beginning of the century, the feudal and restrained religion, centred on the old Catholic families, had begun to be challenged by the first Irish immigrants, and by new styles of devotion from the Continent. These challenges became much greater in the course of the century, and the pattern of English Catholicism was further altered by the influx of converts from the Oxford Movement in the 1840s and 1850s. Tensions inevitably arose between Irish and English, converts and old Catholics, liberals and ultramontanes, and, whilst many of these were revealed in disputes over ecclesiastical organization and missionary strategy, they were also reflected in the contrast between the quiet devotion of the older English Catholicism, and the more exuberant worship and intense piety advocated by foreign missionaries, like Father Gentili, and supported by the Irish poor. The passing of Catholic Emancipation in 1829 finally opened the way for these new forms of piety to be put into practice, though the old Catholic community remained conservative and suspicious of change, and of their Protestant neighbours, for long afterwards.[1]

These devotional changes had their effect on Catholic eschatology. Mission preaching to the masses of lapsed Irish Catholics was revivalist in tone, and tended to stress the dangers of hell fire and paint lurid pictures of the torments of the damned. Gentili's missions always included an exposition of the Four Last Things.[2] Devotions associated with purgatory became common later in the century. At the same time, however, Catholics were not immune from the debate about hell which troubled so many Protestants, and some at least were sensitive to the ethical problems raised by the doctrine of eternal punishment. The fact, however, that purgatory was an integral part of eschatology, meant that the sharp contrast between heaven and hell could be made less harsh by a reinterpretation of the doctrine of purgatory. Such a change of emphasis did in fact occur

---

[1] For tensions within nineteenth-century Catholicism cf. Sheridan Gilley: 'The Roman Catholic Mission to the Irish in London', *Recusant History*, 10, 1969, 123–41.
[2] G. B. Pagani, *Life of the Rev. Aloysius Gentili, LL.D.*, 1851, pp. 218–19.

in the middle and later years of the nineteenth century, often in connection with the new purgatorial devotions. Those responsible for it were, in large measure, the Oxford Movement converts, men formed in a different tradition from the Counter-Reformation scholasticism of the Roman schools and of high intellectual calibre. But their contribution can only be properly appreciated when it is set against the background of the older English Catholicism, and the Liguorian devotion of the Continent.

ESCHATOLOGY IN THE 'GARDEN OF THE SOUL' AND LIGUORIANISM

The *Garden of the Soul*, composed by Bishop Challoner in 1750, reflects the characteristic restrained piety of the English Catholics, amongst whom it became the most popular devotional book. In comparison with later devotional writings, such as those of F. W. Faber, the *Garden of the Soul* contains few passages concerned with the future life, and even the discussion of hell is confined largely to the traditional language of *contrapasso*, the assigning of an appropriate punishment in hell to each sin. 'The Eyes for lascivious looks shall be afflicted with the horrid Vision of Hell and Devils. The Ears for delighting in vicious Discourses shall hear nothing but Wailings, Lamentations, desperate Howlings; and so of the rest.'[3] It is characteristic of the temper of English Catholicism that Challoner does not go into great detail about 'the rest', but is content to affirm that the pain of the loss of God would outweigh all physical sufferings, and to ask his readers to consider what the eternity of hell really means: 'if a Flea in your Ear, or the Heat of a little fever makes one short night so long and tedious, how terrible will the Night of Eternity be, accompanied by so many torments?'.[4] The *Garden of the Soul* is unusually restrained in its descriptions of hell, and forbears from anatomizing the details of physical torment compared, for example, with the contemporary work of St. Alphonsus Liguori. Although the full impact of Liguorianism was not felt in England until after R. A. Coffin's translations of Liguori's works in the 1850s, it was one of the most important devotional traditions in continental Catholicism in the early nineteenth century, and the difference in temper between Liguorian works and the *Garden of the Soul* highlights the contrast between English Catholicism and continental developments.

[3] *Garden of the Soul*, 1741 ed., pp. 53–4.   [4] p. 54.

The fullest exposition of Liguorian eschatology is to be found in *Preparation for Death*, which Liguori wrote in 1758 as the final section of *The Eternal Truths*. In Coffin's translation this is prefaced by a short instruction on the use of the meditations and colloquies that follow, which emphasizes the importance of reflection on the Last Things as an incentive to Christian living. The moment of death has special significance for Liguori, and he urges preparation for it by the regular practice of a special spiritual exercise:

Oh, how important is that last moment, that last gasp, that final closing of the scene! An eternity of every joy, or of every torment, is at stake—a life for ever happy, or for ever unhappy ... My brother, if you believe that you must die, and that you can die only once, so that if you then make a mistake, that mistake is for ever and irremediable, how is it that you do not resolve to begin from this very moment ... to do all that you can to secure yourself a happy death?[5]

Like many devotional writers, Liguori lamented the fact that most men seemed oblivious of the momentous issues of salvation and damnation, and lived as if death, judgment, heaven, and hell were merely poetic fables, and he reminded his readers that they were truths of the faith, and despite the unheeding carelessness of men, and the apparent prosperity of the wicked, God's judgment would inevitably come. 'Thus in the midst of the valley a great pit will be opened, into which the devils and the damned shall fall together; and they shall hear,—O God!—those gates close after them which will never more be opened, never, never, for all eternity.'[6] In his account of eternal punishment Liguori went into considerable detail on the nature of hell. Hell is located in the middle of the earth; punishment takes the form of a highly developed *contrapasso*; and Bonaventure's belief that the stench of one of the bodies of the damned would be enough to destroy all mankind is cited with approval! As for the fire of hell, Liguori allowed his imagination full play:

... the unhappy wretch will be surrounded by fire like wood in a furnace. He will find an abyss of fire below, an abyss above, and an abyss on every side. If he touches, if he sees, if he breathes, he touches, he sees, he breathes only fire. He will be in fire like a fish in water. This fire will not

---

[5] Alphonsus Liguori, *The Eternal Truths: Preparation for death*, (ET. R. A. Coffin), 1857, pp. 19–20. Cf. p. xiv.
[6] pp. 81, 121, 185.

only surround the damned, but it will enter into his bowels to torment him. His body will become all fire; so that the bowels within him will burn, his heart will burn in his bosom, his brains in his head, his blood in his veins, even the marrow in his bones: each reprobate will in himself become a furnace of fire.[7]

Nevertheless, Liguori declared, these pains were as nothing to the pain of the loss of God.[8]

But whilst Liguori was prepared to indulge his imagination on a detailed analysis of the torments of hell, he refuses to do the same with the pleasures of heaven; they cannot be described by those who only have knowledge of earthly pleasures. It is hard to see why such arguments could not equally apply to hell.

It was not only in the details of his teaching and the character of his writing that Liguori's theology had some influence on the changes in eschatology during the nineteenth century, he was also influential through his work in the realm of moral theology. Here Liguori developed the theory known as Aequiprobabilism. This stated that, in cases where the moral law was doubtful, it ought to be followed, if the doubt concerned only whether a particular moral law had or had not ceased to apply, but that the easier option might be followed where there was a doubt whether the law had ever existed. Although, strictly speaking, this doctrine was only applicable in moral decisions, it could clearly be applied to dogmatic questions, in a Church which depended on authoritative pronouncements for the establishment of its orthodoxy, and as such it was a principle to which those wishing to uphold a generous view of the number of the saved appealed.[9] In this debate the principle could be applied in the consideration of three main questions: Are those outside the Church in a state of invincible ignorance? If they are in a state of invincible ignorance, does this mean that the Church can assume their ultimate salvation to be probable? Is it legimate to side with the minority opinion in this matter, which has never been declared illegitimate, even if an examination of the relevant authorities reveals that the majority view is rigorist? Aequiprobabilism, as well as the

---

[7] pp. 189–90. Cf. Aquinas, *Summa Theologica*, III, (Supp.), Q. 97, Art. 7.

[8] pp. 191–2.

[9] There was, and is, no doctrinal definition of the number of the saved, though the maxim *extra ecclesiam nulla salus* has been generally followed. Jean-Baptiste Massillon, a French Oratorian who preached a famous sermon *On The Fewness of the Elect* in 1704, was one of the most notable upholders of a rigorist position, but in practice the Roman Church has been more hopeful.

laxer theory of Probabilism, made it possible for the view of the minority of theologians to be regarded as a real option, when many Catholics became troubled about the question of the number of the saved towards the end of the nineteenth century.

THE ESCHATOLOGY OF THE OXFORD MOVEMENT CONVERTS

(i) J. H. Newman

Newman's eschatology as a Tractarian was, as we have seen firmly rooted in his intense personal awareness of 'two and two only absolutely self-evident beings, myself and my Creator', an awareness which revealed itself in moral terms in a sense of the holiness of God and a horror of sin. This same awareness continued to be the foundation of his theology after his conversion, though its expression was somewhat altered by Newman's now explicit commitment to orthodox Catholic eschatology, particularly to a belief in purgatory. A mind as sensitive as Newman's, however, could not remain indifferent to harsh presentations of eternal punishment, and the problems of theodicy, and consequently we do not only find in his Catholic writings the development of the teaching of his Tractarian days, there is also a search for ways in which the pains of hell and purgatory might be made more acceptable to the conscience of the age, without diminishing the holiness of God.

In the sermons which Newman preached soon after his conversion we already find the outline of the eschatology which he popularized in the *Dream of Gerontius* (1865) firmly established. In a sermon of 1848 Newman spoke of judgment as a necessary condition of human life and described the particular judgment of each man after death as 'the stillest, awfullest time which you can ever experience', the moment when eternity hangs in the balance and after which there can be neither change nor reversal.

O who can tell which judgment is the more terrible, the silent, secret judgment, or the open glorious coming of the Judge. It will be most terrible certainly, and it comes first, to find ourselves by ourselves, one by one in His presence, and to have brought before us most vividly all the thoughts, words and deeds of this past life. Who will be able to bear the sight of himself?[10]

Even holy souls, he suggested, would find the sight of Christ as judge an intolerable torment, and would willingly throw themselves

[10] J. H. Newman, *Faith and Prejudice and other unpublished sermons*, New York, 1956, pp. 34–5.

into purgatory to satisfy the divine justice. They would realize how great an evil sin was: 'It circles round us and enters in at every seam, or rather at every pore. It is like dust covering everything, defiling every part of us, and requiring constant attention, constant cleansing.'[11] In a sermon on 'The Neglect of Divine calls and warnings', Newman again spoke of judgment.[12] He took as his basic theme the sin of presumption, whereby men considered that they could sin with impunity and yet escape the judgment of God. To those who despised the grace given them by God the place of divine judgment could be nothing but a place of terrible revelation, and Newman imaginatively portrayed the sinful soul confronted by its righteous Judge.

Oh, what a moment for the poor soul, when it comes to itself, and finds itself suddenly before the judgment-seat of Christ! Oh what a moment, when breathless with the journey and dizzy with the brightness, and overwhelmed with the strangeness of what is happening to him, and unable to realise where he is, the sinner hears the voice of the accusing spirit, bringing up all the sins of his past life, which he has forgotten or which he has explained away, which he would not allow to be sins, though he suspected that they were . . . And, oh! still more terrible, still more distressing, when the Judge speaks and consigns it to the jailors, till it shall pay the endless debt which lies against it! . . . And the poor soul struggles and wrestles in the grasp of the mighty demon which has hold of it, and whose every touch is torment. 'Oh, atrocious!' it shrieks in agony, and in anger too, as if the very keeness of its affliction were proof of its injustice. 'A second! and a third! I can bear no more! stop, horrible fiend, give over; I am a man and not such as thou, I have not on me the smell of fire, nor the taint of the charnel-house! . . . I know what human feelings are; I have been taught religion; I have a conscience; I have a cultivated mind; I am well versed in science and art . . .'[13]

A judgment such as this was, Newman insisted, the reality, before which the world's pious panegyrics were worthless deceptions.

In 'The Neglect of Divine calls and warnings' Newman attempted to show the fate of the sinner; by contrast the sermon 'Purity and Love' is concerned with the judgment of the soul which has seriously tried to love God, and it is thus closer to the theme of *Gerontius*.

[11] p. 36.
[12] Faber told Newman that Fr. Dalgairns could not stomach this sermon. (F. W. Faber to J. H. Newman, 11 Dec. 1849. Birmingham Oratory, Newman MSS., Faber–Newman 18.)
[13] J. H. Newman: *Discourses to Mixed Congregations*, 1881 ed., pp. 38–9.

How different is the feeling with which the loving soul, on its separation from the body, approaches the judgment-seat of its Redeemer! It knows how great a debt of punishment remains upon it, though it has for many years been reconciled to Him; it knows that purgatory lies before it, and that the best it can reasonably hope for is to be sent there. But to see His face, though for a moment! To hear His voice, to hear Him speak, though it be to punish! . . . I will fear no ill, for Thou art with me. I have seen Thee this day face to face and it sufficeth; I have seen Thee and that glance of Thine is sufficient for a century of sorrow in the nether prison. I will live on that look of Thine, though I see Thee not, till I see Thee again, never to part from Thee. That eye of Thine shall be sunshine and comfort to my weary, longing soul; that voice of Thine shall be everlasting music to my ears. Nothing can harm me, nothing shall discompose me: I will bear the appointed years till my end come, bravely and sweetly.[14]

It was through the *Dream of Gerontius* that these ideas reached a far larger audience.[15] The poem enjoyed great popularity, and its wide appeal was to be found, as Newman's friend J. M. Capes realized, in the fact that it put 'into shape the conviction of innumerable men and women who are as fervently Protestant as can be conceived but who find in some such relief as is here embodied, the only possible solution to the mysteries of life and death'.[16] *Gerontius* was Newman's picture of an ideal Christian death, with the dying man being supported in his last agony by his friends; but it was also the picture of a man, whose life could be described as good but not exceptional, reaching the point of death. Gerontius is indeed Everyman, but he is Everyman as believer. A sympathetic and discerning critic like R. H. Hutton considered it to be not only one of the most unique and original poems of the nineteenth century, but the one least in accord with the temper of the times, 'the most completely independent of the *Zeitgeist*'.[17] Whilst there is certainly a contrast with the agony of doubt reflected in Tennyson's *In Memoriam*,

---

[14] pp. 81–2.

[15] For a more detailed discussion of the *Dream of Gerontius* against the background of Newman's earlier eschatology, cf. Geoffrey Rowell: 'The Dream of Gerontius', *Ampleforth Journal*, 73, ii, 1968, 184–92.

[16] *Fortnightly Review*, N. S. iii, 1868, 345. Newman wrote appreciatively about this review: 'Some parts of it struck me as very *just*. I have often been puzzled at myself, that I should be particularly fond of being alone, and yet also was particularly fond of being with friends—yet I know both one and the other are true, and though I can no more reconcile them than you can, you are the first, as far as I know, who has noticed an apparent inconsistency to which I can but plead guilty.' (Newman MSS., J. H. Newman to J. M. Capes, 16 Mar. 1868, (75 Verses, 1868, f. 24).)

[17] R. H. Hutton: *Cardinal Newman*, 1891, p. 244.

Gerontius summed up much that Victorian believers wished to affirm about the future life, as can be seen by its frequent quotation by writers of all Christian denominations.

In his account of the future life in *Gerontius*, Newman was not concerned to give detailed answers to questions about its nature, but to speak of man's ultimate encounter with God. Therefore, when the soul of Gerontius, perplexed by the nature of its relation to the material universe and by the continuing experience of time, asks the angel for guidance, it is only answered by a reference to its relationship with God. This was the only true understanding of life, after, as well as before, death. Newman was well aware of the symbolic character of eschatological language; as the angel tells Gerontius:

> ... thou art wrapped and swathed around in dreams,
> Dreams that are true, yet enigmatical;
> For the belongings of thy present state,
> Save through such symbols come not home to thee.[18]

The quality of Gerontius' experience of God, on which Newman placed most emphasis, was its bitter-sweet character, the combination of the relationship of the loving soul with its Redeemer and the sinner in the presence of the Holy God. Gerontius is warned that 'the flame of Everlasting Love doth burn ere it transform,'[19] for the vision of God does not bring immediate and unqualified joy.

> ... thou wilt hate and loathe thyself; for, though
> Now sinless, thou wilt feel that thou hast sinned,
> As never thou didst feel; and wilt desire
> To slink away, and hide thee from His sight
> And yet will have a longing eye to dwell
> Within the beauty of His countenance.
> And these two pains, so counter and so keen—
> The longing for Him, when thou seest Him not;
> The shame of self at thought of seeing Him,—
> Will be thy veriest, sharpest purgatory.[20]

These last couplets contain the essence of Newman's understanding of purgatory. Judicial categories are replaced by an emphasis on the holiness of God and the unworthiness of man, which removes the possibility of unfruitful speculation as to the amount of satisfaction God requires, and is at the same time closer to the Patristic imagery

[18] J. H. Newman: *Verses on Various Occasions*, 1867, p. 320.
[19] p. 322.   [20] pp. 329–30.

of the purifying fire of judgment. It is quite distinct from many of the post-Tridentine developments of Catholic eschatology. Purgatory is a place of preparation for heaven, not a lesser hell, where souls are tortured by demons. It is far removed from the kind of crude literalism which was current in much Catholic literature of the time, like the article in the *Catholic Institute Magazine* for 1857, which argued seriously for hell being located in the centre of the earth and volcanoes being the entrances to it.[21]

Even with his sophisticated eschatology Newman was aware of the agony that a serious belief in hell could cause to sensitive consciences. In 1849 he told Capes that the doctrine was for him 'the great crux in the Christian system', which he accepted as a trial of his faith, for true to his Tractarian past, he held that faith could never be easy. At the same time he kept looking for ways of making a distinction between what was vital to the doctrine and the peripheral imagery in which it had been expressed. In this connection, in a way reminiscent of Maurice, he emphasized man's ignorance of the nature of eternity.

It is not infinite time. Time implies a process—it involves the connection and action of one portion of time upon another—if eternity be an eternal *now*, eternal punishment is the fact that a person *is* in suffering; he suffers to-day and tomorrow and so on for ever—but not in a continuation—all is complete in every time,—there is no memory, no anticipation, no growth of intensity from succession.[22]

Further hints about Newman's views on eternal punishment may be found in his novel *Callista* (1855), in which Callista's protests at the notion of hell are met by an appeal to her knowledge of her own present unhappiness. It is this Caecilius argues, which makes the doctrine of hell credible.

Every day adds to your burden. This is a law of your present being, somewhat more certain than that which you just now so confidently asserted, the impossibility of your believing in that law. You cannot refuse to accept what is not an opinion but a fact. I say this burden which I speak of is not simply a dogma of our creed, it is an undeniable fact of nature. You cannot change it by wishing . . .[23]

If this is the case as regards life in the present, it is suggested, it is the more so beyond death, where all external objects, upon which a man

[21] Op. cit., p. 538.
[22] Wilfrid Ward, *The Life of John Henry Newman*, 1912, i, 246.
[23] J. H. Newman, *Callista*, 1962 ed., (Universe Books), pp. 121-2.

relies in this world, will have been removed, and all that will be left will be man's craving for God. Yet, as Newman had pointed out in the *Parochial and Plain Sermons*, 'heaven would be hell to an irreligious man'; a man whose actions had consistently amounted to a rejection of God, was a man who had put himself in a position where his craving for God could never be satisfied. But there was another side to Newman's eschatology as is clear from his sermon on the 'Neglect of Divine calls and warnings', in which he permitted himself what amounted to a prayer of protest against eternal punishment:

O most tender heart of Jesus, why wilt Thou not end, when wilt Thou end, this ever-growing load of sin and woe? When wilt Thou chase away the devil into his own hell, and close the pit's mouth that Thy chosen may rejoice in Thee, quitting the thought of those who perish in their wilfulness? But oh! . . . if the world must still endure, at least gather Thou a larger and a larger harvest, an ampler proportion of souls out of it into Thy garner, that these latter times may, in sanctity and glory, and the triumphs of Thy grace, exceed the former.[24]

It became a frequently quoted passage by those searching for evidence of leanings towards universalism in contemporary Catholic writers.

Newman again discussed eternal punishment in the *Grammar of Assent*, and the arguments are well summarized in a letter Newman wrote to the Reverend H. W. Probyn-Nevins, a vacillator between Anglicanism and Roman Catholicism, in 1872.

As to that awful doctrine I observe (1) that it is a negative one, namely, that the lost will never go to heaven, that there will be no restitution. What eternity in itself involves positively in its idea, we have no notion of whatsoever. (2) Succession of thought, the sense of succession of time, is not logically involved in the idea of eternity . . . (3) Taking punishment to mean pain, there is an infinite number of punishments in degree. There is nothing to show but that, in a multitude of cases, the only punishment will be the *poena damni*, that is the loss of heaven. (4) There is nothing to make it necessary to believe that one and the same individual will for ever have one and the same degree of punishment. (5) Theologians of weight have advocated, and have been allowed to advocate, a gradual mitigation of punishment for the lost. (6) And many ancient Missals contain a Mass for the alleviation of their pains.[25]

[24] *Discourses to Mixed Congregations*, pp. 41–2.
[25] Newman MSS., J. H. Newman to H. W. Probyn-Nevins, 4 June 1872, (Answers to Enquirers, 11, f. 56). Cf. the *Tablet*, 1 Apr. 1893.

But whatever the alleviations Newman proposed, he remained convinced of the cardinal point that eternal punishment was a vital Christian doctrine.

It is the turning point between Christianity and pantheism, it is the critical doctrine—you can't get rid of it—it is the very characteristic of Christianity. We must therefore look matters in the face. Is it more improbable that eternal punishment should be true, or that there should be no God: *for if there be a God there is eternal punishment*, (a posteriori).[26]

From the earliest days the only two Calvinist tenets, which Newman claimed to have taken root in his mind, remained with him, 'the fact of heaven and hell, divine favour and divine wrath, of the justified and the unjustified'.[27] The Augustinian drama of the conflict of the two cities was so deeply embedded in Newman's understanding, that, whilst he might modify his beliefs as to the extent to which these cities might be identified here on earth, he could never have any sympathy with those who denied that they existed at all, whether by an insistence that in the end the two were one, or merely by blurring the issues of the struggle. For Newman held, to use von Hügel's language, that

as soon as we hold the difference between various kinds of acts and dispositions to be always potentially, and often actually or essentially, of more than simply social, simply human importance, we are insisting upon values and realities that essentially transcend space and even time.[28]

(ii) H. E. Manning

Manning made an important contribution to the discussion of eschatology after he joined the Roman Church, by his translation in 1858 of the *Treatise on Purgatory* of St. Catherine of Genoa. Catherine (1447–1510) had stressed the unity of human life before and after death, and held that, from what man knew of God's purifying love in his quest for sanctity on earth he could already know something of the nature of purgatory, though of the ultimate states of heaven and hell he could say little. What was certain was that the three states were all concerned with one reality, the relation of the human soul to God. She spoke of the souls in purgatory as having, in a moment of vision and insight, recognized their relationship to God for what it was, and 'plunged' into the purgative

---

[26] Ward, *Life of Newman*, 1, p. 246.
[27] J. H. Newman, *Apologia*, (World's Classics), p. 6.
[28] F. von Hügel, *Essays and Addresses*, (1st Series), 1921, p. 207.

state in order to be fitted for the full relationship of love in the bliss of heaven.[29] As for those who were condemned to hell, Catherine believed that their sufferings were not infinite in amount, nor was their will entirely malign.

The sweet goodness of God sheds the rays of His mercy even in hell. A man who has died in mortal sin deserves a punishment infinite in pain and infinite in duration, but God in His mercy has made it infinite only in duration, and has limited the amount of pain; He might justly have inflicted a far greater punishment than He has.[30]

Likewise she believed that a gradual improvement took place in purgatory, rather than the soul, with its nature already fixed, making the appropriate satisfaction to God. Manning approved of this understanding of purgatory as being congruous with God's dealings with men on earth.[31] Catherine's purgatory was, as von Hügel pointed out, 'intrinsic and ameliorative' rather than 'extrinsic and vindictive',[32] and as such it met many of the perplexities and difficulties of nineteenth-century believers. Although Manning did not comment on Catherine's work to any great extent, the fact that he considered it important enough to translate and publish is a strong indication that he was sympathetic to its doctrine.

(iii) F. W. Faber

In the devotional writings of Newman's fellow Oratorian, F. W. Faber, with their florid style and ultramontane flavour, there is to be found a considerable discussion of eschatology. To a much greater extent than the other Tractarian converts, Faber stressed the significance of death. Not only was it the biological end of human existence, it was the seal set on a man's whole life, the only human action which was absolutely and completely irreparable. Indeed, a man's death could be called 'the interpretation of his life'.[33] Faber shared the traditional Christian view, that death was a punishment for sin; it was, he wrote, a punishment which consisted in the dissolution of the body coinciding with a time of severe temptation. For this reason alone it was a Christian duty to inform a dying man

---

[29] The notion of the 'plunge' seems to have as its background the Platonic mythology of the cleansing waters of the Acherusian lake, and this notion of the waters of purgatory also occurs in Newman and Faber. Cf. F. von Hügel: *The Mystical Element in Religion*, 1909, ii, 207.

[30] St. Catherine of Genoa; *Treatise on Purgatory*, (ET. H. E. Manning), 1858, p. 7.

[31] p. 28.

[32] Von Hügel, *Mystical Element*, ii, 243–4.

[33] F. W. Faber, *Spiritual Conferences*, 1859, p. 59.

of his condition, and to fail to do so was to risk serious consequences. 'Many souls are now in hell from this selfish cruelty. Mothers have thus sent their children there, not seeing that it was to spare them-selves, rather than their children, that they have been so barbarously silent.'[34] Nevertheless, critical as he believed the moment of death to be, Faber refused to endorse the common view that a sudden death was a sure indication of God's righteous judgment on a sinner. A lingering death, he wrote, could as easily indicate this, for it might well lead to a simple longing to die without a corresponding desire for God; but again it might be a substitute for purgatory. Death was not to be isolated from life: 'As the life is, so shall the end be. Can we say less than that death is the whole significance of life?'[35] On these terms, where apparently 'good' lives have ended in 'bad' deaths, it was only possible to regard such men as destined for hell, though he was not clear as to what exactly constituted a 'bad' death. But, regardless of this, the uncertainty of the moment of death, and of how a man would act when faced with it, were to be taken as a spur to godly living, and Faber believed that those who did so, would find the thought of death both joyful and liberating.

O grave and pleasant cheer of death! How it softens our hearts and without pain kills the spirit of the world within our hearts! It draws us towards God, filling us with strength and banishing our fears, and sanctifying us by the pathos of its sweetness. When we are weary and hemmed in by life, close and hot and crowded, when we are in strife and self-dissatisfied, we have only to look out in our imagination over wood and hill, and sunny earth and starlit mountains, and the broad seas whose blue waters are jewelled with bright islands, and rest ourselves on the sweet thought of the diligent, ubiquitous benignity of death.[36]

All doctrine and devotion, Faber believed, was meant to serve the end of sanctification, and this led him to criticize some popular devotional exercises of preparation for death. Practices such as laying oneself out as a corpse for a few moments, going through the rite of Extreme Unction mentally, or assisting imaginatively at one's own funeral, only too easily became, in his eyes, a sentimental playing at death. True preparation for death should take the form of an abiding sorrow for sin, without a descent into scrupulosity, coupled, as was characteristic of Faber, with a devotion to the Virgin, for 'all agree that deathbeds form a department of the

---

[34] pp. 68–9. [35] p. 81.
[36] p. 109. Cf. *Notes on Doctrinal and Spiritual subjects*, 1866 ed., ii, 362.

Church . . . which belongs to her officially'.[37] The sentimentality, which Faber believed affected devotions of preparation for death, he also considered to be the hallmark of contemporary piety, which was reluctant to look hell in the face and lacked any true seriousness. Himself believing that hell was a powerful incentive to virtue, he was scathing about those who adopted refined devotions themselves but advocated the preaching of hell to the lower classes.

In a prison, in a hulk, a convict settlement, or among the exceeding poor, we are at liberty to use hell. It is a vulgar subject for vulgar minds. Alas! if our languishing upper class piety did but so much as dream of the realities of grace which there are among the exceeding poor, it might blush for the child's play of devotion with which it strives to gild its worldliness without subduing self . . . I see real, good, solid, wholesome work to be done in real, good, wholesome souls, by frequent meditation on hell; and I cannot bring myself to sacrifice it to the sickly insincerities and dishonest arrogances, out of which so large a proportion of temptations against the faith arise.[38]

In his own devotional writings he portrayed hell in lurid imagery:

Once more let us go to the damned and learn—they would give all the world for five minutes at the feet of a priest! Now count up the sins of your past life—look at that damned soul—how it struggles—oh, how sick it is with fire,—how the flames roar through that crowded dungeon. See! how it tosses and bounds! what convulsions—oh, horrible! Then will you make up your minds that you will not go to hell? Lift up your hands— now on your knees—look at the crucifix—now say with me aloud—Oh, Jesus mercy![39]

But for all his protest against sentimental devotion, and his belief in the traditional hell, Faber taught that a man should think ten times of heaven for every thought of hell, despite the difficulties of realizing what the joy of heaven involved. The very vagueness of the imagery associated with heaven was, he maintained, a positive thing; had the joys of heaven been more fully revealed, they would have seemed incredible, and so would have been a temptation to faith.

In *The Creator and the Creature* Faber discussed the problem of the number of the saved.[40] After considering the differing stand-points of a number of theologians, he concluded, that, although there could be no doubt that opposite views had been maintained, it was

[37] p. 129.   [38] pp. 366, 374–5.
[39] *Notes on Doctrinal and Spiritual subjects*, ii, 369.
[40] *Modern Review*, iii, 1882, 182.

likely that the majority of Catholics would be saved. He put forward four points in favour of this opinion. First, the rigorist view had frequently been derived from opinions concerning the fate of un-baptized infants, which were now no longer considered tenable. Secondly, fears which militated against a complete commitment to a holy life had been aroused by non-Christians arguing that Christian-ity taught that only a small minority would be saved, and it was essential that such fears should be allayed. Moreover, if it were true that the majority of Catholics were in hell, it made nonsense of talking of the victory of the love of God, and, as a final argument, Faber suggested that the severity of the pains of purgatory counted in favour of a large number being saved. In a passage which became a favourite quotation of those supporting every kind of mitigating view, Faber wrote:

God is infinitely merciful to every soul . . . no-one has ever been, or ever can be, lost by surprise or trapped in his ignorance; and, as to those who may be lost, I confidently believe that our Heavenly Father threw His arms around each created spirit, and looked it full in the face with the bright eyes of love, in the deliberate darkness of its mortal life, and that of its own deliberate will it would not have him.[41]

Purgatory was, in fact, the keystone of Faber's argument for the salvation of the majority of Catholics; as he put it, 'difficulties are perpetually drifting that way to find their explanation'.[42] He clearly distinguished between a purgatory conceived of as a non-eternal hell, and that portrayed by writers like St. Catherine of Genoa, a volun-tary flight into suffering, which 'turns on the worship of God's purity and sanctity'. Because he was aware that the advocacy of the latter view could lead to charge of lax teaching being made against him, he insisted on the severity of the pains of purgatory, which were worse than all martyrdoms and suffused the whole soul.[43] With his Marian interests he believed that the Virgin had a special function in connection with purgatory, though he seems a little confused as to its exact nature. It was, however, legitimate to call her 'Queen of Purgatory' and to regard her prayers for those suffering there as especially efficacious. One of his hymns deals with this topic.

> Oh turn to Jesus, Mother! turn,
> And call Him by His tenderest names;

[41] *The Creator and the Creature*, 1858, p. 393.
[42] p. 376.   [43] *Notes*, ii, 389–90.

Pray for the Holy Souls that burn,
This hour amid the cleansing flames.

In pains beyond all earthly pains,
Favourites of Jesus! there they lie,
Letting the fire wear out their stains,
And worshipping God's purity.

See, how they bound amid their fires
While pain and love their spirits fill;
Then with self-crucified desires
Utter sweet murmurs, and lie still.

Pray then, as thou hast ever prayed;
Angels and Souls, all look to thee;
God waits thy prayers, for He hath made
Those prayers his law of charity.[44]

Awful as the sufferings of purgatory were, they were born with a perfect contentment, because the souls in purgatory were one in intention with the will of God, were consoled by angels, and were unable to commit the slightest imperfection. In a meditation on purgatory he spoke of its characteristics as 'heroic virtue' and 'beautiful tranquillity'.

Make a composition of place—flames sobbing on the shore of purgatory, like the chafing of the tide upon the rocks—awful dreary light of the far-stretching land of fire—angels, white as falling snow when the sun shines on it, winging their way about—in all that land no sin, nothing but heroic virtues and beautiful tranquillity.[45]

It is clear from this survey of Faber's eschatology in his devotional writings, that he stands with Newman and Manning in his concern for sanctification, and his preference for the ameliorative purgatory of St. Catherine of Genoa, even when his more exuberant temperament leads him into more detailed and curious speculation. It may well be that his more pronounced early Evangelicalism is connected with the greater interest he shows in death in his discussion of eschatology; though this is also noticeable in writers like the Anglo-Catholic, George Nugée, whose Lent lectures for 1853, *The words from the Cross applied to our own deathbeds*, emphasize the importance of the moment of death in a similar way to Faber's devotional writings.[46] But, despite the idiosyncracies of his theology,

[44] *Hymns*, 1862, pp. 164–5.   [45] *Notes*, ii, 391.
[46] Cf. Nugée, op. cit., pp. 38–9; 80–1; 92.

he was welcomed as a significant ally by those seeking to mitigate the harshness of a vindictive purgatory and a theology which taught the fewness of the saved, and was regarded as one of the chief influences behind a more liberal eschatology by those who defended the stricter view.[47]

PURGATORIAL DEVOTION

The growing preoccupation with the question of the number of the saved, and the elaboration of the doctrine of purgatory to support a liberal answer, was accompanied by the development of devotions concerned with purgatory. Manning commended this spirituality in his book *The Internal Mission of the Holy Ghost*, and it found more particular expression in the foundation of the religious order of the *Auxiliatrices des âmes du Purgatoire*, or, as they were generally known in England, the Society of the Helpers of the Holy Souls. The order was founded in Paris in 1856 by Eugénie Smet, with the blessing of both the Archbishop of Paris and the curé d'Ars, and its special character was marked by a fourth vow, of the practice of the devotion known as the Heroic Act of Charity, being added to the three traditional ones of poverty, chastity, and obedience. The devotion had begun in the eighteenth century, and bound the person undertaking it to a 'complete surrender for the souls in Purgatory of all the merits I can acquire'.[48] Quite early in its existence the society was asked to found an English house, and on his death-bed Faber is supposed to have made a plea for them to set one up.[49] In the 1860s both Manning and Bishop Grant of Southwark urged the Mother Foundress to do this, but nothing was actually begun until 1872, when two sisters arrived in England. Newman sent a contribution towards the foundation and many of the hierarchy promised their support.[50] By 1877 they were well established, and the Jesuit, George Porter, was able to cite them as one of the supreme examples of faith in an age of doubt, for 'none have seen the tortures of the Holy Souls, none have heard their lamentations' except by faith.[51]

[47] F. X. Godts held Faber particularly responsible for the widespread acceptance of a more liberal eschatology. cf. *De Paucitate Salvandorum, quid docuerunt sancti*, Bruges, 1899, p. 15.
[48] It had first been advocated by Gaspar Oliden, a Theatine priest. Cf. J. Morris, *Two Ancient Treatises on Purgatory*, 1893, pp. 106–8.
[49] G. Fullerton, *The Life of Mère Marie de la Providence*, 1875, p. 174. For details of the early history of the society cf. C. C. Morewood, *Eugénie Smet*, 1927.
[50] Letters in the archives of the Helpers of the Holy Souls.
[51] MS. sermon, H. H. S. archives.

We find further traces of the popularity of purgatorial devotion in the volume of meditations, *The Prisoners of the King*, published by Fr. H. J. Coleridge in 1878. Coleridge supported the view that many who died outside the visible church would be found in purgatory, and, like Newman and Faber, he interpreted the particular judgment as a sudden light enabling the soul to see with astonishing clarity its position in the eyes of God.[52] Like Faber he considered the age over-sentimental, and spoke in favour of imaginative pictures of physical torture in purgatory as salutary reminders of the seriousness of God's judgment.

It will be better hereafter to have quailed in terror before some picture of Purgatory in which the most fearful torments have been depicted in the grossest way, in which the souls are represented as writhing on spits in the midst of flames, torn to pieces by devils, screaming in agony, and afflicted by some special visible weapon of torture in every limb and every sense, than to have persuaded ourselves that these sufferings of which the saints of God think so much are light and short, and that it can be no such very terrible thing to fall into the hands of the Living God in the day of His Judgment.[53]

Coleridge himself is described as 'a man of great refinement and a sensitiveness that was somewhat excessive', and it may be that he reacted in this way to such pictures, but the *Tablet*'s judgement was probably more accurate, that the chief result of such pictures was 'in frightening children and young persons with horrid dreams (so), that, when they outgrow these childish horrors, they come to hate and turn away from, if not to scoff at, all that in any way calls back the hideous nightmare'.[54]

Coleridge was one of many Catholic writers who utilized supposed private revelations in describing man's future state. The clearly fanciful character of many of these revelations made them a favourite target for attack by Protestant writers. Professor Salmon, for instance, declared in an article in 1883, that appeals to such writings disproved any claim by the Church of Rome to provide an absolute security of faith. The occasion of Salmon's article was the condemnation by the Archbishop of Paris of a notorious weekly review, *Le Libérateur des âmes du purgatoire*, which had propagated many weird opinions purporting to be based on private revelations, such as the location of the vent-holes of hell and purgatory at the north

[52] Op. cit., pp. 9–10.   [53] pp. 199–200.
[54] The *Tablet*, 23 Nov. 1878, p. 651.

pole.[55] Salmon argued that, since the Pope was clearly incapable of distinguishing between different private revelations, those who had joined the Church of Rome in search of doctrinal certainty had been sadly deluded.[56]

'POPULAR ESCHATOLOGY'

Alongside of the comparatively sophisticated eschatology of men like Newman and Faber there existed a large number of crude, popular works, dwelling on the physical agonies of hell and sometimes illustrated with representations of various tortures. Some of these were new editions of much older tracts. For instance, F. Pinamonti's seventeenth-century work, *Hell Opened to Christians to caution them from entering into it*, was reprinted in 1807 with horrific woodcuts, and was available for most of the century. Newman referred disapprovingly to it being given away in Birmingham in 1870, and there was an edition published in Ireland as late as 1889.[57] The nineteenth century, however, produced its own horrific tracts, of which the series of *Books for Children* by the Reverend Joseph Furniss contains what are perhaps the most extreme examples.

Furniss was the son of a Sheffield master cutler, who was ordained after attending the colleges at Oscott and Ushaw in 1834, and later became a member of the Redemptorist order.[58] In 1847 he began the children's mission work, which was to occupy him for the rest of his life. In his mission preaching we are told that he concentrated to a great extent on hell, and that the important sermon on the topic was always carefully prepared. On the night before he preached it, in an attempt to encourage a large attendance, he would say:

[55] *Contemporary Review*, xliv, 1883, 510–12. Cloquet, the editor of *Le Libérateur*, continued to propagate his views in a new periodical, *Le Purgatoire d'après les révélations des Saints*.

[56] In 1887 Father Ignatius Ryder replied to Salmon. He argued that the Roman Church had never claimed to be able to deal with doctrine other than that contained in the revealed deposit of faith, and insisted that in reading accounts of purgatory it was important to look beyond the imagery. He suggested that the torments seen by a St. Brigit, might be only applicable to the 'lower' part of purgatory. (H. I. D. Ryder, *Essays*, [ed. F. Bacchus], 1911, pp. 43, 53). For a modern Catholic statement on the question of private revelations cf. Karl Rahner: *Visions and Prophecies*, E.T. 1963.

[57] Newman MSS. J. H. Newman to J. B. Mozley, 14 Mar. 1870. (Copied Letters, 70, f. 125). James Docherty has shown the close links between Pinamonti and the sermon on Hell in James Joyce's *Portrait of the Artist as a Young Man* (*Modern Philology*, lxi, 1963, 110–119).

[58] For biographical details cf. T. Livius: *Father Furniss and his work for children*, 1896. The Redemptorists were founded by Alphonsus Liguori in 1732.

My dear children, we are going to make a long journey tomorrow. We are all going out of the Church. We are going to see something very wonderful. Be in good time, or you will be too late, and you won't be able to go, you will be left behind—meaning in spirit that they were all to go down to hell.[59]

J. R. Thrane has called the accounts of hell in Furniss's tracts 'penny-dreadful word-paintings of phosphorescent charnel-house horrors', and an examination of them certainly confirms this description.[60] In the tract which gained the greatest notoriety, *Sight of Hell*, Furniss portrayed hell as an enclosure in the middle of the earth, shot through with streams of burning pitch and sulphur, deluged with sparks and filled with a fog of fire.[61] It resounded, he wrote, with the shrieks of millions of millions of tormented souls, 'roaring like lions, hissing like serpents, howling like dogs, and wailing like dragons'.[62] Each of the damned was not only externally tormented by the fire, but also had fire coursing through his veins.

The fire burns through every bone and every muscle. Every nerve is trembling and quivering with the sharp fire. The fire rages inside the skull, it shoots through the eyes, it drops through the ears, it roars in the throat as it roars up a chimney. So will mortal sin be punished.[63]

Furniss went on to describe six dungeons, each with its appropriate torture—a burning dress, a deep pit, a red-hot floor, a boiling kettle, a red-hot oven, and a red-hot coffin. In the fifth dungeon a tormented child is seen:

The little child is in the red-hot oven. Hear how it screams to come out; see how it turns and twists itself about in the fire. It beats its head against the roof of the oven. It stamps its little feet upon the floor . . . God was very good to this little child. Very likely God saw it would get worse and worse and never repent and so it would have been punished more severely in hell. So God in His mercy called it out of the world in early childhood.[64]

It was hardly to be expected that such sadistic descriptions designed for children would pass without comment, particularly as Furniss was a popular mission preacher and his tracts had a wide

---

[59] Livius, p. 59.   [60] *Modern Philology*, lvii, 1960, 172ff.
[61] *Sight of Hell*, n.d., p. 6.   [62] p. 8.   [63] p. 15. cf. Liguori, *q.* above, pp. 155–6.
[64] p. 21. There is a similar position adopted in a very different context in Islamic theology, where the Mutazilites tell alAshari that God prevented a child who had failed to reach heaven from growing up, because He had foreseen that he would be a sinner. Cf. J. W. Bowker: *Problems of Suffering in Religions of the World*, Cambridge, 1970, p. 126.

circulation.[65] Thomas Scott, himself an ex-Catholic and a publisher of free-thinking tracts, published a broadsheet attacking Furniss, and the historian, W. H. Lecky, censured Furniss in his *History of European Morals*.[66] Lecky's protest led to the publication of a pamphlet by G. Fitzgibbon, arguing against the granting of any state aid to Roman Catholic schools, a pamphlet which led the *Irish Ecclesiastical Record* to invite him to attend one of Furnisss' missions, where he would see: '. . . hundreds of sweet, bright-eyed, intelligent, happy children throng with eagerness to the sermon, and when the sermon was over, and the preacher of God's terrors passed through the church, he would have seen these little ones, not shrinking from him in dread, but importuning him with smiles, for a word or a blessing'.[67] A fellow Redemptorist, T. E. Bridgett, argued that the hell Furniss preached was no different from that preached by Christ himself, and was a doctrine which had produced works of love and mercy throughout the world.[68]

The crude pictures of a writer like Furniss are a clear reminder of what both those who protested against the whole idea of eternal punishment and those who, still believing in it, sought to mitigate its apparent harshness, were combating. They are a reminder that very different interpretations of eschatology could exist within the Roman Church, and explain something of the attraction which the writings of a Catherine of Genoa had for those who were repelled by the sadistic frightfulness of works like *Sight of Hell*.

PARTICIPATION OF CATHOLICS IN ESCHATOLOGICAL DEBATES

Although, as we have seen, Catholics often had as great an interest as other Christians in the general debate about eschatology it was not always easy for them to join in the public discussion of the topic. Nevertheless, some contributions were made, and Newman in particular had a considerable influence, both through his public writings and through private letters of advice, as, for instance, at the time of the controversy over the Athanasian Creed.[69] In 1871 there

[65] The *Catholic Encyclopaedia* claims that about 4,000,000 of his works had been sold in English-speaking countries.
[66] T. Scott: *Hell*, n.d., p. 8; Lecky: op. cit, 1869, ii, 237n.
[67] *Irish Ecclesiastical Record*, viii, 1872, 245; G. Fitzgibbon: *Roman Catholic Priests and national schools*, 1872.
[68] T. E. Bridgett: *Blunders and Forgeries*, 1890, pp. 155–6.
[69] Cf. G. W. E. Russell: *Malcolm MacColl*, 1914, pp. 294–5.

was an important correspondence with E. H. Plumptre.[70] This began after Plumptre had sent Newman a copy of a sermon he had preached in St. Paul's on 30 April of that year, in which he had argued that the majority of men, being neither wholly good nor wholly evil, were capable after death of change and reformation, and had quoted the *Dream of Gerontius* in support of his theory.[71] Plumptre had argued for a purgatory which was a fresh opportunity of salvation, and in his reply Newman pointed out that any idea that man's probation continued after his earthly life was over was unacceptable to Catholics. Newman himself believed that it was preferable to speak of the varying degrees of grace and sanctity amongst the saved, and to believe that even those who died without any apparent sign of faith did often have some faith and repentance, than to adopt any idea of a probation after death.[72] In subsequent letters Plumptre attempted to defend his position by citing the cases of those who died as infants, and the difficulty of believing that there was a point at which the door was irrevocably shut on those who had failed to attain sanctity on earth.[73] Newman, on the other hand, thought that to speak of 'probation' implied the possibility of failure as well as success, and suggested that Plumptre was too much inclined to think of the future life in terms of a gradual continuation of earthly life, and to neglect the catastrophic elements—resurrection, judgment, heaven, and hell.[74] Plumptre replied that his eschatology restored a proper significance to the Last Judgment, for at that point what each man was in relation to God would be made final and irreversible.

Protestants and Catholics alike, for the most part, think of that judgment as passed, at the moment of death. The soul knows its doom, then passes to Heaven or Hell or Purgatory, has no real scrutiny to expect when the Judge shall sit upon his throne, while, on this view, the righteous award will be bestowed, according to the tenor of each man's whole being, through all the stages of his existence, and not only according to the short years, or days, or minutes of his earthly life. Does not that give a more, not a less, worthy conception of that to which we look forward as the great completion of God's dealings with our race?[75]

---

[70] 1821–91. Brother-in-law of F. D. Maurice; Dean of Wells 1881–91.

[71] E. H. Plumptre: *The Spirits in Prison and other studies on the Life after Death*, 1884, p. 24 and pp. 1–28 *passim*.

[72] Newman MSS., E. H. Plumptre to J. H. Newman, 26 July 1871 (Plumptre, 98, f. 1.); J. H. Newman to E. H. Plumptre, 26 July 1871 (Plumptre, 98, f. 3.).

[73] Newman MSS., E. H. Plumptre to J. H. Newman, 27 July 1871, (Plumptre, 98, f. 4.).

[74] Newman MSS., J. H. Newman to E. H. Plumptre, 1 Aug. 1871 (Plumptre, 98, f. 6).

[75] Newman MSS., E. H. Plumptre to J. H. Newman, 4 Aug. 1871 (Plumptre, 98, f. 7).

Plumptre's doctrine does not really solve the problem, unless a man's probation after death is held to be in some way more adequate than his life on earth, in which case a man's earthly life appears as no more than an appendage to the true time of decision after death, though for those who succeed in their probation on earth there is the prospect of a spiritual millenium between their death and the Last Judgment. The correspondence was inconclusive, but it was later used by Plumptre as the substance of an article in the *Contemporary Review* in 1878 as part of a series of comments on F. W. Farrar's *Eternal Hope*. At much the same time there was a considerable contribution to public discussion of eschatology in H. N. Oxenham's *Catholic Eschatology and Universalism* (1876).[76] Oxenham was a defender of traditional eschatology, but supported the more liberal views put forward by men like Faber and Newman. In his discussion of the number of the saved he attempted to show that the question was not properly a doctrinal question at all, as it depended on a multitude of historical, moral, and practical variables, of which there was no means of any one having any knowledge, though he personally inclined to the more merciful view, and cited the works of Faber and Lacordaire with approval. He quite firmly rejected ideas of a second probation as raising more questions than they answered.[77] A criticism of his book by the universalist, Andrew Jukes, provoked a sharp reply from Oxenham, in which he declared that contemporary disbelief in eternal punishment was not to be considered as the result of new insights into the meaning of Scripture but as the consequence of the naturalism of 'the classical or Pagan Revival', associated with Swinburne, Pater, and J. A. Symonds.[78] He told Gladstone in a letter of 1878 that he found the tone of many universalist writers decidedly offensive:

[They] assume that what has certainly been the belief of Christendom

---

[76] H. N. Oxenham (1829–88), convert to Rome in 1857; close friend and translator of J. J. I. von Döllinger; was instrumental with F. G. Lee and Phillipps de Lisle in foundation of the Order of Corporate Reunion. (Cf. 'Vicesimus': *H. N. Oxenham*, 1888). The *Tablet* (12 Aug. 1876, p. 204) described Oxenham's book as 'solid and orthodox'. When a modified second edition appeared in 1878, the *Tablet* reviewer was less appreciative: 'We ourselves believe that the majority of Catholics are saved. But as for the doctrine advanced by Mr. Oxenham, that the majority of the human race will inherit the Kingdom of Heaven, though not prepared to say that it has never had any theologian worthy of the name in its favour, yet we fear that it cannot even be said to be probable.' (25 Jan. 1879, p. 108; cf. 1 Feb. 1879, p. 143; 8 Feb. 1879, p. 175).
[77] H. N. Oxenham, *Catholic Eschatology*, 1878 ed., pp. 25, 58, 71.
[78] *The Christian Apologist*, 1876, pp. 105–6.

from the Apostles' days to our own is an obsolete barbarous anachron-
ism . . . Twenty years ago I doubt if any Anglican clergyman would have
embarked on openly averring what had always been looked upon as
heretical on this point, and when Maurice first did so, it was in a diffident
and tentative tone—not to say without an ambiguity of drift very unlike
the confident contempt for the received Catholic doctrine now expressed . . . The religious difficulty has mainly originated in the denial of
purgatory and prayer for the dead, and now by a strange nemesis, those
who would have no Purgatory will have nothing but Purgatory for any-
body![79]

It was a just comment.

R. F. CLARKE AND ST. G. J. MIVART

As a final example of conflicting views of eschatology within Roman
Catholicism we should briefly consider the Mivart affair. In 1892,
Professor St. George Mivart, a Roman Catholic zoologist, who had
won considerable approbation for his informed criticism of Darwinism, published a series of articles in the *Nineteenth Century* under the
title 'The Happiness in Hell'. In some respects his arguments
resembled those put forward in the *Rambler* in 1856 by the liberal
Catholic, R. P. Simpson, who had caused a mild furore at that time
by his suggestion that there were graduations of suffering in hell,
from the depths of despair to what might be called 'Elysian happiness'. Mivart's articles were, however, more strongly marked by
evolutionary ideas. He argued that the lost could be divided into two
categories, those who never had possessed a supernatural beatitude
and those who had forfeited it. To imagine that both groups were
subject to the same penalty, and suffered the sensible pains of hell,
was, he believed, incompatible with elementary justice, and he
suggested that the condition of the damned was one of gradual
amelioration. Lost souls experienced a kind of contentment in following the lower aims which they had deliberately chosen, even though
they were never able to advance to the higher and fuller satisfaction
of the vision of God. Even Augustine, he noted, had affirmed that
existence remained better than non-existence for the lost, and that
they consciously preferred it.[80]

In some respects Mivart's argument did not go much beyond that

[79] British Museum Add. Mss., 44, 456, f. 319. H. N. Oxenham to W. E. Gladstone,
16 May 1878.
[80] *Nineteenth Century*, xxxii, 1892, 899–919.

used by Newman to reconcile men to the idea of eternal punishment, though it was less cautiously expressed, and had evolutionary overtones. The first reactions to the articles were generally favourable, and a correspondent in the *Tablet* hailed Mivart's views as a victory over those who dealt glibly in damnation and scattered 'hell about with a pepper-castor'.[81] But Mivart was a layman indulging in theology; he was known as a scientist with a possibly dangerous interest in evolution; and he was dealing with a topic which had become a matter of extreme sensitivity. It was not, therefore, altogether surprising when an attack was launched on Mivart by a strong defender of traditional eschatology, Fr. R. F. Clarke. When Clarke, a Jesuit, had published a full defence of Thomist eschatology in the *Month* ten years previously, he had shown that he had little use for contemporary moral sensitivity to eternal punishment. 'When men talk', he had written, 'about a Moloch gloating over the agony of the creatures he pretends to love, of a Juggernaut's car crushing his worshippers, they are not arguing; they are indulging in the catch-penny strain of sentimental anthropomorphism.'[82] He was firmly convinced of the deterrent value of hell, and, as usual, this was the point where men like Mivart appeared to be most dangerous.

To minimise is, if possible, more dangerous than to exaggerate, and it is ruinous if it has no sound basis of fact . . . The fear of hell is a powerful deterrent to many educated as well as uneducated, and many a sin would be committed were it not for the wholesome dread of eternal misery before the sinner's eyes. For this very reason I cannot help regarding Professor Mivart's teaching as very very mischievous as well as false.[83]

Clarke's attack alerted the authorities in Rome. The *Civilta Cattolica* described Mivart's views as leading to religious anarchy, and Cardinal Vaughan asked Mivart to subscribe to a statement of belief in eternal punishment, which rejected as 'false and heretical all doctrines which teach that the souls in hell may eventually be saved, or that their state in hell may be one which is not punishment'.[84] Mivart refused to sign and soon afterwards left the Church. Looking back in the controversy in 1900 he wrote that all he had attempted to do 'was limited to such a criticism of Catholic doctrine

[81] *Tablet*, 17 Dec. 1892.
[82] The *Month*, xliv, 1882, 313–14. For Clarke (1839–1900), the first Master of Campion Hall, Oxford, cf. the *Month*, xcvi, 1900, 337–42.
[83] The *Nineteenth Century*, xxxiii, 1893, 83–92.
[84] Cf. *Tablet*, 25 Mar. 1893, p. 448.

and such a statement of its terms and propositions as might show that the Church's teaching about hell, rightly understood, contains nothing which cannot be seen to accord with right reason, the highest morality and the greatest benevolence'.[85] In this he was in some ways attempting the same task as the Modernists. Von Hügel saw his condemnation as making the situation more difficult for them and wrote to Maurice Blondel that it had put everything for the moment, and perhaps for ten years to come, into the hands of the Philistines.[86]

Baron von Hügel, in his great study of mysticism, based on the life and writings of St. Catherine of Genoa and her associates, pointed to a changed attitude towards the idea of purgatory and the principle of ameliorative suffering as one of the most striking phenomena in the history of religious thought since 1750. Not only were non-Catholics prepared to entertain the idea, but within the Roman Church itself there was a move towards 'a truly Purgative Purgatory'. An emphasis on punishment for sin, and satisfaction, Von Hügel suggested, had been largely replaced by a purgatory whose chief characteristic was the slow and painful removal of a bad disposition.[87] The new understanding was more organic and evolutionary and so attractive both to those who wished to emphasize sanctification, and those whose thought was influenced by contemporary philosophies of progress. It also appealed to those who favoured reformatory theories of punishment, though, as we have seen, the leading exponents of the doctrine, the former Tractarians, Newman, Manning, and Faber, were primarily concerned with sanctification and the easing of certain difficulties for religious belief. It was true that, even quite late in the century, the old style of preaching a vindictive punishment after death still existed, but the tide had set firmly against it. The *Tablet*, reviewing a book called *Heaven Opened* in 1880, compared it favourably with the work of Pinamonti, and was thankful that the emphasis was laid on the hope of reward, rather than on the fear of punishment.

Hell, purgatory, and heaven, it was increasingly emphasized, were states rather than places, and concerned with the relationship of the

[85] J. W. Gruber, *A conscience in conflict: the life of St. G. J. Mivart*, New York, 1960, p. 179.

[86] R. Marlé: *Au coeur de la crise moderniste: le dossier inédit d'une controverse*, Paris, 1960, p. 31.

[87] F. von Hügel: *The Mystical Element in Religion*, ii, 230–1, 241–5.

human soul with a holy God. To be banished to hell or to have to suffer in purgatory, was no longer to be considered as a matter of being subject to the relentless operation of the divine justice, but as God himself experienced by those who had consciously turned away from him, or who had only feebly attempted to live in relationship with him. As a result of this more personal understanding, the phrase *extra ecclesiam nulla salus* could be used in a wider context. Men could affirm that God rejected nobody who had not first consciously rejected him, and with the concept of purgatory to hand it became in some respects easier for Catholics than for Protestants to affirm that their eschatology was neither arbitrarily exclusive or immoral. The decreasing number of defenders of the older view, like F. X. Godts, could only complain bitterly that the tares of the age were to be found in the laxity which had developed through ignorance of the true faith.[88]

[88] F. X. Godts, *De Paucitate Salvandorum*, pp. 13–14.

UNIVERSALISTS and the upholders of everlasting punishment both assumed the immortality of the soul; indeed without it their theories would have been untenable. The assumption is not surprising as the doctrine had long been treated as an integral part, not only of Christian theology, but also of natural religion. There had been occasional theologians who had regarded the body as so integral a part of man's nature that man's future life could only be thought of as a re-created man inhabiting a re-paradised earth, but they had been an unorthodox minority. Almost invariably those who had maintained this position had been either Socinian or unorthodox in some other way, and their views had little influence amongst the majority of Christian thinkers.[1] Darwin's theory of natural selection, however, with its emphasis on the development of man from the animal world, was a powerful challenge to older ideas of the uniqueness of man as a being endowed with an immortal soul, and so provoked considerable discussion of the validity of the common assumption of man's immortality. Yet, such was the power of the earlier tradition of both Christianity and natural religion, that, even within liberal Theist circles, immortality was for a long time one of the few points of belief which was stoutly defended.

It would be easy, in the light of the Darwinian challenge, to assume that the emergence of a school of thought which denied the natural immortality of the soul was a direct consequence of Darwinism. This, however, was not the case. Despite the adoption of the theory of 'conditional immortality', as it was generally known, by a number of leading scientists, the history of the movement shows that its roots were more theological than scientific. At least that is the case as far as those who held it as a systematic doctrine were concerned. Conditionalist language, however, as J. H. Leckie pointed out, was often used by scientists and philosophers who certainly did not hold a systematic conditionalism. Leckie distinguished four groups:

---

[1] Joseph Priestley was perhaps the most notable exponent of this position. Some earlier advocates of this view are listed by J. T. Rutt in the *Christian Reformer*, i, 1834, 98–103.

There is the purely *scientific, evolutionary theory*, such as is elaborated by
M. Armand Sabatier, and is at least suggested by Professor Henry
Drummond. (2) There is a *philosophical form* of this doctrine of which the
great exponent is Rothe. With him also may be mentioned Ritschl, and,
some would add, Bergson. (3) There is a *general tendency towards Conditionalism*, which is expressed in varying degrees of definiteness. We may
find this tendency illustrated by writers so unlike each other as Lotze,
Matthew Arnold and Father Tyrrel. (4) Lastly there is a *theological and
systematic form* of this speculation; represented by Edward White,
Pétavel, Menegoz, Haering, and other professional divines, as well as by
scholars and preachers like Huntingdon, Bushnell, Lyman Abbott,
Beecher, Joseph Parker, R. W. Dale, and ever so many besides.[2]

Leckie wrote this of conditionalism as it was in 1918, but in its
earlier stages the movement was of a purely theological character.
It emerged as one of the attempts to find a mediating position
between the extremes of universalism and eternal punishment,
and, in particular, it was influenced by a revulsion from the cruder
forms of missionary theology. Its exponents relied heavily on a
learned, though not always discriminating, appeal to Scripture,
and were to be found for the most part amongst Congregationalists
and Anglican Evangelicals. In the latter part of the century it not
only gained notable scientific adherents, but also attracted adventists
and millenarians.

The basic doctrine of the conditionalists was that God created
man mortal but with a capacity for immortality. At the Fall of man
God passed a sentence of death on man, but in his mercy did not put
it into effect, so that, with the coming of Christ, immortality might
once again be offered to man. This immortal life was only to be
gained by faith in Christ, though an increasing number of conditionalist divines allowed that those non-Christians who lived
according to their own highest lights would be given the opportunity
of responding in faith to Christ and so sharing in his immortal life.
Those who did not have faith in Christ were unfitted to receive the
gift of immortality, and so were annihilated. Those of the school who
were more strongly influenced by Darwinism believed this annihilation to occur at death, but for other conditionalists, who insisted on
the biblical language about the 'second death', and the homiletic
value of retributive punishment as an ethical sanction, annihilation
occurred after the wicked had been punished according to their deserts.

[2] J. H. Leckie, *The World to come and final destiny*, Edinburgh, 1918, p. 226.

In support of their theology the conditionalists were able to point to a certain amount of evidence from the Bible and the history of Christian doctrine. They stressed the late development of the idea of a future life in the Old Testament, and argued that the creation narratives in Genesis indicated an immortal life which was always a divine gift, and never regarded as man's inalienable possession. In the New Testament they treated any contrast between 'life' and 'death' ontologically rather than qualitatively, and, in support of their argument that it was only through Christ that immortality was offered to men, they relied heavily on the text of 2 Timothy 1:10, with its reference to Christ bringing 'life and immortality to life through the gospel'. In the Patristic period they looked to Irenaeus, who had spoken of God bestowing on believers 'as a free gift, everlasting life', and had maintained that it was the vision of God which was the source of man's immortality.[3] The writings of Arnobius supplied further Patristic evidence. In the later history of Christian doctrine they cited Duns Scotus, with his insistence that the immortality of the soul was a truth of revelation and not to be proved by reason alone, and the Renaissance philosopher, Pietro Pomponazzi, who had denied the natural immortality of the soul. Richard Whateley, the Oriel 'Noetic', who later became Archbishop of Dublin, was rather curiously also claimed by the conditionalists as a precursor of the movement, probably because he had advocated the doctrine of the sleep of the soul between death and the Last Judgment, and had stressed the resurrection of the body.[4]

EARLY PROTAGONISTS OF CONDITIONALISM

Henry Hamlet Dobney (1809–84) and Edward White (1819–98) were two of the earliest advocates of conditionalism. Dobney was a Baptist, and White a Congregationalist, and it was amongst the Congregationalists that the doctrine took its firmest hold. The looseness of organization and the breadth of doctrine tolerated within Congregationalism undoubtedly contributed to this, and it is noteworthy that the more homogeneous and disciplined Methodist groups were resistant to conditionalism.[5] The generally Calvinist theology of Congregationalists, with its doctrine of divine decrees,

[3] *Adv. Haer.* iv. 38. 2–3.
[4] Cf. R. Whateley, *The Future State*, 1829, pp. 41–5, 66, 68, 77–8.
[5] The Congregational Union was founded in 1831, and adopted a moderately Calvinist declaration of faith in 1833, but this was not regarded as binding on member churches.

may also have made it easier to adopt a view which made immortality dependent on God's election of men to it, than the generally Arminian theology of Methodism, with its idea of universal redemption. Such an argument should not be pressed too far, however, as it is possible to cite numerous instances of conditionalists using phrases borrowed from Darwinism, like 'survival of the fittest', to describe their doctrine, which come close to a theology of justification by works.

It was in 1844 that H. H. Dobney, then in charge of a Baptist congregation at Maidstone, published his *Notes of Lectures on Future Punishment*. He had originally held orthodox Calvinist views on eternal punishment, but, after preaching an unusually vehement sermon on the text 'These shall go away into everlasting punishment', he had begun to ponder their validity. As he proceeded with his investigation the debate appeared to centre on the question of immortality, and by the end of his inquiry he had come to the conclusion that a universal and uncontingent immortality could not be established by reason apart from revelation; that the Bible did not teach that all men would inevitably live for ever; and that 'the general drift of Scripture was that the righteous only, or the good, or, as Christ said, "they that were worthy to attain it", were those to whom immortality would be a blessing, and they would be "the heirs of God and co-heirs of Jesus Christ in the prerogative of endless life"'.[6] Dobney did not reach these conclusions without considerable mental anguish, and in later years he wrote of how he had 'wallowed on the floor of [his] locked study in agony, lest I should, on the one hand, give up and oppose a mighty truth, or on the other, refuse clearer light'.[7]

In his book Dobney took a firm stand against all doctrines which he considered might lead to antinomianism. Violation of the law, he wrote, was the only thing which could introduce anarchy into an ordered universe, and God was therefore justified both in threatening punishment and in carrying out that threat against those who broke his law. Such an action could not be interpreted as God's resentment against an affront to himself, or an abandonment of his goodness, but only as the expression of God's desire for the ultimate happiness of his creatures.

[6] H. H. Dobney, *Judas*, 1872, Appendix, pp. 114–17.
[7] Ibid., and H. H. Dobney, *Jephson*, 1888, Introductory sketch by H. Simon, pp. xi–xx.

And thus we are calmly and rationally conducted to this point,—that Punishment is inevitable, when Law is broken. It is not wrath, it is not fury, it is not passion, it is all wisdom and goodness: only not that indiscriminate goodness which some love to ascribe to God; not weakness, but an enlarged and all-comprehensive regard to the interests of the whole.[8]

Dobney wished to maintain both that God's punishment was strictly retributive, and not a paternal chastening, and also that it bore a definite relationship to human life, and was not simply dependent on a divine fiat, as were universalist and predestinarian schemes.[9] He was highly critical of the traditional arguments for immortality. Those based on the immateriality of the soul he dismissed as proving too much, for they could as easily be used to support belief in pre-existence and the immortality of animals as the immortality of human beings. The argument from man's universal desire for immortality could, he pointed out, only show the existence of that desire, it could not prove that the desire had any counterpart in reality. Not all, he wrote, who desired happiness thereby possessed it. The inequalities of the present life could, he argued, be redressed by supposing that all men survived death for a period, and need not indicate man's immortality.[10]

Dobney's work provoked mixed reactions. It was virulently attacked in the *Evangelical Magazine*, the editor believing that 'these mushroom divines must be put down'.[11] Dobney was strongly defended, however, by Henry Dunn, the secretary of the British and Foreign Schools' Society, who was later the author of a conditionalist work, and by Dr. John Pye Smith, the liberal Congregationalist theologian, who was tutor of Homerton College.

Despite his early advocacy of conditionalism Dobney did not play a significant part in the later development of the movement, and was mainly revered for having been one of the first divines to systematically adopt the theory. In 1864 he contributed to the *Essays and Reviews* debate in an open letter to Archbishop Longley, which contained an interesting passage in which he attempted to turn the tables on those who suggested that the opponents of eternal punishment had a sneaking sympathy for sin. Might it not be, he asked, that the upholders of everlasting punishment also had an unacknowledged bias?

---

[8] H. H. Dobney, *Notes of Lectures on Future Punishment*, 1844, p. 43.
[9] pp. 13, 58.   [10] p. 64.   [11] *Judas*, Appendix, p. 116.

If the one party be charged with a morbid tenderness that shrinks from what is just, or an undue reliance on their own sense of what is becoming the Most High, or conceited love of singularity, or pride that finds its gratification in daring to oppose the common belief, may not the other party be suspected of a lazy acquiescence where there ought to be robust investigation, or an undue deference to the opinion of others, or a timid wish to be found with the majority, or a fear lest any less terrible dogma should weaken the hold, of morality and religion on many, or even an insensibility to suffering that it is hoped they may themselves escape? Nothing is easier than to impute unworthy motives to those who differ from ourselves, but nothing is more idle.[12]

It must rather be emphasized, Dobney argued, that the penalty threatened by God was a righteous one, and, like Maurice, he taught that men had to recognize that it was sin, and not the penal consequences of sin, which they ought to dread.[13]

At the same time as Dobney published his *Lectures on Future Punishment*, Edward White, then a young Congregationalist minister in Hereford, brought out two books setting out a conditionalist theology, *What was the Fall?* and *Life in Christ*. White had been born in south London in 1819 and, as a child and a young man, had attended the York Street Congregational Church in Walworth, whose minister, George Clayton, was a strict Calvinist and one of the leading Congregationalist divines of the day. The Calvinism of Clayton's preaching made a strong impression both on White, and on the young Robert Browning, who was also a member of the congregation. Although the preacher rarely worked out in any detail the doctrine of the divine decrees, White believed that 'thoughtful children knew very well what doctrines underlay the surface-teaching in families, schools and churches'. The doctrine of election and reprobation was 'taught in a quiet and respectable way' but its implications caused White considerable pain. 'It nearly drove me mad with secret misery of mind, in thinking of such a God', he wrote. 'From fourteen years old and upwards our faith depended very much on the art of not thinking on the hateful mystery.'[14]

[12] H. H. Dobney, *A Letter to his Grace the Archbishop of Canterbury on that portion of his recent pastoral letter which affirms 'The everlasting suffering of the lost'*, 1864, p. 9.

[13] p. 31. Dobney in later years appears to have become a universalist, possibly on Mauricean grounds. Cf. The *Rainbow*, xiv, 1877, p. 35n.

[14] F. A. Freer, *Edward White, his life and work*, 1902, pp. 5–7. White also attended the sermons of Thomas Binney, which he found more congenial. Binney did not believe in everlasting punishment. (cf. E. P. Hood, *Thomas Binney*, 1874, p. 6.)

In 1836 White went up to Glasgow University, but only remained two years, and left without proceeding to a degree.[15] It was shortly after he returned to London that he discovered on a Holborn book-stall the work which was to confirm him in his conditionalist views, James Fontaine's *Eternal punishment proved to be not suffering but privation and Immortality dependent on spiritual regeneration*. The book was, as White recognized, not especially learned, and was in many respects uncritical, yet it made powerful points against the high Calvinist scheme, and underlined neglected aspects of the biblical understanding of man. From it White learnt to appreciate the difference between the Hebraic view of man as an 'ensouled body' and the characteristic body–soul duality of Greek thought. This emphasis on biblical anthropology, as well as Fontaine's employment of it as part of his argument against the doctrine of eternal punishment, became a characteristic part of conditionalist theology.

Fontaine argued that it was untrue that existence was, in every circumstance, a blessing. It was so, he suggested, only when it was derived from God, and consequently there could be no blessing in existence for those who were alienated from God for all eternity. He considered eternal punishment to be an unreal threat: 'it being *impossible* to know the extent of eternal punishment, it cannot be man's duty to know it; it cannot be God's will in respect of him'.[16] Eternal punishment was, Fontaine argued, quite disproportionate to the offence committed, and theologians who dared to suggest that ninety-nine out of every hundred souls were damned, only increased the natural, moral revulsion from the doctrine, and turned God into an essentially unlovable author of eternal misery.[17] Against this, Fontaine put forward the view that the end of man was likeness to God, and as men approached in moral likeness to God through obedience to God's commands, so at the same time their actions tended to immortalize them.

Our appetites, our faculties, and our moral relations, each subserve to the perfection of our nature, and prepare us for God's presence: it is the right employment of these, by virtue of the spiritual life Christ offers us, that procures us immortality. All the duties of life have an immortal tendency: well performed they make us more like God, and so fit us for His presence.[18]

[15] Freer, p. 11.   [16] J. Fontaine, *Eternal punishment* . . . , 1817, p. x.
[17] p. xii.   [18] Ibid.

As a result of this, although at the Last Day both the righteous and
the wicked were raised, only the righteous were raised 'in power',
possessing immortality, and the wicked consequently cease to exist,
in fulfilment of the sentence passed on Adam, which was not eternal
torment but death.[19] Like the eighteenth-century High Churchman,
Henry Dodwell, Fontaine also argued that the life possessed by the
righteous was only given to man through baptism in which he was
born again.[20]

Edward White was well aware that his adoption of Fontaine's
conditionalist theory might lead to his exclusion from Congregationalist pulpits, though it was not in fact until 1851 that the crisis
came.[21] In 1840 he served for a time in Cardiff, and two years later
moved to Hereford, and it is from this period that his letters to John
Foster on the themes of eternal punishment and annihilation date.
Foster (1770–1843) was a former General Baptist minister, who had
turned to literary pursuits, and was known for his essays and his
frequent contributions to the *Eclectic Review*.[22] Although a confessed
Calvinist, he had come to believe that many of those who spent time
and trouble expounding the torments of hell were often callous and
insensitive men, and that the effect of such preaching was largely to
increase the anxieties of those who were already timid, scrupulous,
and melancholic.[23] In his correspondence with White, Foster based
his objections to hell on moral rather than on scriptural grounds, and
he queried whether orthodox divines had ever adequately reflected
on the eternity which they so glibly expounded. Against the picture
of an infinite Being demanding infinite punishment for those who
offended him, he wrote, must be set the diminutive nature and
understanding of man, and those who believed that the punishment
was justified because the damned continued to sin in hell, must be
shown that, even if this were the case, the punishment would still be

[19] p. xviii. Fontaine used the distinction made by St. Paul in I Cor. 15:45. between the
first Adam who became εἰς ψυχὴν ζῶσαν ('an animate being') and Christ, the second
Adam, who became εἰς πνεῦμα ζωοποιοῦν ('a life-giving spirit'), to show that Scripture
used the word 'soul', without implying immortality. C. K. Barrett comments on the
Pauline use of πνεῦμα (spirit) and ψυχή (soul), that both animate the body, but 'it is
characteristic of πνεῦμα in biblical thought that it is not only alive but gives life'. (*From
First Adam to Last*, 1962, p. 74).
[20] p. xxii, cf. F. Brokesby, *Life of Henry Dodwell*, 1715, ii, 608.
[21] Freer, pp. 13–14.
[22] He was a melancholy man, and when young was supposed to have frequently shut
himself up in a barn with a copy of Edward Young's *Night Thoughts*. Cf. *DNB*.
[23] J. E. Ryland *Life, and Correspondence of John Foster*, 1846, i, 100, 137.

an infinite one for a finite sin, and so disproportionate.[24] Foster himself tended towards universalism, believing that Scripture indicated that there were degrees of punishment, and so allowed a principle of discrimination, which might also point to a punishment of limited duration. Although Foster confessed that he had not seriously considered White's theory of conditional immortality, he told White that he believed that its value lay in the absolute distinction that it made between the terms eternal life and eternal death.[25] It was this willingness of Foster to call in question the accepted view, rather than his endorsement of White's position, which encouraged White to write a summary of the conditionalist theory which he published as an anonymous tract, *What is the Fall?*, in 1844.[26]

White's pamphlet attracted little notice except for a condemnation by the *Evangelical Magazine*, but the following year he published a larger work in his own name, *Life in Christ*, which was described as 'four discourses upon the scripture doctrine that immortality is the peculiar privilege of the regenerate'. This caused a minor storm in Dissenting circles, and White himself wrote that it had not been seriously examined but the hysterical condemnation had led to his exclusion from every Nonconformist pulpit in the country.[27] Although he found himself more and more at the centre of theological controversy, he was sufficiently well established at Hereford to remain there until 1851, when he moved to London, and established his own congregation in a chapel in Hawley Road, Kentish Town, which had formerly belonged to the Countess of Huntingdon's Connexion.[28]

One of the most influential supporters of White's doctrine was Sir James Stephen, the Regius Professor of Modern History at Cambridge, who kept the works of both White and Dobney in circulation in the university.[29] Stephen himself found the doctrine of eternal punishment morally repulsive, but did not go much beyond putting forward considerations which would count against an easy acceptance of it. He maintained that he did not wish to question the reality of future punishment, but only whether it was divinely revealed that retribution would be eternal and whether it was permissible to

[24] ii, 405–9, 411.   [25] pp. 413, 415.   [26] Freer, pp. 19, 24.   [27] p. 25.
[28] pp. 27–28, 33. White's departure from Hereford was not the result of his conditionalist theology, but because, having come to hold the doctrine of believer's baptism, he had been re-baptized by Dr. Gotch at the Broadmead Chapel in Bristol. At this time he also maintained the doctrine of the pre-millennial advent of Christ.
[29] p. 26.

believe in the ultimate annihilation of the wicked. He believed that the doctrine of eternal punishment had been greatly elaborated by ecclesiastical tradition, and had been made to appear more cogent than it really was by the unconscious bias of biblical translators.[30]

Such a sympathetic reaction as that of Stephen was rare at the time. More typical was the attack on White and Dobney, made by the Baptist theologian, John Howard Hinton, in the *Eclectic Review*. Hinton republished this later in an expanded version under the title *Athanasia*. The conditionalists struck at the doctrine of immortality because they believed it to be the linchpin of the doctrine of eternal punishment, but Hinton believed that their concern with eternal punishment had prevented them from considering the evidence for and against man's natural immortality as calmly as they should have done. Hinton accepted the conditionalists' contention that man's immortality, according to Scripture, was a gift from God, and not a necessary attribute of his being, but he differed from them in holding that it was a gift that had been bestowed on all men once and for all at their creation. It was not a gift made through Christ to a selected number. Were the conditionalist contention, that only some men were immortal, true, he argued, a physical as well as a moral change would be required at the moment of conversion. He denied that the New Testament references to 'life' and 'death' were to be taken ontologically, and suggested that the conditionalist theory, that the annihilation of the wicked would take place after a period of torment, would make annihilation appear more as a relief than as the ultimate point of suffering.[31]

The publication of conditionalist works in the 1840s also sparked off a short-lived conditionalist movement in Scotland. William Glen Moncrieff, the pastor of a small Independent church at Musselburgh, and a member of the Morisonian (Evangelical Union) group, read Dobney's *Lectures on Future Punishment* in 1848. Being convinced by Dobney's arguments he published his own defence of the position in a series of *Dialogues on Future Punishment* the same year. His work stirred up some local controversy, and he was attacked in the *Christian News* by the minister of the Brighton Street Chapel in Edinburgh. Moncrieff published two further discussions of conditionalism in 1852, and the following year attempted to found a conditionalist periodical under the title of the *Expositor of Life and*

---

[30] J. Stephen, *Essays in Ecclesiastical Biography*, 1853 ed., ii, 502–3.
[31] J. H. Hinton, *Theological Works*, iii, 1864, 1, 7, 28, 30.

Immortality, but it only survived for sixteen months, and with its failure Moncrieff left Scotland for Canada. He seems to have been the only known Scottish adherent of the movement, for in 1875 William Laing could write that 'with the exception of W. G. Moncrieff, not a single minister of any sect has borne witness to this truth of life in Christ'.[32]

MISSIONARY THEOLOGY

The list of reasons in support of conditionalism, which Edward White drew up in 1853, contained the statement that conditionalism furnished 'an answer to the difficulty occasioned by reflecting on the pagan world as abandoned to ignorance, yet destined to eternal torment'.[33] This problem and the moral dilemma it posed, increasingly concerned theologians of all traditions as missionary work spread, and the knowledge of non-Christian peoples grew. Although the usual missionary appeal refrained from a detailed exposition of the fate of the heathen, and was content to refer to them as 'perishing', the implications of this kind of missionary preaching were apparent to all who cared to think about them. Baptist Noel, an Anglican Evangelical who became a Baptist, in his book on missions, illustrates this general kind of missionary appeal.

Whatever may be the results of mission, or whatever the apparent impracticability of the work, God has said that missionaries must be sent, and Christians send them. To these efforts they are no less prompted by the world's necessities. Millions are now perishing in ungodliness and immorality because they know not Christ, who might be saved by the preaching of the Gospel. They are now miserable and the Gospel would instantly ameliorate their lot; they are exposed to the curse of God, and the Gospel would bring them under His blessing: how can Christians believe this and leave them to perish?[34]

Others, like the Congregationalist Richard Winter Hamilton, were more insistent.[35] Hamilton regarded the question of the salvation of the heathen as a matter of fact, not feeling: are the heathen of such a character that their salvation is possible? In Hamilton's eyes only one answer could be given: no matter how poetically their virtues might be described, everything was vitiated by their sin of idolatry.

[32] *Bible Echo*, ii, 1875, 290–1.   [33] Freer, pp. 40–1.
[34] B. Noel, *Christian Missions*, 1842, pp. 346–7.
[35] Hamilton's Congregational lectures, *The Revealed Doctrine of Rewards and Punishments*, (1847), were one of the most unrelieved statements of everlasting punishment published in the nineteenth century.

Were his virtues rare and rich . . . this crime would taint them all . . . This is, of all crimes, the most detestable in the catalogue of crimes. It is never palliated. It is never spared. Wrath holy and indignantly pursues it. That wrath fulminates, like lightning on some bleak cloud from heaven against it. Denouncement cannot be more distinct and unrelaxing. 'No idolators shall inherit the kingdom of God.'[36]

Because the doctrine of hell was used to encourage missionary effort, and indeed in some circles was treated as the sole *raison d'être* of evangelism, it is not surprising that to attack hell was seen by many as an attack on missionary work and evangelism. Yet awareness of the numbers of those outside the pale of Christianity made it more and more absurd to regard all outside the Christian faith, or even more outside particular denominational expressions of it, as damned.[37] As Edward White realized, nothing less than the character of God was at stake: 'There is nothing less than an INFINITE MORAL DIFFERENCE between the character of a Being who WILL torture a Caffre man or woman, or ignorant, wicked Cossak or Negro, through boundless eternity, and that of one who will NOT.'[38] Thus realizing what was at stake, White published an attack on popular missionary theology in 1855. He questioned the whole grounding of missionary activity in the doctrine of hell, and proposed conditionalism as a juster and more acceptable alternative. Not only, he wrote, would this changed theology manifest more accurately the nature of God, it would go some way towards alleviating the doubts which stemmed from the conflict between the love of God and eternal torment.

To be told that God is a father, that God is just, and that God IS love,—yet that He will for ever torment, whether in literal or figurative fire, the ancient American Indians, and poor tattooed savages of the South Seas,—and, at the same time, to be warned that it is dangerous and damnable 'pride of reason' to ask questions on such matters, produces a state of mind which cannot be favourable to religious stability . . . Under most persons'

[36] R. W. Hamilton, *Missions, their authority, scope and encouragement*, 1842, p. 97. Even in Home Missions in England missionaries sometimes found the doctrine of eternal punishment too harsh and rejected it. In 1850 Mr. Clark, the missioner of the London City Mission at Richmond, was relieved of his position for doubts on the subject. *Minutes of Meetings of the governing committee of the London City Mission*, vi, 1850, 36–7.

[37] The Unitarian *Christian Reformer* concluded, on the basis of figures in the *Congregational Almanac*, that for one soul saved 50–100 were damned (vii, 1840, 101).

[38] E. White, *The Theory of Missions: or a Scriptural Inquiry into the Doctrine of the Everlasting Torment of the Barbarous Nations and countless Ignorant Heathen of ancient and modern Times*, 1855, p. 21.

faith, accordingly, lies a deep substratum of unbelief, which occasionally breaks out in a sort of volcanic eruption and earthquake. Numbers of our religious men are afraid of their own thoughts; and therefore denounce thinking on the mysteries of God as dangerous. This cannot but operate injuriously on spiritual religion, for believing grows out of questioning.[39]

Conditionalism was realistic, White believed, because it brought home the threatenings of God in a way that pictures of eternal torment could never do. Eschatology thus became credible again, for White wrote, when 'HELL seems unreal . . . then HEAVEN loses its power also'.[40]

Conditionalists remained interested in missionary theology. In 1869 White could write of an 'immense revolution' in religious opinion on 'the probable destiny of the ignorant, idolatrous nations of the earth'. 'It is the rarest thing to find even a secretary of a missionary college who will, *when firmly pressed*, declare his unfeigned assent and consent to the opinion on this question of the founders of our missionary societies.'[41] By 1869 he even considered the danger to lie elsewhere. Because it was so widely admitted that Scripture allowed varying interpretations of the words referring to punishment, purgatorial and universalist theories were being openly considered in missionary training colleges, and, it was claimed, this had resulted in a lack of urgency in the missionary movement, which no longer seemed to attract candidates of the highest calibre.[42] Conditionalism with its warning of the annihilation of the wicked, seemed to be in a position to restore the note of urgency to missionary work, whilst avoiding the harshness of supposing that God had condemned large numbers of men to eternal torment.[43]

---

[39] p. 70.   [40] p. 72.

[41] 'Missionary Theology', *Rainbow*, vi, 1869, 298.

[42] After the 1876 conference of conditionalists White claimed that copies of the conference report had been distributed to some 50,000 English-speaking missionaries. The General Superintendent of the Wesleyan Missions in south-east Africa became a convert, and was forced to resign his post in 1878. (E. White, *The Endless Life*, 1882, p. 30; Freer, p. 146). For missionary testimony to the virtues of conditionalism cf. Freer, pp. 343–6 and G. G. Stokes, *Evidence of missionaries as to the practical effect of . . . the doctrine of 'Life in Christ'*, 1882.

[43] The theology of missions was also a subject of controversy in America, though conditionalism never succeeded in winning the position that it did in England as an alternative missionary theology. As in England it was the Congregationalists who were the most divided, and the battle was chiefly fought on the committees of the American Board of Control of Foreign Missions (A.B.C.F.M.), which was largely dominated by Congregationalists. As D. E. Swift has shown in his study of the controversy, optimistic views of human nature, a tendency to think in terms of development, and a faith in the

THE MAJOR WORKS OF CONDITIONALISM

It was not until the 1870s that conditionalism made a major impact on theological debate in England, and this was in part connected with the more widespread and public questioning of the doctrine of eternal punishment at that time. This more intense debate was the occasion of a number of considerable works setting out the conditionalist position. Some of these showed a considerable acquaintance with recent German biblical scholarship, though many of them depended more on a minute exegesis of the Bible, treated in a very literalist way, than on the latest conclusions of critical scholarship. The authors of these works also drew on a number of earlier publications which had supported the conditionalist position, including the early works of Dobney and White.

One of the most important and systematic of these earlier writers was an American, C. F. Hudson. His book, *Debt and Grace as related to the doctrine of a future life*, was one of the most considerable defences of the conditionalist position, and even today has value for its discussion of the problems of theodicy. Not only did it have a considerable influence on English conditionalists, it also antedated the *Origin of Species*, and is thus a full statement of conditionalism which does not draw on Darwinism to reinforce its case. Hudson attempted both to show that conditionalism was a more satisfactory doctrine in terms of theodicy than eternal punishment and to explain why it was that the doctrine of eternal punishment had survived for so long as the orthodox Christian doctrine. He stated the conventional conditionalist position that ideas of natural immortality were alien to the earliest traditions of Christianity, and it was only as a result of

---

powers of reason, became characteristic of much American theology in the nineteenth century. Against this the defenders of eternal punishment maintained a static theology, which relied on proof texts, and viewed the Atonement as an objective fact, through which grace had been made available for the salvation of mankind provided men made use of the appointed means of regeneration. Frequently there was a connection between a belief in the low moral state of the heathen and a belief in their general damnation, and A.B.C.F.M. missionaries, who believed in hell, made much of horrific descriptions of such practices as suttee. By contrast liberal theologians stressed development and change, and saw the Atonement as a reconciliation achieved through the transforming power of God's love. They spoke of 'Christ-centred' influences being brought to bear on all men in this life or the next. Cf. D. E. Swift: 'The Future probation controversy in American Congregationalism', (Yale doctoral thesis, 1947) for further details of the American debate.

their becoming accepted as Christian doctrine that a problem of eternal evil had been created. He regarded arguments which attempted to show that hell was a just condition because the damned continued to sin there, as amounting to dualism, and he characterized theologies which claimed that good and evil were solely what God declared them to be as tantamount to atheism. Any righteousness which God demanded of a man, or any punishment he imposed upon him, must, Hudson argued, be finite, for the simple reason that man was finite. Conditionalism met this criterion, whereas the doctrine of everlasting punishment did not.[44]

In his consideration of why, if it were not the original Christian doctrine, everlasting punishment had so long been accepted as Christian orthodoxy, Hudson blamed the dominance of Augustinian ideas. Although they were not responsible for the original emergence of the doctrine, they had supplied its defenders with cogent arguments for it, and by speaking of immutable laws, rather than a trusting reliance on the goodness and power of God, they had convinced men that hell was to be regarded as the natural and inevitable consequence of wickedness.[45] This way of looking at things, he continued, had been further encouraged, by the confusion arising from a loose use of language. Words like 'time' and 'eternity' had been bandied about with little consideration of what the words involved, and confusions between 'immaterial' and 'invisible', and 'immortal' and 'eternal', had led to a dualist understanding of man. This dualist anthropology, he suggested, was paralleled by the moral dualism of a tradition, which, despite its references to sin as 'non-being', in fact assigned to sin an absolute power of its own. Anselm's doctrine of the Atonement, with its stress on satisfaction, had, he maintained, only underwritten this tendency. The sense of human depravity, exegetical confusion, the emotional appeal of hell-fire preaching, and the strong belief that men were to be moved more by fear of pain than love of pleasure, had all played their part, Hudson suggested, in the establishment of everlasting punishment as Christian orthodoxy. Although Hudson succeeded in pointing to definite weaknesses in Augustinian theodicy, his arguments in favour of conditionalism were less strong, and a reader is left with the

[44] C. F. Hudson, *Debt and grace as related to the doctrine of a future life*, Boston, 1858[2], pp. 60, 74.

[45] Cf. Hick's criticism of Augustinian theodicy, *Evil and the God of Love*, 1966, pp. 262–3.

impression that conditionalism is to be accepted as a way out of an impasse rather than for any more positive merits of its own.

There were a series of important conditionalist publications in the 1860s. Henry Dunn, the secretary of the British and Foreign Schools Society, who had defended White and Dobney against the attacks of the *Eclectic Review*, published *The Destiny of the Human Race* in 1863, in which he set out a millenarian version of conditionalism. In the winter of 1863–4 William Ker, the vicar of Tipton in Staffordshire, delivered a series of parochial lectures on popular ideas of immortality, everlasting punishment, and the state of souls after death, in which he advocated a conditionalist position. 1864 also saw the first issues of the *Rainbow*, a journal edited by William Leask, the minister of a Congregational chapel in Dalston, which soon became almost entirely devoted to articles in support of conditionalism. J. B. Heard's *The Tripartite Nature of Man* (1866), a scholarly study of biblical anthropology, and Henry Constable's *The Duration and Nature of Future Punishment* (1868) were other notable contributions. These writers are valuable for an understanding of conditionalism. Dunn, for instance, criticized contemporary thought about the future state for its excessive individualism compared with biblical thought, and he suggested that such individualism led to a trust in one decisive moment, conversion or baptism, for salvation, and to the neglect of sanctification.[46] Ker's conditionalism, like that of the *Rainbow*, was linked with apocalyptic speculation, and in common with many conditionalists of this wing of the movement, he saw the emergence of spiritualism as a sign of the predicted apostasy of the last times.[47] He also speculated on the life enjoyed in heaven by those on whom immortality was bestowed, stating that men's bodies would be incorruptible, glorious, powerful, and spiritual, and would be able to travel with the speed of light through the immensities of space.[48] Ideas of this kind, and Ker's suggestion that were Satan to exist eternally the smoke of his torment would be a perpetual source of annoyance to the blessed, is a reminder of how literally the words of Scripture could be interpreted in some conditionalist circles. It was perhaps the penalty conditionalism paid for basing so much of its theology on proof texts, and even men of considerable theological

[46] H. Dunn, *The Destiny of the Human Race*, 1863, pp. 6, 568.

[47] Cf. the *Rainbow*, ii, 1865, 235.

[48] W. Ker, *The popular ideas of immortality, everlasting punishment and the separate state of souls brought to the test of Scripture*, 1870[2], p. 59.

ability, like Edward White, were prepared to allow extremely literal interpretations and millenarian speculations, without wholly approving of them, simply because their own position was so closely connected with a detailed appeal to the actual words of Scripture.

In contrast to Dunn and Ker, Henry Constable made use of Darwinian arguments to support his conditionalist theology. Fossils, he suggested, provided an analogy of God's working in the moral world:

We find in nature that death and destruction are God's usual agents in removing from their place things animate and inanimate, as soon as they cease to discharge the part for which they were intended . . . Whole races of living things have long ceased to exist:

> 'From scarpèd cliff and quarried stone,
> She cries, a thousand lives are gone.'

In our view God does but apply to higher races for their sin that which He has applied to lower races who knew no sin.[49]

The idea of 'the survival of the fittest' underlay much of what Constable wrote, and he had the curious conception that, after the wicked had been destroyed, hell would 'add its fossil remains to those of the quarries of earth'.[50]

The issues raised by these various works became a matter of public controversy in the 1870s, a decade which was generally marked by severe questioning of established orthodox doctrine. The 'Life in Christ' controversy, as it became popularly known, can be said to have begun with a discussion between Dr. Angus, Andrew Jukes, and Edward White in the columns of the *Christian World*. White marked his return to the public debate by a vigorous defence of conditionalism. He pointed out that, in his teaching and preaching on the subject, he had been careful to avoid the word 'annihilation', which, he believed, 'merely entangled the question with metaphysical arguments on the abolition of substance', and obscured the conditionalist emphasis on 'the dissolution of the tripartite nature of man'.

Our idea of the death of a man is, that it is fundamentally the dissolution of his complex being, the destruction of that life, which consists in the union of the parts. It is evident that this breaking up of humanity, or

---

[49] H. Constable, *The Duration and Nature of Future Punishment*, 1876 ed., p. 211.

[50] p. 212. Thomas Binney wrote appreciatively of Constable's book and the conditionalist movement. Cf. *Bible Echo*, i, 1874, 35–6.

destruction of its life, may be effected in two different ways—either by the separation of the elements of man's being, or by the destruction of the very materials of his existence. There may be two 'deaths', one in which the body is broken up, and the spirit which informed it taken away from it, while both the dust and the spirit remain in being—and another in which not only the life and individuality of the complex man is dissolved and destroyed, but also the very elements of conscious being are reduced to nothing. What we have taught is that both these modes of death are spoken of in Scripture and are called the first and second death.[51]

It was because they distinguished these two varieties of death that White, and those conditionalists who adopted his particular scheme, objected to the label 'Annihilationists', which, they considered, classified them with materialist non-believers in their understanding of death. Despite their objections, however, it remained a common name for adherents of the conditionalist school.

By the time of the correspondence in the *Christian World* White was no longer a suspect figure, but had achieved some standing in Congregationalism. The interest created by the debate in the religious press convinced him that he should rewrite his early work, *Life in Christ*, and he began this task at the end of 1873. The book appeared in October, 1875; there was a reprint the following year; and in 1878 a revised and expanded edition appeared, of which 10,000 copies were eventually sold.[52]

Life in Christ, which von Hügel described as a 'strange mixture of stimulating thought, deep earnestness and fantastic prejudice', was the most important publication of conditionalism.[53] In it White drew on current evolutionary theory to emphasize the close connection between man and the animal world, which, he believed, had undermined all the old arguments for natural immortality.[54] If evolution was true it meant that man's future was limited by 'the horizon which contains the animal race; since an immortal life cannot be supposed to have sprung from a perishable source', and he believed that attempts to save man's immortality by suggesting that the animating principle was immaterial were misguided, for the same principle might be applied to amoebae and zoophytes.[55] Nevertheless, he argued, man

[51] Freer, pp. 72–3.   [52] pp. 76–7.
[53] Von Hügel, *The Mystical Element in Religion*, ii, 229n.
[54] *Life in Christ*, 1878 ed., pp. 5–6.
[55] pp. 8, 23. The *Spectator* published a number of articles in support of animal immortality at this time and the Revd. J. G. Wood's *Man and Beast: Here and Hereafter* (1878) contains a variety of curious speculations on the subject.

did possess language, morality and religion, which clearly differentiated him from the animal world, and pointed in a different direction. Morality, in particular, required some kind of life beyond death, though not necessarily an immortal one, in order that appropriate rewards and punishments might be distributed and the moral law be clearly asserted. It was, however, on the biblical understanding of man that he placed most weight. Scripture, he wrote, never once placed 'the eternal hope of mankind on the abstract dogma of the Immortality of the Soul', nor declared 'that Man would live for ever because he is naturally immortal'.[56] Because the Bible, like modern science, regarded the body as an integral part of man, death could only be seen as the breaking up of the unity of man, which would have been a man's total destruction, had not God demonstrated in Christ another and contrary principle. For although, when Christ died, his humanity was broken up and 'destroyed', 'a divine and spiritual energy remained, around which God built up again the dissolved Humanity, and made that so restored God-man the Life of the World'.[57] White's belief that the Resurrection of Christ was exactly parallel to the promised resurrection of man led him to take issue with all who maintained that man's resurrection had already occurred, whether they did this by treating resurrection as a synonym for spiritual rebirth, or by holding that ἀνάστασις should be translated as 'survival' rather than as 'resurrection'.[58] With his belief in a 'physical' resurrection, went a belief in the physical punishment of the wicked, and he argued that the widely held view that future punishment consisted only in the fire of man's anguish at his separation from God was the consequence of false ideas of endless punishment, and verged on docetism. Sodom and Pompeii were taken by him as examples of God's use of physical punishment.

Why the bodily resurrection of the wicked at all if there be no future judgment on the body? Why should such physical retribution from the hand of God hereafter be regarded as more incredible than the manifold inflictions of contemporary providence? If it has not been contrary to fact that God should judge wicked men by the body here,—why hereafter?[59]

He went on to appeal to science as providing evidence of a close link between the material and the spiritual.

[56] p. 77.

[57] pp. 94, 97, Cf. J. B. Heard, *The Tripartite Nature of Man*, 1866, p. 107.

[58] pp. 329-30. The American, George Bush was the chief advocate of translating ἀνάστασις as 'survival', Cf. his book, *Anastasis*, 1844.

[59] p. 352.

Not only, White maintained, was conditionalism a more accurate account of biblical teaching, it was also liberating in both faith and practice. It was the exact parallel in the moral realm of the idea of natural selection. 'The New Testament', he wrote, 'does not teach the survival of the *strongest*, but the survival of the *fittest*; and these are they who "labouring and heavy laden", embracing righteousness and trusting in and taking hold of the Redeeming Love, "look for the mercy of God to eternal life" '.[60] Far from encouraging materialist views of man, lowering man's estimate of the gravity of sin, and depriving natural theology of one of its cardinal doctrines, as its critics suggested, conditionalism was more credible than the older orthodoxy, and thus more practically influential than belief in eternal punishment. White's primary concern was the scriptural basis of conditionalism, but, once this was established, he went on to argue that conditionalism met materialism on its own ground. It did not need to win a metaphysical battle about human nature before men might be persuaded to believe in Christ, and it did not need to catalogue the horrors of eternal punishment in order to frighten men into belief. In any case White believed that hell-fire preaching no longer made a serious impact.

You cannot reach any in these days, except the most ignorant and thought-less with the threat of endless physical misery; and, if you could, the impression would be but transitory. Multitudes hear these menaces with-out a pang, and 'take sittings' to listen to them, if eloquently set forth by a tragic preacher.[61]

Conditionalism deterred more by threats of a specific and certain punishment, than by threats of a disproportionate retribution. The decline of belief in hell, White suggested, had been partly the result of the spread of Benthamite ideas of punishment, and an emphasis on prevention and reformation. Against this, White insisted that retribu-tion was the ground of all divine punishment, even though it was not a retribution which was to be equated with passionate vengeance.[62]

Thus, for all its appearance of novelty, *Life in Christ* was a con-servative book. It basically attempted to find better reasons for affirming a strongly biblicist faith of a Calvinist variety, and only made use of Darwinian language when it could be made to serve that purpose. Its particular theological stance was largely directed at overcoming the doubts caused by the doctrine of eternal punishment

[60] p. 479.   [61] pp. 480–1, 483, 497.   [62] pp. 491, 501–3.

and only incidentally may it be said to have shown new theological insight.

Conditionalist eschatology did create some difficulties of its own, particularly in respect of the doctrine of the intermediate state between death and the end of the world, and conditionalists differed considerably amongst themselves on this matter. Edward White connected it with the immortality given through Christ. It had been brought into being through him, and for good and bad alike it was one of the results of the new dispensation.[63] Others disagreed. The notion of a disembodied state seemed to them to conflict with the full humanity which was characteristic of the future life. Henry Constable thus preferred the doctrine of the sleep of the soul and argued strongly that Christianity had no doctrine of an intermediate state.

Ghost-lands on the earth or under the earth have no place in the healthy teaching of Scripture. We have in heathendom bodiless souls rolling stones up steeps, and longing for draughts of water, and suffering agonies on wheels. But these are old wives fables. We have no mimicry of them in the Word of the Living God.[64]

Such a denial of the intermediate state, he believed, restored the resurrection to its rightful place.

Resurrection, the grandest act in God's dealings with man, is not the aimless, objectless, purposeless thing that our Platonic theology has made it. It gives life to man, to one man eternal life for his endless joy in praising God, to another man life, for judgment and righteous retribution.[65]

The majority of conditionalists differed from Constable, however, and argued that it was impossible to eliminate a surviving soul from the biblical record. Edward White went so far as to suggest that the intermediate state might provide an opportunity for the evangelization of the ignorant, and would ensure that the second death, in which the soul would be destroyed, would have a special terror.[66]

CRITICS AND SUPPORTERS OF CONDITIONALISM

Although conditionalism had many supporters within Congregationalism, as well as outside, there were probably more Congregationalists who were attracted to views of a Mauricean or uni-

[63] p. 96.
[64] H. Constable, *Hades, or the intermediate state of man*, 1873, p. 97.
[65] p. 90. H. S. Warleigh, in his tract, *Extinction* (1871), supported Constable, with the exception that he believed that in the case of Christians there was no sleep of the soul.
[66] *Life in Christ*, pp. 308–12.

versalist character. James Baldwin Brown, a man who owed much to A. J. Scott, Thomas Erskine, McLeod Campbell, and Julius Hare, as well as to Maurice himself, was the leading exponent of Mauricean theology.[67] P. T. Forsyth, who was greatly influenced by him, referred to him as 'recognising the growing demand of the future for a social salvation', and it was this social emphasis, and his strong belief that Christ died for all men and was the 'Brother of the human race and not of a chosen few', which led him to speak out against conditionalism.[68]

Baldwin Brown's particular criticism of conditionalism can best be seen against the background of his theology as it is set out in his book *The First Principles of Ecclesiastical Truth* (1871), in which he argued that Augustinianism and Calvinism both err in taking their assertion of the primacy of grace to the point where they deny that those who did not agree with their particular understanding were outside the Christian faith.[69] He ascribed the decline of Calvinism during the nineteenth century to the growth of a universal view of history, which had 'no place for a theology which treats pagan nations as outside the love and care of God'. Moreover, he argued, utilitarianism, by its emphasis on the greatest good of the greatest number, had had little use for systems which were only concerned with the good of small numbers of the elect, and unitarianism had also made its protest against any moral division of God. As a consequence, he noted, that, even with Evangelicalism, there was a growing reluctance to trade on a theology of fear.

I believe that one very important reason for the low estate into which, in these recent days, the evangelical community has fallen, in point of intelligence, highmindedness and charity, is connected with the theology of fear in which we have so largely dealt . . . We have endeavoured systematically to frighten men into the kingdom of heaven by terrors; or, we have sought to allure them by the promise of safety and joy . . . We have spoken to men, not of health, soundness, life, but of safety, and the root which we render salvation, meant life before it meant soundness, and soundness, health before it meant safety.[70]

Whilst Brown saw that conditionalism was a reaction from the doctrine of eternal torment which he too repudiated, he believed

[67] Freer, p. 354, *Spectator*, 27 Oct. 1877; E. Baldwin Brown, *In Memoriam James Baldwin Brown*, 1884, pp. 31–2.
[68] P. T. Forsyth, *Baldwin Brown*, 1884, p. 8; E. Baldwin Brown, op. cit., p. 25.
[69] J. Baldwin Brown, *First Principles of Ecclesiastical Truth*, 1871, p. 353.
[70] p. 360.

that it suffered from too many weaknesses to be accepted as a true theological understanding. He charged conditionalists with putting a powerful weapon into the hands of atheists and materialists by asserting that man was not essentially distinguishable from the animal creation, and considered that the idea that the soul survived death without being necessarily immortal was far more incredible than the doctrine of immortality.

The notion of a soul immortal enough to live through death, but not immortal enough to live on for ever, is too childish to be entertained beyond the little school of literalists who delight in it. The world outside will be content to believe that that which proves its powers to live through death claims its immortality.[71]

But his overriding objection was the exclusivism of conditionalism, which he regarded as only Calvinism disguised in the new dress of an 'immortal caste'.

This doctrine of annihilation seems to me to be very closely connected with the idea—which has ruled largely in the region of theological thought since the early days of the Church, though tempered and lightened in its bearings, until Calvinism arose, by 'the power of the keys'—that Christ came to seek and to save the elect few ordained to believe in Him, while the rest were left unpitied to rot in the corruption of sin and to settle down into the everlasting night. The fewness of the saved, the multitude of the lost, are notions which we constantly meet with in this literature; and there is too often a tone of lofty superiority to poor sinners, and exclusive thought and care for the righteous, as if the Universe existed for them alone, which seems to me to be rebuked by almost every word and work of our Lord.[72]

Moreover, the destruction which conditionalists claimed to equate with punishment, seemed to Brown to be a merciful release after a period of torment.[73]

However, like Maurice before him, Brown endeavoured to point out the features of conditionalism which he believed to have a permanent validity. One such point was its way of speaking of man's future life as 'Life in Christ', but, Brown emphasized, this life was not the preserve of an 'immortal caste', but a truth of the universal church. It was concerned, not with existence, but with that which made existence blessed. Again the idea of destruction pointed to a truth, but it was the destruction of sin, not of the sinner.[74] Brown

[71] J. Baldwin Brown, *The Doctrine of Annihilation in the light of the Gospel of Love*, 1875, pp. 64–5.
[72] p. 83, cf. p. 70.   [73] pp. 87–8.   [74] pp. 106–7, 123–4.

himself was prepared to accept the name of universalist, in that he hoped for a universal restoration in which all men would freely fulfil God's command, but he stressed that it was a free response with which he was concerned, and so it was a universalist hope, rather than a belief in a Divine decree of universal salvation.[75]

Both Brown and the conditionalists were Christocentric in their theology, but their Christocentrism took different forms. For Brown, following Maurice, Christ was the one in whom the relationship of man to God was normatively defined, and it was into that relationship that God perpetually willed to bring men, even when they refused to acknowledge him, or lived in ignorance of him. The quality of this underlying relationship was such that it endured beyond death. For Edward White Christ was indeed at the centre, in that it was only through him that men could find salvation, but he believed the salvation which Christ offered to involve an ontological change, which separated men into two fixed and unchangeable categories. They also differed in their treatment of the Bible. Brown had little interest in the balancing of texts, and endeavoured to treat the Bible as a whole, whereas White had a far more textual and detailed approach.[76]

Besides the Congregationalist, Baldwin Brown, there were also Methodist critics, who, from their Arminian position, disliked the conditionalist division of men into two classes, the mortal and the immortal. They were also sceptical of the close connection conditionalists made between the body and the soul, considering it surprising, that were this the case, there was no bodily evidence of the immortalization of the soul, which conditionalists appeared to believe took place at a particular moment of the believer's earthly life.[77]

The supporters of conditionalism were also notable. R. W. Dale, the famous preacher who was minister of Carr's Lane Chapel in Birmingham, announced his conversion to conditionalism in 1874. He believed that conditionalism was not only 'a restatement of the relation of the human race to the Lord Jesus Christ', but 'a reassertion, in a more definite and emphatic form, of the ancient doctrine of the church concerning the nature and necessity of regeneration'.[78] Two years later, in 1876, there was the first of a series of conditional-

---

[75] pp. 128-9. Cf. *Life in Christ*, pp. 285-8.   [76] pp. 15-16.
[77] 'Conditional Immortality', *London Quarterly Review*, l, 1878, 149, 158. Universalism was also criticized. Cf. *Minutes of Wesleyan Conference*, 1878, p. 275.
[78] A. W. W. Dale, *Life of R. W. Dale*, 1898, p. 313; cf. pp. 110, 149.

ist conferences at the Cannon Street Hotel in London, and its report
was widely circulated, especially amongst missionaries.[79] The
speakers at it illustrated a variety of conditionalist themes. Henry
Constable attacked the doctrine of immortality as a manifestation of
human pride; William Leask outlined the relationship of conditionalism and missionary theology; and Arthur Mursell showed how
secularists used the doctrine of eternal punishment as a damaging
weapon against Christianity.[80] Influential laymen also announced
their agreement with conditionalist views, including three M.P.s,
Sir Thomas Chambers,[81] Henry Richard,[82] and Samuel Smith.[83]
Some scientists were also sympathetic. P. G. Tait, one of the authors
of the influential, popular work, *The Unseen Universe*, held White's
work in high esteem, though it is uncertain whether he ever distinctly
committed himself to the doctrine.[84] Henry Drummond, however, in
the section concerned with eternal life in his book, *Natural Law in
the Spiritual World*, adopted the conditionalist view, that Christianity
had never been more misguided than when it had attempted to prove
that man was naturally immortal on the basis of physiological
evidence or philosophical speculation.[85] Science, Drummond wrote,
held that eternal life was 'uninterrupted correspondence with a
Perfect Environment'. Christianity maintained that its essence was
the knowledge of God, a knowledge which might be interpreted as
correspondence with God,[86] and for the Christian, the possibility of
that correspondence rested on Christ alone. It was Christ who had
claimed to give men life, and this claim had to be taken literally.[87]

It was not, however, the biologist, Drummond, but a mathematician, Sir George Gabriel Stokes, who became the leading
scientific advocate of conditionalism.[88] For Stokes conditionalism

[79] Conference Report, 1876. The chair was taken by Lt.-Gen. Goodwyn, and
amongst conditionalists present were: H. Constable, J. B. Heard, W. Leask, S. Minton,
A. Mursell, J. F. B. Tinling, and Edward White.

[80] *Report*, pp. 15, 23, 43. Cf. D. Wardlaw Scott, *Two Sermons*, 1885, p. 36.

[81] Liberal M.P. for Hertford. Cf. *Bible Echo*, i, 1874, 87.

[82] Secretary of the Peace Society and a leader of Welsh nationalism. Chairman of the
Congregational Union, 1877.

[83] M.P. for Flintshire, and later for Liverpool, where he was a cotton merchant.
A Presbyterian. Cf. S. Smith, *My Life-work*, 1902, pp. 97–102; Freer, pp. 126–8.

[84] C. G. Knott, *Life and scientific work of Peter Guthrie Tait*, 1911, pp. 238–9, 242–3.

[85] H. Drummond; *Natural Law in the Spiritual World*, 1890 ed., pp. 226–7.

[86] p. 215.   [87] p. 235.

[88] Lucasian Professor of Mathematics at Cambridge. He began consideration of the
problem of conditionalism in 1851. Cf. J. Larmor, *Memoir and scientific correspondence
of Sir G. G. Stokes*, i, 1907, 46–7, 82.

meant that man's immortality was 'not by nature but by grace', and his ability to receive it through Christ was closely parallel to the original position of Adam, for in both cases immortality was dependent on obedience.[89] He dismissed as nonsense the argument put forward by some believing scientists at the time, who spoke of man's spiritual powers as subject to the law of the conservation of energy, and as therefore surviving death. Stokes could discover no evidence that will and mechanical energy were mutually convertible.[90]

The adherents of systematic conditionalism were almost entirely to be found within the Augustinian-Calvinist tradition, and placed a high value on the verbal inspiration of the Bible. Despite the eighteenth-century example of Henry Dodwell, who had maintained a close connection between baptismal regeneration and the gift of immortality, there seem to have been no High Anglican conditionalists. The reason for this is probably to be found in the fact that they already had their own ways of modifying the rigours of eternal punishment, through the advocacy of some form of purgatory. Likewise Broad Churchmen moved towards universalism, rather than towards the elaborate theories of conditionalism, though they were capable of adopting evolutionary language in much the same way as conditionalists.

As with all theologies which stress the absolute sovereignty of grace, there was a tension in conditionalism between the desire to say that immortality was the free gift of God, and the wish to avoid any charge of apparent arbitrariness in the bestowal of the gift. Thus at the same time as conditionalists affirmed that immortality was 'Life in Christ alone', they argued for 'survival of the fittest' as the heart of New Testament teaching.

It is perhaps surprising, in the light of John Hick's recent distinction between Augustinian and Irenaean theodicies, that a theology which belonged so definitely to the Augustinian and Calvinist tradition should appeal so frequently to Irenaeus for its Patristic support. But conditionalism was essentially a mitigated Augustinianism, its characteristic doctrine being intended to alleviate the harshness of an Augustinian theodicy pressed to its conclusions. Irenaeus, with his stress on immortality as a gift of God, was a valuable witness for conditionalists, even though they did not

[89] G. G. Stokes, *Conditional Immortality a help to sceptics*, 1897, pp. 14, 27.
[90] p. 33. For Edward White's estimate of Stokes, cf. Freer, p. 275.

adopt his full theological outlook.[91] Those conditionalists who drew on contemporary evolutionary theory, however, did approach much more closely to the Irenaean view, and emphasized the possibilities of growth and development open to man in a way which is reminiscent of what Hick has called the 'vale of soul-making' theodicy. But those who equated the immortalization of man with the moment of his conversion were far removed from this understanding and held a theology more akin to Calvin's divine decrees.

Conditionalism also has links with the incarnational emphasis and the stress on *Christus consummator*, which dominated so much of later nineteenth-century theology. White asked in *Life in Christ*, 'Is it not THAT THE VERY OBJECT OF THE INCARNATION IS TO IMMORTALISE MANKIND?',[92] and conditionalists generally presented a theology of Christ as an immortal being entering the world, and bestowing this immortality on those who in faith responded to him, thus stressing the Person rather than the Work of Christ. They perhaps made a more important contribution, however, in their re-examination of biblical anthropology. Although their scholarship may at times be criticized, and the literal interpretations they drew from the evidence regretted, they did succeed in showing that the biblical understanding of man was more complex than many had realized, and certainly did not coincide with the popular dualist picture. J. B. Heard, whose work, with the possible exception of the German Old Testament Scholar, F. J. Delitzsch, was the most notable conditionalist contribution in this field, hoped that the new understanding of the biblical picture of man would lead to a fresh exploration of other aspects of biblical theology.[93] The Christocentrism of conditionalism is an example of how this could happen. It set not only eschatology, but the whole of theology, in a new context. As Leckie pointed out: 'Conditionalism is formidable in this respect, that it, more than any other eschatological speculation, influences the entire theology of those who adopt it, and would, if generally received, profoundly modify the whole Christian view of the world and of life'.[94] Nevertheless conditionalist Christocentrism and appreciation of biblical anthropology were

[91] For Irenaeus' understanding of immortality in the context of his whole theology, cf. G. Wingren, *Man and the Incarnation, a study in the biblical theology of Irenaeus*, Edinburgh, 1959, pp. 204-7.
[92] *Life in Christ*, p. 204.
[93] J. B. Heard, *The Tripartite Nature of Man*, p. 336
[94] *The World to come and final destiny*, p. 219.

significant in spite of, rather than because of, the basic conditionalist doctrine, though they were noteworthy in a nineteenth-century context in which man's inherent capacity to transcend himself was so often emphasized. In the end conditionalism can best be judged, as Leckie saw clearly, as a theory devised to meet certain difficulties, though raising many others, and as a valuable protest against a sentimental indifferentism.[95]

[95] pp. 250–1.

Appendix to Chapter IX

CONTINENTAL SUPPORTERS OF THE DOCTRINE OF CONDITIONAL IMMORTALITY

THE most notable advocates of the theory of conditional immortality on the Continent in the nineteenth century were French and Swiss divines. In Germany universalism was more prevalent, despite the anathematizing of it in the seventeenth article of the Augsburg Confession. This universalism was particularly characteristic of those who had been influenced by idealist philosophy or radical pietism.[1] There were, however, a number of German conditionalists, of whom Richard Rothe (1799–1869) was probably the chief. Their conditionalism was not the ontological conditionalism that was prevalent in England, but a soteriological conditionalism, a faith that all men could be saved on condition that they 'converted themselves'.[2]

Emmanuel Pétavel-Olliff (1836–1910) was the leading conditionalist on the continent. He was the son of a Swiss pastor, A.-F. Pétavel, who had been brought into contact with Edward White through helping his father with his correspondence, particularly in connection with a group interested in the future of the Jews and the second coming of Christ, to which both White and the elder Pétavel belonged. White's sister, Ellen, was married to M. Ranyard, a close friend of the Pétavels, and this provided a further contact.[3] In 1863 Emmanuel Pétavel became minister of the Swiss Church in London, where he remained until 1866, staying at first with the Ranyards, and later at Brixton, after his marriage to Susanna Ollif whom he had first met at an Evangelical Alliance meeting in Geneva in 1861.[4] When he returned to Switzerland he settled at Neuchâtel.

---

[1] For an account of universalism on the Continent cf. Gotthold Müller, 'Die Idee einer Apokatastasis ton panton . . .', *Zeitschrift für Religions- und Geistesgeschichte*, 1964.

[2] Cf. R. Rothe, *Dogmatik*, (Zweiter Teil, zweiter abteilung), Heidelburg, 1870; C. I. Nitzsch, *System der Christlichen Lehre*, Bonn, 1844[5], p. 404; W. Schmidt, *Christliche Dogmatik*, ii, Bonn, 1898, 517.

[3] Ellen Ranyard (1810–79). Founder of the London Bible Women's Mission and author of many tracts under the pseudonym 'LNR'.

[4] E. Pétavel-Ollif, *Souvenirs et mélanges* (Biographical account by H. Norbel), Lausanne, 1913, pp. 31–42, 93–4.

The influence of Pietism, with its universalist tendencies, had already been felt in the Neuchâtel theological school, particularly through the work of Ostervald and Oliver Petitpierre. Pétavel, however, came to adopt a conditionalist position, which he had first met in Edward White, after he had made a detailed study of the sense of the word 'destroy' in Scripture. In 1869 he gave his first exposition of this position in a paper, *La Loi du progrès*, which was later expanded into a book, *La Fin du mal*, which he published in 1872.[5] Pétavel's work was noticed by the philosopher, Charles Renouvier, in the *Critique philosophique* in 1873, and there was considerable discussion of Pétavel's ideas in the journal. It was noted that Charles Lambert, a French mathematician, who had been engaged in the survey for the Suez canal, had anticipated some of Pétavel's positions in his *Système du monde moral* (1863). Lambert had been more influenced by Darwinism than was the case with Pétavel, and had argued that man was not immortal by nature, but only became so according to the way in which he used his liberty. He believed this process to be exactly the same as that of natural selection in the physical world.[6] Renouvier himself argued that conditionalism, because it rested man's hope of immortality on moral obligation rather than on metaphysical arguments, approximated to the critical philosophy of Kant, as well as emphasizing the judgment of God.

When Renouvier and Pillon started a supplement to the *Critique philosophique*, known as the *Critique religieuse*, there was further discussion of the issue. Dupont-White wrote an article maintaining that immortality was only credible when it was maintained on the basis of an explicit revelation founded on miracle.[7] Renouvier, in a more detailed consideration of the question, argued that conditional immortality was entirely in accord with what was known of the working of natural laws, and also with the moral emphasis of Kantian philosophy, and he believed Pétavel to have made a substantial contribution to the understanding of man.[8]

In 1880 Charles Byse, a pastor of Swiss extraction working in Brussels, published a translation of White's *Life in Christ*. This aroused considerable interest amongst members of the Reformed

[5] pp. 107–8. Translated into English in 1875 under the title *The Struggle for Life*, chosen because of its obvious Darwinian reference.
[6] M. Méry, *La Critique du christianisme chez Renouvier*, Gap, 1963, i, 388.
[7] *Critique religieuse*, i, 1879, 51, quoted in Méry, i, 391.
[8] Méry, i, 392, 396.

Church in France, and discussion of it was a feature of the annual gatherings of pastors in 1880, 1883 and 1884. The great German scholar, Dorner, told Byse how greatly he appreciated the work.[9] The Belgian Christian Missionary Church, to which Byse was attached, regarded the work with grave suspicion, however, and began proceedings against him, which lasted through 1882 and 1883, until he was eventually forced to leave his pastorate, though against the wishes of the majority of his own congregation.[10] Other works appeared in support of conditionalism. Auguste Sabatier, Charles Babut, and César Malan, the younger, published books in France and Switzerland. Jonker did likewise in Holland, and Oscar Concorda's *Pro Immortalitate* (1883) shows that there were even conditionalists in Italy. Pétavel himself published a learned defence of conditionalism in 1891, which was translated into English as *The Problem of Immortality* and was warmly welcomed by Edward White as a work of erudition and piety.[11]

Pétavel's book was in many ways the most thorough statement of conditionalism which appeared, and in the preface contributed by Charles Sécretan, a distinction is made between Pétavel's position and that of Henry Drummond. Sécretan argues that Christianity belongs to the moral order, which is dependent on free will, and 'nature ends where liberty begins'. It is, therefore, an error to 'confound the survival of the worthiest with the survival of the fittest'. Determinist systems, whether mechanistic naturalism or religious predestinarianism, were he believed, alike inimical to the highest man could achieve, and he saw in conditionalism a faith which took its stand on the ground of freedom.[12] Pétavel believed that 'a system of dogmatics without eschatology' was like a building without a roof, and he recognized that, at the time of writing, eschatology was more and more neglected. Eternal punishment had become increasingly incredible, and it had only been replaced by a vague universalism in the liberal theology of the day. Conditionalism he believed to be a genuinely contemporary, as well as a truly Christian eschatology, for it was 'the meeting-point of . . . biblical Christianity, rationalist Christianity, Kantism, and evangelical transformism'.[13] He attributed the growth of the movement to the

[9] E. Pétavel, *The Problem of Immortality*, E.T., 1892, p. 24n.
[10] Freer, p. 178.
[11] Pétavel, *Souvenirs et mélanges*, p. 136.
[12] Pétavel, *The Problem of Immortality*, 1892, p. xi.
[13] p. 33.

increased knowledge of the biblical philology, which had led him to adopt it, but he also gave considerable weight to the philosophical arguments in its support put forward by Renouvier and the neo-critical school. By 1902 he could write to C. H. Oliphant:

Evolutionary thought is compelling attention to that theodicy which alone can give a cap-stone to the edifice of selective purposes and progress in history and biology. I think we must place most stress upon the philosophic argument, less upon the exegetic, owing to the changed attitudes to the Bible.[14]

Unlike White, who believed in a once and for all moment of immortalization equivalent to conversion, Pétavel spoke of a progressive immortalization, a concept which, although conceivable in moral terms, is a little difficult in ontological. In support of his conception he placed great emphasis on the sacraments, as the Fathers had done, as 'the medicine of immortality'.

As with Baptism, so it has been with the Lord's Supper. Under the influence of Platonic ideas, the meaning of the symbol has been obscured. The meaning of the practice having been lost, the supper, too became a magical operation, a sort of fetish . . . Lest they should lose their nobility and vitality in the ritualism, the sacerdotalism, and the sacramentalism of certain sects, the evangelical communities ought to seek in the primitive doctrine of *ontological life in Christ* the key of these important symbols.[15]

[14] *Souvenirs*, p. 336.
[15] *The Problem of Immortality*, pp. 187–8.

X   Conclusion

MR. GLADSTONE's comment, at the end of the nineteenth century, that the doctrine of hell had been 'relegated . . . to the far-off corners of the Christian mind . . . there to sleep in deep shadow as a thing needless in our enlightened and progressive age', is a reminder of the change which had taken place in Christian eschatology during the century.[1] It is true that the doctrine of hell had not been removed from the official theological confession of any denomination, but men were no longer deprived of office for teaching a tentative universalism or regarded with suspicion for espousing the doctrine of conditional immortality.[2] The hell-fire sermons of the great preachers no longer carried conviction, and their descriptions of the details of eternal torment, far from bringing men to reflect on how perilous was their situation and how vital was the issue of salvation or damnation, were more likely to seem full of unwarranted speculation and morally offensive. The Bible, after several decades of controversy and criticism, no longer occupied the position of unquestionable authority which it had once held, and even where men were still concerned to profess a biblical religion, there had been too much discussion of the texts concerning eternal punishment for them to be altogether unaware of the difficulties surrounding their interpretation. At the same time the whole question of the future life itself, and man as a being with an immortal soul, had become much more problematical, and this, which had previously been an implicit, if not an explicit, assumption of all religious teaching, was beginning to be pushed to one side. As early as 1872, as has already been mentioned, Mark Pattison contrasted the situation of the eighteenth-century defenders of natural religion, who assumed the soul as a fact, with that of his own generation, who had to prove it.[3] The *Nineteenth Century*'s 'Modern Symposium' of 1877 also bears witness to a

---

[1] W. E. Gladstone, *Studies subsidiary to the works of Bishop Butler*, 1898, p. 206.

[2] There was a late exception in the case of Dr. Joseph Agar Beet, who, under pressure from the Wesleyan Methodist Conference of 1904, resigned his chair at Richmond, as a consequence of his book, *The Last Things*, originally published in 1897. Cf. Beet's preface to the revised edition of the book (1905).

[3] Mark Pattison, 'The Argument for a Future Life', *Metaphysical Society Papers*, xxv, 4. Cf. above, p. 4.

growing uncertainty about the existence of the soul and the possibility of a future life. Absolute disbelief in a future life as a consequence of the attacks of a materialist science was not, however,
common, and it is surprising what little effect the early developments of psychology had on belief in an immortal soul.[4] Idealist
philosophy, with its concern to interpret reality in terms of mind,
was undoubtedly a powerful counterweight to materialism in this
context, and it is noteworthy that J. R. Illingworth, in his influential
Bampton Lectures of 1894, *Personality Human and Divine*, could
not only claim that 'critical philosophy' had 'distinctly strengthened
the claim . . . of human personality to be a spiritual thing', but could
also assert that physical science had in no way weakened that claim.[5]
But, if there were few who completely abandoned belief in the
possibility of a future life, there were many for whom the idea had
become much vaguer. The old assurances and the definite doctrines
of orthodox Christian eschatology had become doubtful, not least
because of the controversies over hell. Although the old language
continued, in part, to be used, it was often in conjunction with a
shadowy hope of a final apotheosis, expressed in terms of romantic
yearnings. Hegelian language about the realization of the World
Spirit was linked with a universalist theology, and sometimes
associated with the evidence of psychic research, or with an orientally
influenced theosophy. Orthodox divines, troubled about hell and
sharing the Victorian faith in progress, at times accepted this
approach; Unitarians and liberal theists notoriously did so. The
doctrine of *Christus Consummator*, emphasized by, above all, Brooke
Foss Westcott, was both orthodox and biblically based, and spoke
powerfully to a generation troubled by evolution and which yet had
a supreme faith and confidence in the ability of man to order the
world and his own future. But the emphasis on Christ the Fulfiller
and the social hope of men could easily degenerate into the cloudy
phraseology of aspiration, and even Westcott was guilty of that at
times.[6] Psychic research, in which there was increasing interest in

[4] Owen Chadwick, *The Victorian Church*, ii, 1970, 34. F. W. H. Myers claimed that
science was neutral but the lack of verification of the future life meant the belief was
being widely abandoned. *Science and a Future Life*, 1901[2], pp. 1–3.

[5] Illingworth, op. cit., Preface, p. vii. For the influence of T. H. Green's idealism on
religious thought cf. Melvin Richter, *The Politics of Conscience*, 1964.

[6] B. F. Westcott, *Christus Consummator*, 1887[2], pp. 12–15, 'Christus Consolator
leads us to *Christus Consummator* . . . Progress is still, as in the first age, the essence of
our faith . . . "Let us be borne on", "borne on" with that mighty influence which

some intellectual circles in the last decades of the century, could likewise be linked with an idealist philosophy, even though, in other respects, its appeal was scientific and empirical. F. W. H. Myers concluded his great survey of the evidence provided by psychic research for a future life, *Human Personality and its Survival of Bodily Death*, not only with a quotation from Plotinus, but also with an enraptured expression of hope, which employed many of the characteristic phrases of an idealist, and quasi-scientific, eschatology.

Science, then, need be no longer fettered by the limitations of this planetary standpoint; nor ethics by the narrow experience of a single life. Evolution will no longer appear as a truncated process, an ever-arrested movement upon an unknown goal. Rather we may gain a glimpse of an ultimate incandescence where science and religion fuse in one; a cosmic evolution of Energy into Life, and of Life into Love, which is Joy ... Inevitably, as our link with other spirits strengthens, as the life of the organism pours more fully through the individual cell, we shall feel love more ardent, wider wisdom, higher joy; perceiving that this organic unity of Soul, which forms the inward aspect of the telepathic law, is in itself the Order of the Cosmos, the Summation of Things ... Far hence, beyond Orion and Andromeda, the cosmic process works and shall work for ever through unbegotten souls. And even as it was not in truth the great ghost of Hector only, but the whole nascent race of Rome, which bore from the Trojan altar the hallowing fire, so is it not one Saviour only, but the whole nascent race of man—nay, all the immeasurable progeny and population of the heavens—which issues continually from behind the veil of Being, and forth from the Sanctuary of the Universe carries the ever-burning flame: *Aeternumque adytis effert penetralibus ignem.*[7]

The First World War, with its millions of dead and futile suffering, made much of the optimistic language of idealist theology sound shallow and unreal; but already, before 1914, there had been signs of an impending change. G. E. Moore's article 'The Refutation of Idealism', published in 1903, the same year as Myers's *Human Personality*, indicated a new outlook, and in 1910 the appearance in English of Albert Schweitzer's *Quest of the Historical Jesus*, shattered easy assumptions about the harmony of the New Testament with contemporary liberal thought, and underlined the eschatological

---

waits only for the acceptance of faith that it may exert its sovereign away, "borne on" by Him whose unseen arms are outstretched beneath the most weary and the weakest...'

[7] F. W. H. Myers, op. cit., 1903, ii, 290–2.

nature of the teaching of Jesus.[8] The demand of faith, its critical nature, and the judgment of God were once more stressed. Nevertheless it was not, and could not be, a return to the old crudities of a debased Calvinism. One of the effects of the nineteenth-century debates had undoubtedly been to make men more widely aware of the imaginative nature of religious language, and to show them that theological understanding was not advanced by subtle interpretations of the undying worm or the unquenchable fire.

Literalism had, however, been a mark of many of the nineteenth-century controversialists. They had also shared other assumptions. One was undoubtedly the place given to scripture. Even universalists generally appealed to Scripture, rightly interpreted, as supporting their view, and were faced with the problem of explaining away awkward, exclusivist texts and references to the Gehenna of fire. Another more or less general assumption was the need for an overriding ethical sanction. If conditionalists were to deny an eternal hell, they had to insist that sin would not go entirely unpunished. If F. D. Maurice wished to emphasize that Christianity was concerned with salvation from sin, rather than with salvation from punishment, he had to convince his readers of the intolerableness of a life in separation from God. If others argued in favour of an enlarged purgatory as a means of avoiding the moral affront caused by the doctrine of hell, it was necessary for them to insist that the purification of hardened sinners would be a painful process.

Although no common, 'revised version' of Christian eschatology emerged during the nineteenth century, but rather a number of different versions, each stressing different elements in the biblical tradition in an endeavour to meet popular criticisms of the doctrine of eternal punishment in particular, there was one notable, common feature, in contrast to the eschatology of previous generations. That was the growing importance of the doctrine of the 'intermediate state'. The term itself was characteristic of the nineteenth century, and, whether it took the form of a tentative reappraisal of purgatory, or of a fore-shortened hell, or as a place of moral progress and expansion of the mind, it represented a move away from a predominantly Calvinist eschatology. Father Faber wrote of purgatory, that 'difficulties are perpetually drifting that way to find their

---

[8] For this change cf. Thomas A. Langford, *In Search of Foundations: English Theology, 1900–1920*, Nashville: New York, 1969, chapters 2 and 3.

explanation',[9] and, what he wrote in a Roman Catholic context, may be taken as a commentary on all nineteenth-century eschatology. An intermediate state became important to those who wished to emphasize the necessity of sanctification before a man could attain to full communion with God. It relieved, to some extent at least, the problems of the destiny of the heathen and of those who had apparently been deprived by their circumstances, capabilities, and environment of all reasonable chance of appreciating the significance and importance of the Christian gospel. It fitted better with a dynamic, evolutionary picture of the universe, than the conception of fixed and unalterable states into which men entered at death. To some extent it relieved the tension between the judgment of the individual and the general judgment at the Last Day, in that it could be represented as a state of preparation for the new order which was to be ushered in at the End of the World. For those who wished to recover the full faith of the age of the Fathers, it was the logical counterpart of prayers for the dead.

The Christian theologian, recognizing the agonies and conflicts of the Victorian debate about hell, is inevitably faced with the question of evaluating the debate theologically. We saw, at the beginning, how orthodox Christian eschatology had only partially succeeded in reconciling the Christian hope for the individual with the Christian hope for the world as a whole, and that, consequently, the relationship of the theology of death and the judgment of the individual to the Last Day and the End of the World had never been satisfactory. It was not, therefore, surprising that the nineteenth-century debate should disclose some of these tensions. The New Testament, the very authority to which so many of the participants in the debate absolutely appealed, itself spoke with a divided voice, if it was treated as a collection of texts to be weighed one against another. In another respect, as the conditionalists in particular recognized, the biblical account of man's nature did not exactly tally with that which had come to be accepted as Christian orthodoxy, as a result of the assimilation of Christian doctrine to the assumptions of Hellenistic thought.

The theological difficulty of the doctrine of hell is not a new one, nor is it as peripheral a question as is sometimes supposed. It strikes right into the heart of the questions of man's freedom and responsibility, his awareness of good and evil and the perilousness of his

[9] F. W. Faber, *The Creator and the Creature*, 1858[2], p. 376.

choosing between them, and it inevitably reflects on the nature and character of God. As John Hick has written, 'there is a tension within Christian thought between the motives that move towards this doctrine of everlasting punishment and the motives that move towards a theodicy'.[10] Hick goes on to argue for the truth of universal salvation as 'the extrapolation of the Christian faith into the future', and says of the doctrine of hell that it 'has as its implied premise either that God does not desire to save all His human creatures, in which case He is only limitedly good, or that His purpose has finally failed in the case of some—and indeed, according to theological tradition, most—of them, in which case He is only limitedly sovereign'.[11] Yet universalism can never be easy, and to assert it absolutely is, in the last resort, to undermine moral seriousness. The teaching of Jesus, as it is reported in the gospels, holds in tension the assertion of God's love and care, and the severity and decisiveness of judgment and future punishment, expressed in traditional Jewish terms.[12] Neither element can be sacrificed without weakening the fabric of Christian theology, but how they are related is not easily shown. Of modern theologians perhaps the one who has explored this area most rigorously is Nicolas Berdyaev, in the chapter on hell in his book *The Destiny of Man*, and it is with his theological reflections that we may most fittingly conclude.

In a sense it can be rightly said that hell is the fundamental problem of ethics, for it is concerned with the ultimate nature and consequences of a man's actions and decisions, and the relation of those actions and decisions to the character and purposes of God. In one perspective, as Nicolas Berdyaev perceptively saw, to believe in hell is to believe in man's spiritual freedom. 'The idea of hell is ontologically connected with freedom and personality, and not with justice and retribution ... Hell is necessary not to ensure the triumph of justice and retribution to the wicked, but to save man from being forced to be good and compulsorily installed in heaven.' Looked at in this way, man might almost be said to have 'a moral right to hell'.[13] It is not, however, the only perspective. Christian theology also affirms the goodness and grace of God, and his love towards men shown in creation and redemption. It looks in hope

---

[10] J. H. Hick, *Evil and the God of Love*, 1966, p. 377.

[11] p. 378.

[12] Cf. A. M. Fairhurst, 'The Problem posed by the severe sayings attributed to Jesus in the Synoptic Gospels', *Scottish Journal of Theology*, 23, 1970, pp. 77–91.

[13] N. Berdyaev, *The Destiny of Man*, 1937, pp. 266–7.

towards the ultimate triumph of God's purpose in creation and redemption, and to speak of the objective existence of an eternal hell in this context is inevitably to compromise God's goodness, and end in an ultimate dualism. The Christian can never rest in such a situation; as Karl Barth argues in the *Church Dogmatics*, there is no eternal covenant of wrath parallel to the covenant of grace.[14] Is it then possible to affirm the seriousness of man's actions and decisions, the irrevocability of them in terms of what a man becomes in the future through the totality of his actions in the past, and at the same time to declare an ultimate hope in the triumph of God's purposes?

Two points have been made in answer to this question, which, although not entirely satisfying, do at least indicate the way to a solution. The first is the suggestion made by Berdyaev, when he insists that hell is to be seen as subjective and not objective. It is the product of man's self-centredness and isolation, yet it is also a state in which man remains, however obscurely, conscious of God as the one who alone can give his life meaning and significance. As Berdyaev writes: 'Hell is the state of the soul powerless to come out of itself, absolute self-centredness, dark and evil isolation, i.e. final inability to love'. It is, he continues, not to be envisaged as 'God's action upon the soul, retributive and punitive as that action may be; it is the absence of any action of God upon the soul, the soul's incapacity to open itself to God's influence and its complete severance from God'.[15] Such a situation, real and terrible as it is, can, however, never be accorded the same ultimate reality as that which belongs to God himself. The Christian lives in faith and hope, and the dimensions of that faith and hope are measured by Christ's descent into hell. It was there that a response was made to the calling of God in the context of absolute human self-centredness and isolation. To hope, therefore, on this basis, in the ultimate triumph of God's purpose, cannot be to provide a neat theological solution; for neat theological solutions, whether they be of hell as the triumph of divine justice, or an optimistic universalism, or predestination by divine decree, are all attempts to rationalize the situation of man's existence before God, involved in the choice of good or evil. It is out of that experience that the knowledge, both of the possibility of hell, and of the ultimate possibility of God has been won; and if, in the end, the Christian hope is in the ultimate triumph of God's love,

[14] K. Barth, *Church Dogmatics*, II, ii (E.T., 1947), 450; cf. Berdyaev, p. 268.
[15] Berdyaev, p. 277.

that hope can never be an easy universalism, but only a hope founded on a love which descended into hell, and triumphed over it in the Resurrection.

The second point concerns the criticism that any form of universalism denies the reality of ethical and moral challenge and decision, and it has been well made by Dr. Ian Ramsey: 'If universalism were true, it has been said, we could all conclude that it would not matter very much in the long run what we did.' 'But', he goes on to point out, 'if, in this way, we did not bother about the challenge of a moral situation, it would be to deny the very significance of the situation from which the discourse started.' By this Ramsey means that the acceptance of a doctrine of universalism, in the sense of 'a final triumph of God's purposes', and 'the final disappearance of Hell', could only spring from the belief that we were 'able to speak consistently *both* of God and his love and his power, and *also* about the cosmic significance of moral decision, the cosmic loneliness and separation it involves and so on'.[16] Such a universalism is in fact rooted in a serious moral concern, and in an awareness that an evil decision made by a man results in alienation from God.

Paul Tillich is another who has attempted to do justice to both the reality of hell, and the ultimate triumph of God's purposes. He makes the point that 'absolute judgments over finite beings or happenings are impossible, because they make the finite infinite'. Man, Tillich argues, can waste his potentialities or fulfil them, though in neither case totally, and he wishes to speak of eternal life as an 'essentialisation' according to the degree in which a man has responded to God as his end. Such an understanding, he argues, attempts to hold together, 'the despair of having wasted one's potentialities', with 'the elevation of the positive within existence (even in the most unfulfilled life) into eternity'. Moreover, because human goodness is ambiguous, and salvation is for all men dependent on divine grace, and because men are not isolated entities, but are linked closely to each other and to the natural world, the elements of Christian tradition, which look to a 'universal participation in the fulfilment of the Kingdom of God' *must* be held together with affirmations concerning the future of the individual. Cosmic and individual eschatology must not be separated.[17]

[16] Ian Ramsey, 'Hell' in *Talk of God*, (*Royal Institute of Philosophy Lectures*, ii, 1967/8), 1969, 224.
[17] Paul Tillich, *Systematic Theology*, iii, 1964, pp. 433-6.

Opinions will differ as to how far such attempts to relate the universalist assertion of the ultimate triumph of God's purposes, and a hell of which the essence is separation from God, have been successful. But it is quite clear that not only discussion of this issue, but all theological language relating to the future life, is not concerned, as it so often has been, with celestial or infernal map-making, but with the nature and ground of the Christian hope. 'Doctrines of Hell', as Ian Ramsey reminds us, 'like all other theistic doctrines, exist primarily to point to God who is, in the last resort, the single topic of all religious discourse'; and, in this context, the affirmation of Hans Urs von Balthasar, that God is the true 'Last Thing' of the creature, in confronting whom man experiences heaven, hell, and purgatory, points to the heart of Christian eschatology.[18] That eschatology must seek to relate what it says of the future of the individual to that which it hopes for the world as a whole. The God of which it speaks, is the God who is disclosed at the boundaries of history, as well as at the boundaries of the individual life.

The nineteenth-century discussions of eschatology moved in many ways towards this approach, and each of the different traditions of eschatological thought, which were elaborated in the course of the century, have insights to offer to those concerned with the task of constructing a contemporary Christian eschatology. From the conditionalists we may learn, that to talk of an eternal life apart from its grounding in God, is not only to make unwarranted assumptions about human nature, but is also to make eternal life a function of that nature, rather than the object of man's hope and a gift of God. Yet, from the course of that debate, lessons may be learnt of the dangers of attempting to say too much, and of juggling with biblical texts. Universalism, with its firm refusal of an ultimately dualist solution to the questions raised by man's experience in the world, points to the final unity of love, which is the ultimate expression of God's nature and purposes; as such it can never be removed from the Christian hope. But, in so far as universalists have so often become vague optimists, that hope cannot be one which refuses to take seriously the moral conflict of good and evil; the fact that actions once committed can never be undone; and the consequences of this for any theology which speaks of forgiveness and

---

[18] Ian Ramsey, p. 225; H. U. von Balthasar, *Word and Redemption*, New York, 1965, 'Some points of Eschatology', pp. 147ff.

ultimate reconciliation. We cannot do without a doctrine of hell, for it stands as a vitally important reminder of the reality and seriousness of the experience of alienation, isolation, and estrangement, and the consequences of evil in human life, though to speak of hell can so easily make God morally obnoxious and repellent. In eschatology, as in other areas of theology, the theologian's path is perilous, as the men of the nineteenth century, who debated the issues with such agony and passion knew to their cost. The least we can say of them is that in their controversies they not only uncovered the confusions of the past, they also opened up perspectives of vital importance for the future.

Bibliography

A. MAIN MANUSCRIPT COLLECTIONS UTILIZED

(a) *Farrar papers.* (Cathedral Library, Canterbury). Large bundle of correspondence concerning *Eternal Hope* and *Mercy and Judgment* (*c.* 125 letters) together with letters on related topics from other bundles.

(b) *Helpers of the Holy Souls' MSS.* (Holy Rood House, 1, Gloucester Avenue, London N.W.1). Small quantity of correspondence relating to the establishment of the order in England. Various sermons preached for the order.

(c) *Liddon MSS.* 1. Correspondence preserved at Pusey House, Oxford. 2. MSS. volume of meditations, *The End of Life*, compiled in 1858, preserved at Cuddesdon College, Oxford.

(d) *Newman MSS.* Correspondence of Newman on various aspects of eschatology extracted from the correspondence preserved at the Birmingham Oratory.

(e) *Pusey MSS.* (Pusey House, Oxford). Letters illustrating the development of eschatological doctrine amongst the Tractarians and their opposition to *Essays and Reviews*.

B. SELECT BIBLIOGRAPHY OF PRINTED MATERIAL (MAINLY NINETEENTH-CENTURY WORKS ON ESCHATOLOGY)

The place of publication of books is London, unless otherwise stated. E.T. = English translation.

ALTHOLZ, J., *The Liberal Catholic Movement in England: the 'Rambler' and its contributors, 1848–1864*, 1962.

ANON., *Sketch and life of Professor Tholuck*, Edinburgh, 1840.

——, *The Recognition of Friends in Heaven, A Symposium*, 1866.

——, *Eternal Punishment: a critique of Canon Farrar's 'Eternal Hope'*, 1878.

——, *That Unknown Country: Or what men believe concerning punishment*, Springfield, 1888.

ASHWELL, A. R., and WILBERFORCE, R. G., *Life of the Right Reverend Samuel Wilberforce*, 3 vols. 1880–2.

AXON, W. E. A., 'On General Gordon's copy of Newman's "Dream of Gerontius"', *Manchester Quarterly*, viii, 1889.

BALDWIN BROWN, E., (ed.), *In Memoriam: James Baldwin Brown*, 1884.

BALDWIN BROWN, J., *First Principles of Ecclesiastical Truth: Essays on the Church and society*, 1871.

——, *The Doctrine of Annihilation in the light of the Gospel of Love*, 1875.

VON BALTHASAR, H. U., *Word and Redemption*, E.T., New York, 1965.

BELCHER, T. W., *Robert Brett, of Stoke Newington. His life and work*, 1889.

BELL, G. K. A., *Randall Davidson, Archbishop of Canterbury*, 1952[3].

BELSHAM, T. W., *A Review of Mr. Wilberforce's Treatise, entitled 'A Practical View of the Prevailing Religious System of Professed Christians'*, 1800 ed.

——, *A Summary View of the Evidence and Practical Importance of the Christian revelation*, 1807.

——, *Memoirs of the late Reverend Theophilus Lindsey, M.A., together with a general view of the progress of the Unitarian doctrine in England and America*, 1873 ed.

BERDYAEV, N. A., *The Destiny of Man*, E.T., 1937.

BETTANY, F. G., *Stewart Headlam: a biography*, 1926.

BICKERSTETH, E. H., *Yesterday, Today and For Ever*, 1866.

BIRKS, T. R., *The Difficulties of Belief in connexion with the Creation and the Fall*, Cambridge, 1855.

——, *The Ways of God; or, Thoughts on the difficulties of belief, in connexion with providence and redemption*, 1863.

——, *The Victory of Divine Goodness*, 1867.

——, *The Atonement and the Judgment: a reply to Dr. Candlish's Inaugural Lecture; with a brief statement of facts in connexion with the Evangelical Alliance*, 1870.

BLAIR, R., *The Grave*, Edinburgh, 1858 ed. (Preface by F. W. Farrar).

BOROS, L., *The Moment of Truth: Mysterium mortis*, E.T., 1965.

BOULGER, J. D., *Coleridge as religious thinker*, (Yale studies in English, 151.) New Haven, 1961.

BRANDON, S. G. F., *The Judgment of the Dead. An Historical and Comparative Study of the Idea of a Post-Mortem Judgment in the Major Religions*, 1967.

BRAMLEY, H. R., *Eternal Punishment: a criticism of Dr. Farrar's*

'*Eternal Hope*'; *read at a meeting of the Oxford Clerical Association*, 1878.

BRIDGETT, T. E., *Blunders and Forgeries: Historical essays*, 1890.

BRODRICK, G. C., and FREMANTLE, W. H., *A Collection of the Judgments of the Judicial Committee of the Privy Council in Ecclesiastical Cases relating to Doctrine and Discipline*, 1865.

BROKESBY, F., *The Life of Mr. Henry Dodwell*, 2 vols. 1715.

BROOKE, S. A., *Life and Letters of Frederick W. Robertson, M.A., incumbent of Trinity chapel, Brighton, 1847–53*, 2 vols. 1880 ed.

BUDD, S., 'The loss of faith. Reasons for unbelief among members of the Secular Movement in England', *Past and Present*, 36, April 1967.

BULTMANN, R., *Life and Death*, (with contributions by G. von Rad and G. Bertram), E.T., 1965.

BURN, W. A. L., *The Age of Equipoise, a study of the mid-Victorian generation*, 1964.

CALL, W. M. W., *Reverberations. Revised, with a Chapter from my Autobiography*, 1875.

CARPENTER, J. E., *James Martineau, theologian and teacher. A study of his life and thought*, 1905.

——, *Studies in Theology*, (with P. H. Wicksteed), 1903.

CARPENTER, L., *An Examination of the Charges made against Unitarians and Unitarianism and the Improved Version . . . by Dr. Magee . . .*, Bristol, 1820.

CARPENTER, R. L., (ed.), *Memoirs of the Life of the Reverend Lant Carpenter*, Bristol, 1942.

CASWALL, E., *The Masque of Mary, and other poems*, 1858.

ST. CATHERINE OF GENOA, *The Treatise on Purgatory*, (E.T. H. E. Manning), 1858.

CHADWICK, W. O., *The Victorian Church*, Part I, 1966, Part II, 1970.

CHANNING, W. E., *Works*, 6 vols. Glasgow, 1840–44[3].

CHANNING, W. H., *Memoir of W. E. Channing with selections from his correspondence*, 1851 ed.

COLENSO, J. W., *Ten weeks in Natal. A journal of a first tour of visitation*, Cambridge, 1855.

——, *St. Paul's Epistle to the Romans: newly translated and explained from a missionary point of view*, Cambridge, 1861.

COLERIDGE, H. J., *The Prisoners of the King. Thoughts on the Catholic doctrine of Purgatory*, 1878.

COLERIDGE, S. T., *Biographia Literaria*, 2 vols. 1847².

——, *Aids to Reflection*, (ed. Rev. Derwent Coleridge), 1854⁷.

——, *The Table-talk and Omniana*, 1917 ed.

CONSTABLE, H., *Hades: or the Intermediate state of man*, 1873.

——, *The Duration and Nature of Future Punishment*, 1876⁵.

CONWAY, M. D., *Autobiography. Memories, memoirs and experiences of Moncure D. Conway*, 2 vols. 1904.

COTTLE, J., *Essays on Socinianism*, (1850).

COX, S., *Salvator Mundi: or, Is Christ the Saviour of all men?* 1877.

——, *Expository Essays and Discourses*, 1877.

——, *The Hebrew Twins, A vindication of God's ways with Jacob and Esau*, (with prefatory memoir by Mrs. Cox), 1894.

CRAGG, G. R., *From Puritanism to the Age of Reason: a study of changes in religious thought within the Church of England, 1660–1700*, Cambridge, 1966 ed.

CUNNINGHAM, J. W., *Sermons*, 2 vols. 1822–4.

DALE, A. W. W., *The Life of R. W. Dale of Birmingham*, 1898.

DARBY, J. N., *The Collected Writings*, (ed. W. Kelly), 34 vols. (1867–1883).

DENISON, E. B., *The Life of John Lonsdale, Bishop of Lichfield*, 1868.

DENISON, G. A., *Fifty years at East Brent. The letters of G. A. Denison. 1845–1896*, (ed. L. E. Denison), 1902.

DESSAIN, C. S., (ed.), *The Letters and Diaries of John Henry Newman*, vol. xi–, 1961–.

[DICKINSON, C.,] *Pastoral Epistle of His Holiness the Pope to some Members of the University of Oxford*, 1836.

DOBNEY, H. H., *Notes of Lectures on Future Punishment*, 1844.

——, *A letter to His Grace the Archbishop of Canterbury, on that portion of his recent pastoral letter which affirms 'the everlasting suffering of the Lost'*, 1864.

——, *Judas, or a Brother's inquiry concerning the Betrayer. A dream*, 1872.

DRUMMOND, H., *Natural Law in the Spiritual World*, 1890 ed.

DRUMMOND, J. and UPTON, C. B., *The Life and Letters of James Martineau*, 2 vols. 1902.

DUNN, H., *The Destiny of the Human Race: a Scriptural enquiry*, 2 vols. 1863.

EATON, D., *Scripture the only Guide to Religious Truth. A narrative of the proceedings of the Society of Baptists in York . . . To which is added a brief account of their present views of the faith and practice of the Gospel*, York, 1800.

ERSKINE, T., *True and False Religion*, Leicester, 1874.

ESTLIN, J. P., *Sermons, designed chiefly as a preservative from infidelity and religious indifference*, Bristol, 1802.

——, *A Unitarian Christian's statement and defence of his principles*, Bristol, 1815.

——, *Familiar Lectures on Moral Philosophy*, 2 vols. 1818.

FABER, F. W., *All for Jesus: or, the Easy Ways of Divine Love*, 1854[4].

——, *The Creator and the Creature: or, the wonders of Divine Love*, 1858[2].

——, *Hymns*, 1862.

——, *Notes on doctrinal and spiritual subjects*, 2 vols. 1866.

——, *Spiritual conferences*, 1859.

FAIRCHILD, H. N., '*La Saisiaz* and the *Nineteenth Century*', *Modern Philology*, xlviii, 1950.

——, *Religious Trends in English Poetry*, iv, 1830–80, New York: Morningside Heights, 1957.

FARRAR, F. W., *Eternal Hope*, 1878.

——, *Mercy and Judgment: a few last words on Christian Eschatology with reference to Dr. Pusey's 'What is of Faith?'*, 1894 ed.

FARRAR, R., *The Life of Frederick William Farrar, sometime Dean of Canterbury*, 1904.

FISKE, J., *The Destiny of man viewed in the light of his origin*, Boston, 1884.

FITZGIBBON, G., *Roman Catholic Priests and National Schools*, Dublin, 1872[2].

FLEW, A., (ed.), *Body, Mind and Death*, New York, 1964.

FONTAINE, J., *Eternal Punishment proved to be not suffering but privation, and immortality dependent on spiritual regeneration*, 1817.

FORSYTH, P. T., *Baldwin Brown. A tribute, a reminiscence, and a study*, 1884.

FOSTER, F. H., 'The Eschatology of the New England Divines', *Bibliotheca Sacra*, xlv, Oberlin, Ohio, 1888.

FROTHINGHAM, O. B., *Transcendentalism in New England. A History*, (Harper Torchbooks), New York, 1959.

FROUDE, J. A., *The Nemesis of Faith*, 1849[2].

FULLER, A., *The Calvinistic and Socinian systems examined and compared, as to their moral tendency, in a series of letters* ... 1794[2].

——, *Socinianism indefensible, on the ground of its moral tendency*, 1797.

FULLERTON, G., *Life of Mère Marie de la Providence, foundress of the helpers of the holy souls*, 1835.

FURNISS, J., *How to teach at Catechism*, iii, 1863.

——, *Sight of Hell*, n.d.

GLADSTONE, W. E., *Studies subsidiary to the Works of Bishop Butler*, 1896.

GODTS, F. X., *De Paucitate salvandorum, quid docuerunt sancti?* (ed. altera) Bruges, 1899.

GOODFELLOW, A., *Farrar and Cox versus Dr. Thomson ; or hell and everlasting punishment unscriptural and unreasonable*, Manchester, 1878.

GORER, G., *Death, Grief and Mourning in contemporary Britain*, 1965.

GRIGGS, E. L., (ed.), *Collected letters of Samuel Taylor Coleridge*, 3 vols. 1956–9.

GRUBER, J. W., *A conscience in conflict : the life of St. G. J. Nivart*, New York, 1960.

GURNEY, A., *Our Catholic Inheritance in the Larger Hope*, 1888.

HAIGHT, G. S., (ed.), *The George Eliot letters*, 7 vols. 1954–6.

HAMILTON, R. W., *Missions : their authority, scope, and encouragement*, 1842.

——, *The revealed doctrine of Rewards and Punishments*, 1847 ed.

HANNA, W., *The Letters of Thomas Erskine of Linlathen*, Edinburgh, 2 vols. 1877.

HÄRDELIN, A., *The Tractarian Understanding of the Eucharist*, Uppsala, 1965.

HART, J., '19th century social reform: a Tory interpretation of history', *Past and Present*, 31 July, 1965.

HARTLEY, D., *Observations on Man, his frame, his duty, and his expectations*, 2 vols. 1749.

HAWEIS, H. R., *The Broad Church : or, what is coming*, 1891.

HEARD, J. B., *The tripartite nature of man ; spirit, soul and body ; applied to illustrate and explain the doctrines of original sin, the new birth, the disembodied state, and the spiritual body*, 1866.

HERVEY, J., *Meditations among the Tombs*, 1813 ed.

HICK, J., *Evil and the God of Love*, 1966.

HINTON, J., *Dying*, Harmondsworth, 1967.

HINTON, J. H., *Theological Works*, 2 vols. 1864.

JONES, H. GRESFORD, 'Universalism and Morals', *Scottish Journal of Theology*, iii, 1950.

JUKES, A. J., *The Second Death and the Restitution of all things*, 1867.

——, *The New Man and the Eternal Life: notes on the reiterated Amens of the Son of God*, 1884[3].

KEBLE, J., *A Litany of our Lord's Warnings (for the present distress)*, Oxford, 1864.

——, *Outlines of Instruction or Meditations for the Church's Season* (ed. R. F. Wilson), 1880.

KENRICK, J., *A biographical memoir of the late Rev. Charles Wellbeloved*, 1860.

KENTISH, J., *The Moral Tendency of the genuine Christian doctrine: a discourse delivered at Exeter, July 6th, 1796*, 1798[2].

KER, W., *The popular ideas of immortality, everlasting punishment, and the state of separate souls brought to the text of Scripture*, 1870[2].

KNOTT, C. G., *Life and Scientific Work of Peter Guthrie Tait, Supplementing the two volumes of scientific papers published in 1898, 1900*, 1911.

LACORDAIRE, J. B. H., *Oeuvres*, 6 vols. Paris, 1861.

LAKE, K., (ed.), *Memorials of William Charles Lake, Dean of Durham, 1869–1894*, 1901.

LARMOR, J., *Memoir and Scientific Correspondence of the late Sir G. G. Stokes*, 2 vols. Cambridge, 1907.

LATHBURY, D. C., *The Correspondence on church and religion of W. E. Gladstone*, 2 vols. 1910.

LEASK, W. (ed.), *The Rainbow*, 1864–87.

LECKIE, J. H., *The World to come and Final Destiny*, Edinburgh, 1918.

LECKY, W. E. H., *A history of European morals from Augustus to Charlemagne*, 2 vols. 1869.

LEE, F. G., *The Christian Doctrine of Prayer for the Departed*, 1872.

LIDDON, H. P., *Life of Edward Bouverie Pusey* (ed. J. O. Johnston and R. F. Wilson), 4 vols. 1893–5.

LIGUORI, A., *The Eternal Truths: Preparation for death* (E.T. R. A. Coffin), 1857.

LIVIUS, T., *Father Furniss and his work for children*, 1896.

LONGLEY, C. T., *A Pastoral Letter addressed to the Clergy and Laity of his Province*, 1864.

LUCKOCK, H. M., *After death. An examination of the testimony of primitive times respecting the state of the faithful dead, and their relationship to the living,* 1879.

——, *The Intermediate State between death and judgment,* 1890.

MACARTNEY, H. B., *'England, Home and Beauty'; sketches of Christian life and work in England in 1878,* [1880]

MACCOLL, M., *The 'Damnatory Clauses' of the Athanasian Creed rationally explained in a letter to the Right Hon. W. E. Gladstone, M.P.,* 1872.

MACINTYRE, A., *Secularization and Moral Change,* 1967.

MAISON, M. M., *Search your soul, Eustace!—A Survey of the Religious Novel in the Victorian Age,* 1961.

MANNING, H. E., *Sermons,* 4 vols. 1842–50.

——, *The Internal Mission of the Holy Ghost,* 1875.

MANSEL, H. L., *Man's conception of Eternity: an examination of Mr. Maurice's theory of a fixed state out of time,* 1854.

MARTENSEN, H. L., *Christian Dogmatics,* E.T., 1865.

MARTIN, J. P., *The Last Judgment in Protestant Theology from Orthodoxy to Ritschl,* 1963.

MARTINEAU, J., *Endeavours after the Christian Life,* 1843–7.

——, *Miscellanies,* (ed. T. S. King), Cambridge, Mass. 1852.

——, *A Study of Religion, its sources and contents,* 2 vols. Oxford, 1888.

[MARTINEAU, J., THOM, J. H., and GILES, H.,] *Unitarianism defended: a series of lectures by three protestant dissenting ministers of Liverpool,* Liverpool, 1839.

MAURICE, F., *The Life of Frederick Denison Maurice,* 1884[2].

MAURICE, F. D., *Introduction to Law's 'Remarks on the Fable of the Bees',* Cambridge, 1844.

——, *The New Statute and Mr. Ward: A letter to a non-resident Member of Convocation,* Oxford, 1845.

——, *The Church a family: twelve sermons on the occasional services of the Prayer Book,* 1850.

——, *Theological Essays,* Cambridge, 1853.

——, *The Word 'Eternal' and the Punishment of the wicked: A letter to the Rev. Dr. Jelf,* Cambridge, 1853.

——, *The concluding essay and preface to the second edition of Mr. Maurice's Theological Essays,* Cambridge, 1854.

——, *The Gospel of St. John. A series of discourses,* Cambridge, 1857.

——, *Lectures on the Apocalypse, or the Book of Revelation of St. John the Divine,* 1861.

——, *What Message have the Clergy for the People of England? A letter to the Rt. Hon and Rt. Rev. the Bishop of London in reference to the controversy on the future state of sinners*, 1864.

——, *Moral and Metaphysical Philosophy*, 2 vols. 1882 ed.

MCFARLAND, T., *Coleridge and the Pantheist Tradition*, Oxford, 1969.

MERY, M., *La Critique du christianisme chez Renouvier*, 2 vols. Gap, 1963[2].

MOMERIE, A. W., *Agnosticism, and other sermons*, Edinburgh, 1884.

MOREWOOD, C. C., *Eugénie Smet, Mère Marie de la Providence, Foundress of the 'Helpers of the Holy Souls'*, 1927.

MORRIS, J., *Two ancient treatises on Purgatory; (A Remembrance oj the Living to pray for the Dead by J. Mumford, and Purgatory surveyed by R. Thimelby)*, 1893.

MORRIS, J. W., *Memoirs of the life and writings of the Rev. Andrew Fuller*, 1816.

MULHAUSER, F. L., *The Correspondence of Arthur Hugh Clough*, 1957.

MÜLLER, G., 'Die Idee einer Apokatastasis ton panton', *Zeitschrift für Religions-und Geistesgeschichte*, 1964.

NEWMAN, F. W., *The Soul, her sorrows and her aspirations. An essay towards the natural history of the Soul as the true basis of theology*, 1849.

——, *Theism, doctrinal and practical; or didactic religious utterance*, 1858.

——, *Life after death? Palinodia*, 1886.

NEWMAN, J. H., *An Essay on the Development of Christian Doctrine*, 1845.

——, *Parochial and Plain sermons*, 8 vols. 1868 ed.

——, *Verses on Various Occasions*, 1868.

——, *Callista, a sketch of the third century*, 1881.

——, *Apologia pro vita sua*, (World's classics ed.), 1964.

——, *Discourses addressed to Mixed Congregations*, 1881[6].

——, *Faith and Prejudice and other unpublished sermons*, New York, 1956.

——, *An Essay in aid of a Grammar of Assent*, New York, 1947 ed.

——, *A Letter addressed to his Grace the Duke of Norfolk on occasion of Mr. Gladstone's recent expostulation*, 1875.

——, *Autobiographical Writings*, (ed. H. Tristram), 1956.

NEWSOME, D. H., 'Justification and sanctification: Newman and the Evangelicals', *Journal of Theological Studies*, N.S., 15. i. 1964.

——, *The Parting of Friends: a study of the Wilberforces and Henry Manning*, 1966.

NOEL, B. W., *Christian Missions to Heathen Nations*, 1842.

NOEL, G. T., *Sermons intended chiefly for the use of families*, 1827².

NUGÉE, G., *The words from the Cross as applied to our own deathbeds, being a series of Lent lectures delivered at St. Paul's, Knightsbridge, 1853*, 1856.

OXENHAM, F. N., *What is the Truth as to Everlasting Punishment? In reply to Dr. Pusey*, 1881.

OXENHAM, H. N., *Catholic Eschatology and Universalism. An essay on the doctrine of future retribution*, 1878.

PALMER, W., *Letters to N. Wiseman, D.D., on the Errors of Romanism, in respect to the Worship of Saints, Satisfactions, Purgatory, Indulgences and the Worship of Images and Relics*, Oxford, 1842.

PATTISON, M., 'The Arguments for a future Life', (*Metaphysical Society Papers*, xxv), 1872.

PEEL, A., *Letters to a Victorian editor, Henry Allon, editor of the 'British Quarterly Review'*, 1929.

PESE, E., 'A suggested background for Newman's *Dream of Gerontius*', *Modern Philology*, 47, 1949.

PÉTAVEL-OLLIF, E., *The Problem of Immortality*, (E.T. F. A. Freer), 1892.

——, *Souvenirs et mélanges*, Lausanne, 1913.

PFLEIDERER, O., *The development of Theology in Germany since Kant, and its progress in Great Britain since 1825*, 1890.

PINAMONTI, G. P., *Hell opened to Christians, to caution them from entering into it, or, considerations of the infernal pains . . . for every day of the week*, 1807 ed.

POULET, G., 'Timelessness and Romanticism', *Journal of the History of Ideas*, 15, 1954.

VAN PUERSEN, C. A., *Body, Soul, Spirit. A Survey of the Body–Mind Problem*, 1966.

PUSEY, E. B., *An Earnest Remonstrance to the author of the 'Pope's Pastoral letter to certain Members of the University of Oxford'*, 1836.

——, *The Day of Judgment. A sermon preached on the Twentieth Sunday after Trinity in St. Peter's Church, Brighton*, Oxford, 1839.

——, *What is of faith as to everlasting punishment?* 1880.

RAHNER, K., *On the Theology of Death*, (*Quaestiones Disputatae* 2), 1961.

RAMSEY, I. T., *On being sure in religion*, 1963.

RIGG, J. H., *Modern Anglican Theology*, 1880³.

ROBBINS, W., *The Newman Brothers: an essay in comparative intellectual biography*, 1966.

ROBERTSON, F. W., *Sermons*, (1st ser., 1899 ed.; 2nd ser., 1897 ed.; 3rd ser., 1874 ed.; 4th ser., 1886 ed.;).

ROWELL, D. G., 'The Dream of Gerontius', *Ampleforth Journal*, 73, 1968.

——, 'The Origins and History of Universalist Societies in Britain, 1750–1850', *Journal of Ecclesiastical History*, 22, 1971.

RYDER, H. I. D., *Essays* (ed. F. Bacchus), 1911.

RYLAND, J. E., (ed.), *The Life and Correspondence of John Foster*, 2 vols. 1846.

SCOTT, D. W., *The Purpose of the Ages, or, the final salvation of all*, 1885.

SCOTT, T., *Hell*, n.d.

SICKELS, E. M., *The Gloomy Egoist. Moods and themes of melancholy from Gray to Keats*, New York, 1932.

SIEVEKING, I. G., *Memoir and Letters of Francis W. Newman*, 1909.

SMITH, S., *My Life-work*, 1902.

SNYDER, A. D., 'Coleridge on Böhme', *Publications of the Modern Language Association of America*, 45, 1930.

STEPHEN, J., *Essays in Ecclesiastical Biography*, 2 vols. 1853³.

STOKES, G. G., *Evidence of missionaries as to the practical effect of presenting Christianity to the heathen in the form associated with the doctrine of 'Life in Christ'*, Cambridge, 1882.

——, *Conditional Immortality, A help to sceptics*, 1897.

SWIFT, D. W., 'The Future probation controversy in American Congregationalism' (Unpublished Yale Ph.D. thesis, 1947).

TAIT, A. C., *A Charge to the clergy of the diocese of London at his visitation in December 1866*, 1866.

TAYLER, J. J., *Christian Aspects of Faith and Duty*, 1851.

TAYLOR, I., *Saturday Evening*, 1832.

——, *Physical Theory of another life*, 1857³.

THOM, J. H., (ed.), *Letters of J. J. Tayler*, 2 vols. 1872.

THOMSON, ALEXANDER, *The Scripture Doctrine of Future Punishment*, Manchester, 1876.

THOMSON, ANDREW, *The Doctrine of Universal Pardon considered and refuted in a series of sermons*, Edinburgh, 1831².

THOMSON, W., *A Pastoral letter to the clergy and laity of the Province of York*, 1864.

TILLICH, P., *Perspectives on 19th and 20th Century Protestant Theology*, 1967.

[TRENCH, M. ed.] *Richard Chenevix Trench, Archbishop. Letters and Memorials*, 2 vols. 1888.

UNDERWOOD, A. C., *A History of the English Baptists*, 1947.

UPTON, C. B., *Dr. Martineau's Philosophy*, rev. ed. 1905.

VAUGHAN, D. J., 'Scottish Influence upon English Theological Thought', *Contemporary Review*, 32, 1878.

'VICESIMUS' (i.e. OAKLEY, J.), *H. N. Oxenham, Recollections of an old friend*, Manchester, 1888.

VIDLER, A. R., *F. D. Maurice and Company. Nineteenth century studies*, 1966.

WALKER, D. P., *The Decline of Hell. Seventeenth-Century Discussions of Eternal Torment*, 1964.

WARD, W. P., *The Life of John Henry Cardinal Newman*, 2 vols. 1912.

——, *Problems and Persons*, 1903.

WARLEIGH, H. S., *A Demonstration of the extinction of evil persons and of evil things, in answer to J. N. Darby and others*, 1871.

[WHATELEY, R.] *A view of the Scripture revelations concerning a Future State laid before his parishioners*, by a Country Pastor, 1829.

WHITE, E., *The Theory of Missions: or, a scriptural inquiry into the doctrine of the everlasting torment of the barbarous nations and countless ignorant heathen of ancient and modern times*, 1855.

——, *Life in Christ: a study of the scripture doctrine on the nature of man, the object of the divine incarnation, and the conditions of human immortality*, 1878 ed.

——, *The Endless Life: two discourses on the history of English opinion on human destiny during the last thirty years*, 1882.

WHITTEMORE, T., *The Modern History of Universalism, from the era of the Reformation to the present time*, Boston, 1830.

WILSON, H. B., *The Communion of Saints*, Oxford, 1851.

WILSON, W., *The History and Antiquities of Dissenting Churches and Meeting Houses in London, Westminster and Southwark*, 4 vols. 1808–14.

WINCHESTER, E., *The Universal Restoration exhibited in a series of Dialogues between a minister and his friend*, 1788.

WOOD, H. G., *Frederick Denison Maurice*, 1950.

WOOD, J. G., *Man and Beast, here and hereafter*, 1878.

WOODS, C. E., *Archdeacon Wilberforce, his ideals and teaching*, 1917.

WRIGHT, R., *An Abridgement of Five Discourses, on different subjects; intended to obviate several objections which have been made to Universal Restoration and calculated to answer other important purposes*, Wisbech, 1798.

——, *An Essay on Future Punishment*, Liverpool, 1814^2.

——, *An Essay on a Future Life*, Liverpool, 1819.

——, *The Resurrection from the Dead an essential doctrine of the Gospel, and the neglect of it by reputed orthodox Christians an argument against the Truth of their System*, Liverpool, 1820.

——, *The Eternity of Hell Torment indefensible : being an examination of several passages in Dr. Ryland's sermon entitled 'The First Lye refuted'*, n.d.

——, *A Review of the Missionary Life and Labours of Richard Wright*, 1824.

INDEX

Index